Cover Art: "Stalemate" by Stan Miyazaki in the collection of the Department of Visual and Performing Arts in Education, The University of British Columbia

Published simultaneously in Canada by Pacific Educational Press, The University of British Columbia, Vancouver, B.C. V6T 1Z5 and in the U.S.A. by Teachers College Press, 1234 Amsterdam Avenue, New York, NY 10027

Canadian Cataloguing in Publication Data

Main entry under title:

Reflection in teacher education

Includes bibliographies and index.
ISBN 0-88865-061-2

1. Teachers - Training of.   I. Grimmett, Peter Philip.
II. Erickson, Gaalen, 1942-
LB1715.R43 1988   370'.7'1   C88-091486-6

Library of Congress Cataloging-in-Publication Data

Reflection in teacher education / edited by Peter P. Grimmett
   Gaalen L. Erickson.
   p. 220 cm.
   Includes bibliographies and index.
   ISBN 0-8077-2949-3
   1. Teachers--Training of--Congresses. 2. School supervision-
-Congresses.   3. Schön, Donald A.   I. Grimmett, Peter
Philip.   II. Erickson, Gaalen L., 1942-
LB1707.R44 1988
370'.72--dc19   88-25995
                                                         CIP

Printed and bound in the United States of America

93 92 91 90 89 88   1 2 3 4 5 6

TABLE OF CONTENTS

Section III: Reflections on Reflection

Conclusion

PREFACE

This book is the outcome of a symposium held at the American Educational Research Association meeting, Washington, D.C. in April 1987. The symposium—"Instructional supervision and teacher education in the twenty-first century: Educating teachers as reflective practitioners"—was sponsored by the Special Interest Group for Instructional Supervision and Division K of the AERA, by the Canadian Association for Teacher Education, and by the Centre for the Study of Teacher Education at the University of British Columbia. Donald Schön of the Massachusetts Institute of Technology gave the key-note address with commentaries coming from Lee Shulman of Stanford University, Gary Fenstermacher of University of Arizona, and Geraldine Gilliss of the Canadian Teachers' Federation. Peter Grimmett of the University of British Columbia chaired and organized the session.

The purpose of the symposium was for Schön to address the question of how instructional supervision can be used to coach preservice and inservice teachers in reflection as a viable component of their professional education. He was also asked to describe how his idea of "a reflective practicum" can be operationalized in teacher education. The format of the session was one which provided for a good deal of dialogue, initially among Schön and the panel and subsequently among members of the audience.

The session did indeed stimulate dialogue. A timely and thorough discussion of how Schön's ideas can be integrated into teacher education began with the commentary and critiques given by Shulman, Fenstermacher, and Gilliss. That dialogue has continued and now finds its expression in the chapters of this book.

Most of the dialogue around these ideas has taken place at universities (notably Canadian ones) that Schön himself has visited. Scholars at Queen's University and the Ontario Institute for Studies in Education each contribute chapters about research that is using Schön's thinking as a sensitizing framework. The University of British Columbia evidences a dialogue in ferment; some scholars conduct research within what could loosely be called the Schön genre while others have powerful critiques of the foundational tenets of Schön's conception of reflection. Much of this dialogue at the University of British Columbia revolves around a program of research on reflection in teacher education coordinated by Gaalen Erickson. This research

1

program is one of four currently in place at the Centre for the Study of Teacher Education.

This book is edited by the Centre for the Study of Teacher Education, and copublished by Pacific Educational Press and Teachers College Press so that members of the international research community can join in the dialogue about reflection in teacher education. It represents a beginning in a most important area of study, and we hope that it spawns much interest and debate about what constitutes reflection in teacher education.

Special thanks are due to Nelda Oman, Cindy Drossos and Anne Linder, the Centre's secretaries, for typing the manuscript, to Ted Riecken, Graduate Assistant in the Centre, for his technical editing of some of the chapters, to Sarah Biondello, the Acquisitions Editor at Teachers College Press, New York, and to Sharon Radcliffe at Pacific Educational Press for her help in bringing this project to completion.

June, 1988

Peter P. Grimmett, Director
Gaalen L. Erickson, Research Program Coordinator
Centre for the Study of Teacher Education
The University of British Columbia

INTRODUCTION

THE NATURE OF REFLECTION AND SCHÖN'S CONCEPTION IN PERSPECTIVE

Peter P. Grimmett
University of British Columbia

Donald Schön's writings (1983, 1987) have aroused a great deal of interest in teacher education. Many scholars of diverse traditions and backgrounds are beginning to craft ideas around the concept of "reflection." Zeichner (1986) describes several of the most common approaches to the preparation of reflective teachers during preservice teacher education: action research, ethnography, journal writing, supervision, curriculum analysis, and the Ohio State version of "reflective teaching." He also notes many of the strategies which distinguish these approaches one from the other. Some specify a set of specific components for the reflective process, while others advocate the use of a particular strategy, such as journal writing, without specifying aspects of the reflective process, while a limited number of approaches attempt to detail the steps of reflection and particular instructional processes to be used. Zeichner also distinguishes among different approaches by the degree to which they are explicitly justified in relation to a theoretical stance. He further classifies approaches according to the level at which a "reflective" intervention is directed. In some cases, entire teacher education programs have been revised, in others only individual courses have been altered without modifying the overall program context. This leads to the important distinction between those approaches which view the development of reflective teachers as a worthy goal in itself and those which assume that changes in the organizational, social, and political context have to occur before reflective teaching in schools is possible.

Tom (1985) attempts to conceptualize inquiry-oriented teacher education. He classifies inquiry-oriented teacher education along three dimensions. First, although teacher educators in this tradition agree that making teaching problematic is central to the process of inquiry, different emphases emerge as the focus of such a process. Some approaches are more narrow in scope, delimiting teaching to its technical aspects, while others are broader in the sense that they focus on making problematical the moral and political context within which teaching is embedded. Tom also distinguishes inquiry-oriented approaches according to the model of inquiry employed. These distinctions are based on the rigor of the model and its projected outcomes, i.e., whether the approach leads merely to the accumulation of knowledge or whether it orients teachers to actions encompassing thought and behavior. His final distinction is ontological. Some approaches view educational phenomena as natural and given to scientific laws while others view reality as being socially constructed.

Both these reviews (Zeichner, 1986; Tom, 1985) highlight a salient point: that, although many teacher educators use similar terms such as reflection and inquiry, and employ approaches which at first glance appear to be similar, there is little shared meaning among the people who write about reflective teaching and inquiry-oriented teacher education. There appears to be even less agreement on what characterizes the content of reflective inquiry and on what kinds of contexts tend to foster such a process. On the other hand, all seem to be persuaded that reflection (however they understand and operationalize the term) is a worthy aim in teacher education. Why is this interest in reflection so current again? One partial explanation for this phenomenon can be found in the thinking and writing of Schön who, more than anyone, has crystallized the essential elements of processes characterized as "reflective." A second partial explanation lies in the "ghost of John Dewey." His influence has been so pervasive (particularly on Schön himself) that no understanding of research in this genre is possible without first acknowledging the common properties enunciated so long ago by this intellectual giant.

The Nature of Reflection

Dewey (1933) characterizes reflection as a specialized form of thinking. It stems from doubt and perplexity felt in a directly experienced situation and leads to purposeful inquiry and problem resolution. Inferences drawn from the observed phenomena of past experience are tested as the basis for future action. Central to the process is the paradox that one cannot know without acting and one cannot act without knowing.

Perplexity in a Directly Experienced Situation

Reflection arises from a directly experienced situation which puzzles or surprises us. It occurs when a state of doubt, hesitation, perplexity, or mental difficulty engulfs the mind. Grappling with a genuine problem or question stemming from sudden change or uncertainty draws out reflection; for the perplexing nature of the experienced situation presents the mind with an unresolved difficulty:

> The function of reflective thought is, therefore, to transform a situation in which there is experienced obscurity, doubt, conflict, disturbance of some sort, into a situation that is clear, coherent, settled, harmonious. (Dewey, 1933, pp. 100-101)

The conclusion arrived at is always tentative and subject to further examination; for reflection impels one to inquiry, the "active, persistent, and careful consideration of any belief or supposed form of knowledge in light of the grounds that support it and the further conclusions to which it tends" (Dewey, p. 9).

Purposeful Inquiry and Problem Resolution

Reflection always leads to a consequence. "Demand for the solution of a perplexity is the steadying and guiding factor in the entire process of reflection" (Dewey, p. 14). It begins with observations made by oneself or others in a directly experienced situation. These observations, in turn, suggest possible courses of action. Together data (observations) and ideas (suggested courses of actions) constitute "two indispensable and correlative factors"

(Dewey, p. 104) of reflection. The observed conditions perplex us, causing suggestions for action to occur. To be reflective, however, immediate direct action is withheld; the perplexity is conceptualized as a problem to be solved and suggested actions are entertained as hypotheses to be tested first by mental elaboration or reasoning and second by overt action. The latter aspect provides for experimental corroboration of the conjectured ideas before any determination of the problem is reached.

Such purposeful inquiry makes demands of the mind. One is not allowed the luxury of jumping to conclusions or being uncritical of ideas. One must be "willing to endure suspense and to undergo the trouble of searching" (Dewey, p. 16) until a consecutive ordering of ideas leads to "a conclusion that contains the intellectual force of the preceding ideas . . . making some idea worthy of belief . . . making it *trustworthy*" (Dewey, p. 47). In so doing, reflective inquiry transforms a perplexing situation into a settled one by providing a tentative resolution to the initial problem.

Future Actions Inferred from Past Experience

Transforming a situation of perplexity into one of clarity and coherence inevitably involves one in making inferences. Dewey describes inference as "the process of arriving at an idea of what is absent [in a given situation] on the basis of what is at hand . . . it involves a *jump from the known into the unknown*" (pp. 95-96). Inference therefore occurs through a suggestion that is aroused by the directly experienced situation. Inference in itself is not misleading; it is the acceptance of untested inferences that distorts and misinforms. Reflection involves the rigorous testing of inferences (suggestions) by mental elaboration and overt action.

> . . . first, the process of forming the idea or supposed solution is checked by constant cross reference to the conditions observed to be actually present; secondly, the idea *after* it is formed is tested by *acting* upon it, overtly if possible, otherwise in imagination. The consequences of this action confirm, modify, or refute the idea. (Dewey, pp. 104-105)

The making of inferences has an anticipatory quality about it. Suggestions for action constitute prognostications or predictions. Problem resolutions develop a definite set towards the future. Reflection, however, involves equal reference to the past. Inferences are drawn from one's past experience and suggestions arise out of the situation as it was experienced. As such, reflection involves looking back as well as looking ahead. Indeed, the closer the process of reflection moves towards a resolution of the felt problem, the more critical it becomes to examine past events and experience.

Such a Janus-like orientation enables reflection to stretch the mind beyond mere information towards the accumulation of wisdom. The acquisition and storing of information does not require reflection; rather, it draws heavily on memory. Transforming such information into knowledge "operating in the direction of powers to the better living of life" (Dewey, p. 64) is the hallmark of reflection and wisdom is its fruit. Such wisdom causes thoughtful persons to be heedful, circumspect, and given to scrutiny rather than rash, unwary, and perfunctory. It also makes them deeply cognizant of the paradox of knowing described by Plato.

Knowing and Acting: The "Meno" Paradox

How can people acquire knowledge of any kind when the world in which we live is characterized (Carter, 1984) as offering only a choice between the 20/20 vision of certainty and indoctrination, and the blindness of relativism and skepticism? Carter's (1984) thesis that *intellectual myopia* acts as the cornerstone of moral philosophy provides one possible answer. For, on the one hand, intellectual myopia celebrates the fact that we are not intellectually blind; on the other hand, such a way of seeing frequently points out weaknesses in other positions without necessarily being able to put anything better in its place. Carter's conception of intellectual myopia mirrors in its essence the paradox of learning in Plato's *Meno*.

Intellectual myopia can be said to characterize the essence of Socrates' actions in his dialogue with Meno. In attempting to open up Meno's mind to the weaknesses inherent in the popular sophistic emphasis on the eloquent skills of the debater rather than on the solidity of the evidence and truth of the arguments, Socrates pushes Meno's understanding of "virtue" to the point where the student is thoroughly perplexed:

> Socrates, even before I met you, they told me that in plain truth you are a perplexed man yourself and reduce others to perplexity. At this moment I feel you are exercising magic and witchcraft upon me and positively laying me under your spell until I am a mass of helplessness . . . My mind and my lips are literally numb, and I have nothing to reply to you. Yet I have spoken about virtue hundreds of times, held forth often on the subject in front of large audiences, and very well too, or so I thought. Now I can't even say what it is. (Plato, 1964, *Meno*, p. 80 a-b)

This sudden recognition by Meno that he has not the least idea of what virtue is causes him to frame the paradox of learning that all students (particularly ones in teacher education) experience at one time or another:

> But how will you look for something when you don't in the least know what it is? How on earth are you going to set up something you don't know as the object of your search? To put it another way, even if you come right up against it, how will you know that what you have found is the thing you didn't know? (Plato, *Meno* p. 80 d)

The paradox of learning consists in a student not understanding what he or she needs to learn and yet only being able to begin the process by acting as if he or she understood. This "launching out" is a necessary precursor to knowing that something exists and to knowing how something functions. This preliminary step is neither blind nor certain; rather it is steeped in the kind of experiential doubt and perplexity that a person's mind inevitably seeks to resolve. As such, the paradox of learning is an essential characteristic of reflection.

The nature of reflection articulated by Dewey and the *Meno* paradox described by Plato appear to be central to Schön's conception of reflection.

Schön's Conception of Reflection

Schön (1983) argues that the knowledge-in-action of practitioners is to be found in the professional actions of practitioners and their reflection on and in such actions rather than in a particular kind of theoretical thinking that he terms "technical rationality" (p. 21). In so doing, he refutes the idea that a science-like corpus of propositional knowledge can "drive" practice, and that it can lead to predictability and control in practical affairs. He prefers to consider "science before the fact as a process in which scientists grapple with uncertainties and arts of practice" (p. 49). Schön's quest for professional knowledge-in-action revolves around a search for "an epistemology of practice implicit in the artistic, intuitive processes which some practitioners do bring to situations of uncertainty, instability, uniqueness, and value conflict" (p. 49).

Practitioners' professional knowledge is displayed, then, in the messy, indeterminate zones of action which do not fit the predominant model of technical rationality. Such knowledge is constructed by practitioners through reflection-in-action (i.e., an action is generated and tested through "on-the-spot experimenting," [p. 141]) and reflection-on-action (i.e., an action planned on the basis of post-hoc thinking and deliberation). Both types of reflection involve some form of experimentation in which practitioners attempt to create meaning of the problematic aspects of a practice situation through "problem setting" and "problem solving":

> In real world practice, problems do not present themselves to the practitioner as givens. They must be constructed from the materials or problematic situations that are puzzling, troubling and uncertain . . . When we set the problem, we select what we will treat as the "things" of the situation, we set the boundaries of our attention to it, and we impose upon it a coherence which allows us to say what is wrong and in what directions the situation needs to be changed. Problem setting is a process in which, interactively, we *name* the things to which we will attend and *frame* the context in which we will attend to them. (Schön, 1983, p. 40) (Emphasis in original)

This reframing of a problem situation enables practitioners to make use of their existing "repertoire of examples, images, understandings, and actions" (Schön, 1987, p. 66). Reflection, thus, engages practitioners in a "conversation" with the problematic situation. Past experiences are brought to bear on the situation; frames are imposed which highlight certain aspects of phenomena at work in the situation; problems are set, the situation reframed, and problem-solving actions are generated. What practitioners essentially "see" in an uncertain situation of practice depends on what they *make* of the practice setting and the way in which they experimentally "converse" with the situation as they have framed it. This reflective exchange with the situation leads to further framing and reframing for "the situation talks back, the practitioner listens, and as he appreciates what he hears, he reframes the situation once again" (Schön, 1983, pp. 131-132). The cyclical nature of this conversation is a fundamental aspect of reflection for new understandings of the situation precipitate further reflection and appreciation:

> In this reflective conversation, the practitioner's effort to solve the reframed problem yield new discoveries which call for new reflection-in-action. The process spirals through stages of appreciation, action, and reappreciation. The unique and uncertain situation comes to be understood through the attempt to change it, and changed through the attempt to understand it. (Schön, p. 132)

Problem setting and a reframing of the puzzling situation are central tenets to the view of reflection-in-action advanced by Schön (1983, 1987). For Schön, the concept of reflection is an integral part of his view of professional knowledge. He is interested in how professionals think in action; how they use their practical knowledge in situations of practice. Contained within Schön's view of professional knowledge are his ideas about the way professionals "frame" problems using their practical knowledge. The way we conceptualize a problem affects the solutions we develop. Schön argues that we often think metaphorically as we frame problems and work toward their solution. Metaphoric thought combined with practical knowledge can lead us to tentative solutions to problem situations that are tested as the practitioner engages in a "reflective conversation" with the situation. In a reflective conversation, hypothesized solutions are tested as they are applied in situations of practice when the situational "back-talk" provides the practitioner with information about his or her proposed solution.

Another fundamental aspect of Schön's conception of reflection is experimentation. Reflective practitioners engage in moves that have to do with the choice of action to be taken. Choosing actions in the indeterminate and messy zones of practice poses practitioners with the "Meno paradox." For Schön (1987), the Meno paradox accurately describes the experience of learning professional practice. The student is attempting to learn things, the meaning and importance of which cannot be grasped ahead of time:

> It [the Meno paradox] captures the very feelings of mystery, confusion, frustration and futility that many students experience in their early months or years of [professional] study. He [the student] knows he needs to look for something but does not know what that something is. He seeks to learn it, moreover, in the sense of coming to know it *in action*. Yet, in the first instance, he can neither do it nor recognize it when he sees it. Hence, he is caught up in a self-contradiction: "looking for something" implies a capacity to recognize the thing one looks for but the student lacks at first the capacity to recognize the object of his search. The instructor is caught up in the same paradox: he cannot tell the student what he needs to know, even if *he* has words for it, because the student would not at that point understand him. (Schön, p. 83) (Emphasis in original)

This initial learning process carries with it a double burden for students of professional practice: at one and the same time they must learn to execute professional practices and to recognize when their execution is at a level of competence. Schön summarizes the learning predicament thus:

> The paradox of learning a really new competence is this: that a student cannot at first understand what he needs to learn, can only learn it by educating himself through self-discovery, and can only educate himself by beginning to *do* what he does not yet understand. (Schön, p. 85) (Emphasis added)

Beginning to act when it is not altogether clear how one should act is the way students of professional practice learn to know-in-action. They must engage in action without knowing in order to discover what needs to be learned. To do so, however, requires of students the "willing suspension of disbelief" until they have access to knowledge, derived through reflection in and on action, upon which to make informed choices. Schön (1987) quotes Quist's (the design studio master) articulation of this expectation:

> It has to be a kind of contract between the two. The teacher must be open to challenge and must be able to defend his position. The student, in turn, must be *willing to suspend his disbelief*, to give the teacher's suggestion a chance to try the suggestion out. The student must be willing to trust that the faculty member has a *programmatic intention which will be pre-empted or ruined by his requiring full justification and explanation before anything is done.* (p. 87) (Emphasis added)

Students must therefore temporarily suspend any misgivings they may hold about the worthwhileness of a programmatic suggestion or intention so that they can begin to act. This is precisely because action is the necessary precursor to reflection. It is in reflection-in- and on-action that the willing suspension of disbelief is temporarily abated until further learning dictates the call for renewed action.

The Meno paradox creates in most students a sense of being at risk. Their autonomy to act as they see fit, the hallmark of professionals, is temporarily disallowed so that they can learn how to function as professional practitioners. In order to gain that sense of competence, control, and confidence that characterizes professionals, students of professional practice must first give it up. As they act and reflect in situations of perplexing uncertainty, mystery, and frustration, that which is given up for the sake of experimenting begins to emerge in their development. Out of the darkness of student unknowing comes the light of professional practical knowledge.

Schön's Contribution in Perspective

The study of reflective practice in teacher education is essentially concerned with how educators make sense of the phenomena of experience that puzzle or perplex them. The purpose of the endeavor, in Donmoyer's (1985) terms, is the pursuit of meaning as distinct from the pursuit of truth or fact. Because teaching involves the interaction of complex human beings capable of creating inordinate ways of giving meaning to phenomena experienced within a socio-linguistic culture, questions of meaning precede questions of truth. That is, how subjects attribute meaning to phenomena is the initial focus of researchers rather than the investigation of the validity of those meanings. The purpose of this kind of research is neither prediction nor explanation; rather, it is to explore phenomenologically how educators create what Shulman (1987) describes as the "wisdom of practice" within what Lieberman and Miller (1984) have characterized as the complex world and dynamic work of teachers.

Elsewhere (Grimmett, Riecken, MacKinnon, & Erickson, 1987) different conceptions of reflection have been categorized according to the ontological dimension of how research-derived knowledge is viewed as contributing to the education of teachers. Put differently, it distinguishes among conceptions on the basis of their answers to the question, is research-derived knowledge seen as a source for mediating action in the sense that the purpose of reflection is to *direct* teachers in their practice; or is such knowledge regarded as *informing* practice in the sense of providing a rich basis for selection as teachers *deliberate* among competing alternatives for action; or does research-derived knowledge constitute one source of information whereby teachers *apprehend* practice as they reconstruct their classroom experiences.

The first category of conceptions of reflection essentially represents it as thoughtfulness about action—thoughtfulness that leads to conscious, deliberate moves, usually taken to "apply" research findings or educational theory in practice. The use of the word "apply" is significant here, for the authors who hold to this conception subscribe to an associated view of educational theory and research findings about teaching that is technical, perhaps even mechanistic, in character. It is a view of knowledge with which one could expect the knower to reflect in order to *direct*, or *control* practice. Among all of the current writers on reflection, those whose works fall into this group are perhaps the most optimistic about positively affecting practice. Another distinguishing feature of this category is the tendency of authors to view "new information" as coming solely from "authorities" who publish in journals—never from the practice situation itself.

A second category of conceptions on reflection in teacher education advances a view of reflection as deliberation and choice among competing versions of "good teaching," consideration of educational events *in context*, and anticipation of the consequences following from different lines of action, taken from these competing versions of good teaching. Contributions in this category are distinguished by their attention to the context of educational events, and the idea that in reflecting about particular events and situations, one deliberates among competing views of teaching and examines each in light of the consequences for classroom practice that each action entails. Thus, there is a tendency for authors to subscribe to an eclectic view of knowledge, the test of which is in the benefit of its consequences for students. The associated expectation placed on the knower is to *inform* practice through reflection.

The third broad category of literature on reflection in teacher education is constituted by works that put forth varieties of the conception of reflection as reconstructing experience, the end of which is the identification of a new possibility for action. In many cases, this literature draws explicitly on a constructivist view of knowledge; reflection is seen as a means by which a practitioner *appreciates*, or *apprehends* practice. It includes conceptions of reflection as the *reorganization* or *reconstruction of experience* that leads to (1) new understandings of action situations, (2) new understandings of self-as-teacher or the cultural milieu of teaching, or, following a critical-theoretical tradition, (3) new understandings of taken-for-granted assumptions about teaching.

The first subsection of the third broad category has features which are common in the degree to which the act of problem setting in an action situation is made problematic itself. Here, reflection is seen as a means by which a teacher can either attend to features of the situation that were previously ignored, or assign new significance to features that were identified previously. In either case, reflection involves recasting situations in light of clarifying questions, reconsidering the assumptions on which previous understandings of the situation were based, and beginning to rethink the range of potential responses that are available to the teacher. Accordingly, reflection is seen in this subsection as a general means by which the knower *appreciates*, or *apprehends* practice situations.

The second subsection of this third category presents conceptions of reflection as the reconstruction of experience, the focus of which is on the individual's view either of himself or herself as a teacher, or of the cultural milieu of teaching. Much of the work is phenomenological or hermaneutic in orientation, aimed at providing interpretive accounts of the way teachers structure their knowledge and "cultural world." The main idea put forth by the investigators is that experience, including one's past and present teaching practices and one's personal biography, is shaped by reflection. Reflection, then, is regarded as a process in which teachers structure and restructure their personal, practical knowledge.

The final subsection of this third category consists of scholarly works that put forth conceptions of reflection as reconstructing taken-for-granted assumptions about teaching. Reflection, according to these authors, enables practitioners to articulate, and ultimately to emancipate themselves from the humanly-constructed social, political, and cultural distortions that frustrate and constrain self-understanding. Critical reflection, then, begins with such questions as, "to what ends, and in whose interest is knowledge being used?"

This categorization of differing conceptions of reflection displays the wide divergence of understandings extant in the field of teacher education. It also provides one way of placing Schön's particular conception in perspective. Schön's view of reflection is not concerned with a conscious thoughtfulness designed to mediate (if not sometimes impede) action, nor is he specifically encouraging practicing teachers to deliberate among competing alternative views of what research suggests constitutes "effective teaching." Rather, his writing is very definitely in the category in which reflection is regarded as the reconstruction of experience, not primarily for purposes of explicating the cultural milieu of the teachers' world or taken-for-granted assumptions and humanly-constructed distortions embedded within the social, political, and moral context of schools, but for purposes of apprehending practice settings in problematic ways. Clearly, the context of Schön's conception of reflection is constituted by action settings which precipitate puzzles or surprises for the professional practitioner. His focus is on how practitioners *generate* professional knowledge in and *appreciate* problematic features of action settings. As such, Schön's contribution to reflection is distinctively important. He builds on and extends Dewey's foundational properties of reflection in a manner that is clearly different from how critical theorists (e.g., Habermas, 1971; Van Manen, 1977), critical action researchers (e.g., Carr and Kemmis, 1983; Smyth, 1986), and investigators of teachers' cultural milieu (e.g., Clandinin, 1986; Connelly and Clandinin, 1985; Elbaz, 1983) conceive of the process of reflection. The reflection that Schön focusses on takes place in the crucible of action. And it is his marked emphasis on the action setting that sets Schön's work apart.

This book is framed around Schön's particular conception of reflection. It has three sections. The first section essentially represents the proceedings of a symposium at the 1987 American Educational Research Association Meeting in which Schön addressed specific education focussed issues for the first time. The second section contains research in education that follows along lines similar to those expressed by Schön; that is, the studies explore reflection in the context of the action setting of practice. The third section is made up of critiques of Schön's thinking, particularly as it is represented in his two major works, *The Reflective Practitioner*, and *Educating the Reflective Practitioner*. Sections I and III contain critiques of Schön's thinking. Some of these critiques dispute that Schön's choice of the context of action is the appropriate one for reflection, some take issue with Schön's use and understanding of "technical rationality," and some question his interpretation of the complexities and artistic features inherent in the action setting of practice.

The framework used in this introduction is designed to place Schön's contribution to our understanding of reflection in perspective relative to Dewey's original formulation of reflective inquiry and other work in education on reflection and reflective teaching. It is also put forward as a tentative interpretive frame for making sense of the different perspectives on reflection which lie behind the critiques contained in this book. It is, however, merely a sensitizing framework. In the final analysis, the reader must decide what to make of Schön's view of reflection as it pertains to education and of the varied perspectives represented by the contributing authors. On the one hand, the debate sparked by this volume could create misgivings in the mind of the reader about Schön's view of reflection in education. On the other hand, the section regarding research currently under way could encourage others to explore this area of study. Whatever conclusions the reader reaches notwithstanding, this book is offered as a starting point for intellectual ferment and excitement as we seek to understand more fully the intricacies of teacher education.

REFERENCES

Carr, C. & Kemmis, S. (1983). *Becoming critical: knowing through action research*. Victoria, Australia: Deakin University Press.

Carter, R.E. (1984). *Dimensions of moral education*. Toronto: University of Toronto Press.

Clandinin, J. (1986). *Classroom practice: Teacher images in action*. Philadelphia: Falmer Press.

Connelly, F.M. & Clandinin, D.J. (1985). Personal practical knowledge and the modes of knowing: Relevance for teaching and learning. In: E. Eisner (Ed.), *Learning and Teaching the Ways of Knowing*. Chicago: University of Chicago Press.

Donmoyer, R. (1985). The rescue from relativism: Two failed attempts and an alternative strategy. *Educational Researcher, 14*(10), 13-20.

Dewey, J. (1933). *How we think: A restatement of the relation of reflective thinking to the educative process*. Chicago: D.C. Heath.

Elbaz, F. (1983). *Teacher thinking: A study of practical knowledge*. London: Croom Helm.

Grimmett, P.P., Riecken, T.J., MacKinnon, A.M., & Erickson, G.L. (1987). *Studying reflective practice: A review of research.* Paper presented at the Working Conference on Reflective Teaching, University of Houston, Texas, October 8-11.

Habermas, J. (1971). *Knowledge and human interests.* Translated by J. Shapiro, Boston: Beacon Press.

Lieberman, A., & Miller, A. (1984). *Teachers, their world, and their work.* Alexandria, VA: ASCD.

Plato. (1964). *The collected dialogues of Plato.* E. Hamilton & H. Cairns (Eds). New York: Bollingen Foundation.

Schön, D.A. (1983). *The reflective practitioner: How professionals think in action.* New York: Basic Books.

Schön, D.A. (1987). *Educating the reflective practitioner: Toward a new design for teaching and learning in the professions.* San Francisco: Jossey-Bass.

Shulman, L.S. (1987). Knowledge and teaching: Foundations of the new reform. *Harvard Educational Review, 57*(1), 114-135.

Smyth, W.J. (1986). *Reflection in action.* Victoria, Australia: Deakin University Press.

Tom, A. (1985). Inquiring into inquiry-oriented teacher education. *Journal of Teacher Education, 36*(5), 35-44.

Van Manen, M. (1977). Linking ways of knowing with ways of being practical. *Curriculum Inquiry, 6* (3), 205-228.

Zeichner, K.M. (1986). Preparing reflective teachers: An overview of instructional strategies which have been employed in preservice teacher education. *International Journal of Educational Research, 11*(5), 565-575.

SECTION I:
EDUCATING TEACHERS AS REFLECTIVE PRACTITIONERS

This section addresses the important question of how the ideas contained in Schön's two books, *The Reflective Practitioner (1983)* and *Educating the Reflective Practitioner (1987)*, can be integrated into teacher education. The four chapters essentially constitute the proceedings of the symposium, held at the annual meeting of the American Educational Research Association in Washington, D.C. in April 1987, which acted as the catalyst for this book.

Schön's chapter on "coaching reflective teaching" represents his first piece of writing to focus specifically on how teachers as professionals can be educated to become reflective practitioners. To do so, he draws on the records of the Teacher Project conducted jointly by Jeanne Bamberger and Eleanor Duckworth. Schön characterizes reflection in teacher education as being represented by teachers who become curious about what children say and do, who "give reason" to classroom events and pupil behavior. Equally, he expects coaches to mirror this form of reflective teaching in their dealings with individual teachers. This *modus operandi* opens up opportunities for coaches and teachers to learn sensibly from past experience in a manner that facilitates the combatting of what Schön refers to as "the normal cynicism" present in schools.

Shulman's commentary begins by contextualizing Schön's thinking in the grand tradition of educational philosophy and the social sciences. He goes on to highlight certain dangers inherent in Schön's dichotomous thinking, specifically challenging the latter's interpretation of the notion of "giving reason" to pupil actions with the point that teachers are also obligated to ensure that pupils' actions are "reasonable." Shulman also attempts to extend Schön's thinking by showing how one can give reason to institutions as well as to individuals. Central to Shulman's critique is the challenge he issues to Schön's basic dichotomy between professional knowledge and technical rationality.

Fenstermacher picks up this point by characterizing Schön's dichotomy as a "Good versus Evil" struggle, in which technical rationality appears to become an evil force. Like Shulman, Fenstermacher criticizes such bifurcated thinking. But Fenstermacher is much more concerned about Schön's use of "epistemology." As a philosopher, Fenstermacher has serious misgivings about Schön's use of a "new epistemology of practice" and remains unconvinced that Schön has warranted grounds for making such a claim. In a similar vein, he also contests Schön's conception of what constitutes "research." At the same time, however, Fenstermacher acknowledges that Schön has introduced a most useful rhetoric for talking about professionals' "knowing-in-action," which he (Fenstermacher) argues can be appropriately studied through investigations of teachers' practical arguments.

The final chapter contains a critique written from a very different perspective. As a practitioner herself, Gilliss is not convinced that what Schön has discovered in other professions, such as music and design, has any relevance to the world in which professional teachers find themselves. Indeed, she argues that, because of the particularly dynamic context of teaching, there is little time for teachers to engage in the kind of reflection that Schön espouses. Further, she questions Schön's contention that "technical rationality" has invaded a minor profession like teaching to its detriment. Gilliss sees little evidence of a permeating sense of technical rationality in teaching (except among some administrators and bureaucrats) and ends by suggesting that what teaching may lack more than anything as a profession is the technical knowledge base Schön appears to discount.

1

COACHING REFLECTIVE TEACHING

Donald A. Schön
Massachusetts Institute of Technology

By reflective teaching, I mean what some teachers have called "giving the kids reason": listening to kids and responding to them, inventing and testing responses likely to help them get over their particular difficulties in understanding something, helping them build on what they already know, helping them discover what they already know but cannot say, helping them coordinate their own spontaneous knowing-in-action with the privileged knowledge of the school.

Instructional supervision I would like to consider as including *any* activity that supports, guides, or encourages teachers in their reflective teaching. It may be undertaken through a variety of formal roles and programs: the venerable role of the principal as "principal teacher," continuing education, inservice training, internships. It may also be undertaken through a variety of informal roles and activities on the part of fellow-teachers, friends, students, and parents.

In all its guises, formal or informal, instructional supervision in the sense I propose can be usefully understood as a kind of coaching. Through advice, criticism, description, demonstration, and questioning, one person helps another learn to practice reflective teaching in the context of the doing. And one does so through a Hall of Mirrors: demonstrating reflective teaching in the very process of trying to help the other learn to do it.

Both reflective teaching and reflective supervision (the term I shall use henceforth) are kinds of research. Research not *about* or *for* practice but *in* practice. To make this sort of research explicitly understandable, to formulate and demonstrate the kinds of rigor appropriate to it, is to contribute to a healing of the breach between research and practice that has long plagued schools of education—as it plagues all university-based professional schools.

In this chapter, I shall illustrate what I mean by reflective supervision, using three examples to suggest three different functions and styles of coaching. In this process, I shall illustrate and describe reflective teaching as well. And finally I shall draw from these examples some implications for the sorts of educational research I would like to see flourishing in schools of education.

Getting Curious about the Things Kids Say and Do

Consider this vignette drawn from the records of the Teacher Project, an innovative approach to inservice training for elementary school teachers, initiated by Jeanne Bamberger and jointly conducted by Bamberger and Eleanor Duckworth.

In late February of the project's first year, Mary, one of the seven teachers then participating in the seminar, brought in a story about George "who asks me very basic questions that are so covered, like chocolate-covered cherries, I'm still having a hard time digging them out." There had been an eclipse of the sun, but George's father had told him, "we didn't have it because it was snowing."

> So he came in and said to me, "What happened to the sun yesterday?" I said, "It was up there." And he said, "But I didn't see it." I said, "It's cloudy out." He walked back to his seat, still mumbling, and I said, "George, what's the matter?" He came back to me and said, "My father said we didn't have whatever that thing was yesterday." I said, "The eclipse?" He said, "Yes, that's it." I asked him "What did your father tell you about it?" "He said we didn't have it because it was snowing."
>
> I told George that we had it; even though it was snowing, you look behind the clouds. He walked back to his seat and about a half hour later he said to me, "My father doesn't lie, we didn't have it."
>
> So I asked him, "George, where do you think the sun is today?" He still couldn't understand it was behind the clouds.
>
> I took a book and put it in front of the window cord and asked him if he could see the cord. He said no, and I explained to him that is how it is with the sun when it is behind the clouds. And he said, "But my father . . . " so anyway. I didn't know what to do. His father told him there was a really big hole in the sky; George asked me if I had seen the diamond ring . . . he said his father said it would take a real big thing to fill that hole.

The next week, Mary came back with "an update on George."

> I had to wait until the next cloudy day, so I didn't get to him until Friday. I was thinking about it for three days, and I thought specifically about something somebody here mentioned, the "where" as meaning location. When I asked him *where* was the sun, meaning the location of it, not whether it is in the sky at all which is what I wanted. Someone thought he might have thought East, West or some location.
>
> I wondered how I could phrase my question to him so he will say, "It's in the sky," which is what I want "to know if he understands." So, when it was a cloudy day on Friday, I said to him, "What happened to the sun today?" And he looked at me like I was from Mars, and said, "It's in the sky." He must have seen the look of relief on my face because he said, "What's the matter?"
>
> I said, "Remember the day of the eclipse when I asked you where the sun was 'when it was snowing' and you said, that you didn't know?" And he said, "Yah." So I said, "Well, where is the sun today?" He said,

20

"I don't know. It's up there somewhere." That's just what he was doing. He was using the *where* for location! Then I said to him, "You know the eclipse we had? Did we have it here?" He said, "Well, no. Well, I guess. Well, I'm not sure." I said, "I guess what I'm asking you is, did it happen in the sky over Cambridge?" He said, "Yah."

I said, "Well, did you see it?"

George said, "No."

I said, "Is that what you mean, we didn't have it because you didn't *see* it?"

George said, "Yah, because I didn't *see* it."

And then I said, "But it *happened*, right?" And he said, "Right." I had been on the wrong track with him. He had wanted a point for the *where,* to say *where* "in the sky" it is. I was thinking he didn't know "that the sun was in the sky."

[later in the discussion]

I said I was confused about the other day "when we discussed the eclipse." But I did ask him about the book I had shown him the other day and the cord behind it, and he said he knew the cord was there but he couldn't see it. So I said, "When I showed you that example of the cord and the book, and then I asked you where the sun was and you said, "I don't know" he said, "Well, I don't know *where* it is. I can't see it." And at this point, we were on the same level, and I said, "You are right, you *can't* see it. And I don't know where it is either."

In this example, Mary begins by seeing George as confused and ends by attributing the confusion to herself. As she attributes a *sense* to George's odd-seeming behavior ("giving him reason," as the teachers called it), she is led to discover a puzzle in behavior she would probably have taken otherwise as a sign of George's ignorance. And her inquiry into the puzzle takes the form of a kind of detective work in which her own questions are as much an object of attention as are George's answers. Her new hypothesis deals with the whole confusing process of communication that includes her initial question, George's answer, and possible alternative interpretations consistent with his "reason." Her experiment consists of the invention of a question that would allow him to distinguish the sun's being in the sky from its being at a particular location in the sky. And when she gets his reassuring answer, she confirms her new understanding of his understanding by using it to clarify the earlier example of the cord and the book.

More generally,

— A teacher attends to an odd, surprising thing a kid says or does: she *allows* herself to be surprised.
— She frames her interpretation of the kid's utterance as a *puzzle* to be solved. She assumes that the kid is making sense and her problem is to discover that sense.
— She gets curious about it, and inquires into the puzzle. She invents on-the-spot experiments through which to explore it.
— As a consequence of these explorations, or in their very conduct, she

helps the kid connect his spontaneous understandings or know-how to the privileged knowledge of the school.

Teaching, in this sense, is a form of reflection-in-action: reflection on phenomena, and on one's spontaneous ways of thinking and acting, undertaken in the midst of action to guide further action.

How might one help a teacher build her capability for and inclination toward reflective teaching? To pose this question is to adopt the stance of a *coach* who tries to help someone *do* something. The moment we take this stance, we set up three levels of attention:

1. The kid's interaction with some phenomenon (George and the eclipse, for example).
2. The teacher's interaction with the kid's interaction with the phenomenon: how does she see and interpret what the kid says and does? How does she think about it, explore it, test her understandings, draw lessons for what she will say and do next?
3. The coach's interaction with the teacher: how the coach understands and responds to the teacher's understandings, feelings, ways of inquiring.

These three levels can be represented thus:

COACH [TEACHER (KIDS' PHENOMENA)]

In reflective supervision, a coach helps, provokes, encourages a teacher to reflect on her own practice. A coach supports her reflection on her own reflection-in-action: that is, her effort to make explicit to herself what she is seeing, how she interprets it, and how she might test and act on her interpretation.

In order to get to the inner relationships, a coach must always pass through the outer one. In other words, a coach gets to the teacher's interaction with kids (and their interaction with phenomena) only through the medium of an interaction with the teacher. And in this interaction, one often finds vulnerability, anxiety, and defensiveness. Why?

Surprise and puzzlement are at the heart of reflective teaching. But this means not having a "right answer," at least for a time. It may even mean foregoing the possibility of a "right answer." And, in the prevailing sense of "control," being out of control. There is a prevailing belief among teachers that one should *know,* that there are right answers, whose source lies *outside* oneself; a belief reinforced by the schools of education—indeed, by the dominant epistemology of practice built into all professional schools in the modern research university.

As one participant in the Teacher Project wrote,

> The magic word is "answer" . . . Everyone else had answers—better answers than I, certainly. The answers were had by authors of books, producers of films and programs, administrative personnel . . . everyone had a "correct" response to anything and everything, a better response than I, because they somehow "knew" more.
>
> There is security in thinking that there is one answer. That somewhere out there, there is one right response to a given situation. If a system has

worked for years under a certain set of assumptions, then one's responsibility is to learn about that system and master it . . . The system is the answer. We must mold ourselves *to fit it. It* is the end, rather than a means to the end.

A teacher who deeply, automatically believes in right answers and believes that she should hold them, and that it is her main business to communicate them to kids, must often feel vulnerable to confusion, uncertainty, being at a loss. She learns strategies to avoid or circumvent such experiences: selective attention, junk categories (e.g., witchcraft, slow learning, poor memory), and unilateral control.

But reflective teaching opens a teacher to confusion, to not-knowing, hence to vulnerability, to anxiety provoked by vulnerability, and to defensive strategies designed (often automatically) to protect against vulnerability.

Reflective teaching opens a person to confusion, to *not*-knowing—therefore, to a rejection of belief in externally given "right answers."

As the teacher quoted above went on to write:

Boy, how silly! What we must do is develop an understanding . . . of the system so that we can explore ways of making it better. Historical precedence does not mean future mold, it means future consideration—something to keep in mind when trying out a new approach.

And she added:

it is risky to try something new . . . it takes self-confidence developed from self-awareness and self-appreciation.

Coaching reflective teaching always involves a threefold task:

— To make sense of, respond to the substantive issue of learning/teaching in the situation at hand,
— To enter into the teacher's ways of thinking about it; *particularizing* one's description or demonstration to one's sense of the teacher's understanding,
— To do these things in such a way as to make defensiveness less likely.

In all such examples, the three components of the coaching task must be combined. The coach joins a teacher in her reflection on her own reflection-in-action, seeks to enter into a kind of collaborative on-the-spot research, and creates a Hall of Mirrors in which coaching illustrates what it is about.

Research issues at stake in this kind of supervision include the following:

— The nature of kids' spontaneous understandings and know-how, the substance of their confusions, difficulties that arise at the juncture of everyday knowledge and school knowledge.
— The structures, strategies, and styles of reflection-in-action involved in reflective teaching; the logic of a teacher's on-the-spot experimentation, the forms of rigor appropriate to it.
— Sources of defensiveness and bases for responses effective in reducing defensiveness.

Research into issues like these can be carried out *in* practice, in the action-present; or it may be carried out *on* practice, after-the-fact, when practice is documented so as to make such research possible. And it can yield two kinds of usable knowledge:

— Carefully documented stories that contribute to usable repertoire.
— Theories that offer perspective on practice; to be tested in the next instance of reflection-in-action.

Learning from Past Experience

How do we draw lessons from past experience that we define as "success" or "failure"? How, for example, do teachers and administrators draw lessons from educational innovations—that others have carried out or that they themselves have initiated? How does a teacher learn from a classroom intervention or event that she considers remarkably successful? What does it mean, in cases like these, to learn *well* from past experience? And how might someone be helped to do so?

My old friend Ray Hainer used to tell a story about his aunt who was a kindergarten teacher in Mansfield, Ohio. This remarkable woman made many different sorts of material available to the children in her class and she encouraged the children to make things, indulging their fancies in any way that pleased them. On one day, there were orange crates, blankets, and a variety of objects, including a pendulum and an old clock face. The children began to pile the orange crates on top of one another. Then somehow they had the idea of making a grandfather clock, and delightedly set to work covering the boxes with a blanket. At the very top, they placed the clock face, and suspended the pendulum from the top-most box. In the midst of this creative scene, the superintendent of schools happened to drop in. He was so delighted with what the children had done, so pleased to see them engaged in constructive play, that he said he would see to it that every kindergarten in Mansfield had similar materials and had the experience of constructing a grandfather clock. Ray's aunt's heart sank as she imagined hundreds of five-year olds in classrooms all over town carefully assembling grandfather clocks in planned spontaneity.

More recently, a student of mine, Kalyn Culler, wrote about her experience as program coordinator in a very successful affirmative action program at Berkeley, the Professional Development Program. ("How we're adding racial balance to the math equation." John Marlowe and Katharyn Culler, *The Executive Educator, April, 1987.*)

This program, designed by Uri Treisman, helped minority freshmen and sophomores to

> excel in a first-year calculus course (a prerequisite for all engineering and physical science majors). Minority students who took part in the program invariably earned grades of B- or better; before the PDP program . . . minority students grades were much lower.

Treisman had taken a detailed look at how students from various ethnic groups were doing at the university. He had discovered that Asian students

24

who did very well, studied in groups, with a great deal of mutual support whereas typical minority students arrived socially unprepared for university life. These students usually had excelled in high school by isolating themselves from their peers; once at Berkeley, they continued to the same thing, attending classes alone and studying alone. Quite simply, they didn't have formal or informal social groups . . . The solution seemed easy enough: Create what PDP labels an "honors/study group approach." Minority students had enough of the skills and all of the desire and ability to succeed at the university level; what they needed, though, was a sense of "academic community" and the "support necessary to raise their performance."

Kalyn spent a good deal of her time, over a period of six years, trying to help other educators replicate the program. This is how she has described her experience:

> I tried to write a manual that would teach a novice about the details of running a program like ours. After several attempts, we abandoned this project. We were unable to capture the complexity of the program. Every boiler-plate manual we produced seemed destined to lead replicators into trouble. Requests for information about the program were answered instead with an invitation to come visit it "in action" and to take away copies of any materials the visitors thought useful. In seven years, I led more than one hundred visitors through a two-day introduction to the program . . . Interestingly, of the three most successful programs we inspired, only one resembled the original in form.
>
> A pattern emerged among the visitors who came to learn about our program. Those who created programs we most respected were more parisimonious about accepting detailed information about how we ran our program. They also asked more questions about what motivated our program design. Those who created programs we claimed less proudly craved every detail about program operation. One team of educators even photocopied attendance sheets! We became wary of people interested in the particulars of our operations, and we became curious about the types of information useful to a sophisticated adaptor—one who could create a program that captured the *spirit* of ours.

Both types of visitors, replicators and adaptors, tried to learn and apply the lessons of the program. But those whose programs were most successful, at least as Kalyn saw them, did not *transfer* the knowledge they had derived from their visit. They *transformed* what they had observed, constructing a new program specific to their own settings from their exposure to the PDP original.

In my terms, they were engaged in a kind of reflective transformation of experience. They were engaged in a kind of "seeing" and "doing" as—seeing their own situation as a version of the one they had observed, doing in their own situation as they had seen the PDP people do. In the original sense of the word metaphor—from the Greek *metapherein,* to carry across—they were engaged in a process of metaphor, carrying a familiar experience over to a new context, transforming in that process both the experience and the new situation.

Their enterprise was one of reflection on reflection-on-action, analyzable according to the following schema:

They observed in this case, the action of others (the schema is just as applicable to cases in which the action is their own). They reflected on their observations and embodied them in a description—very likely a *story*, for story-telling is the mode of description best suited to transformation in new situations of action. They observed, reflected and described, treating their story not as a record of a "method" to be mechanically replicated but as a metaphor for the construction of a new program.

Similarly, a reflective teacher builds her repertoire or teaching experiences, holding examples like the story of the Grandfather Clock, or George and the eclipse, above, not as methods or principles to be applied like a template to new situations, but as stories that function like metaphors, projective models to be transformed and validated through on-the-spot experiment in the next situation.

How may we be helped to learn from past experience in the mode of reflective transformation? We can encourage one another to tell stories about experiences that hold elements of surprise, positive or negative. Stories are products of reflection, but we do not usually hold onto them long enough to make them into objects of reflection in their own right. When we get into the habit of recording our stories, we can look at them again, attending to the meanings we have built into them and attending, as well, to our strategies of narrative description. We can get curious about what makes a "good story" —a story that is faithful to past experience, coherent in its own right, and evocative for future reflection-in-action. We can pay attention to the assumptions and ways of framing experience built into our stories—something that we are very much helped to do when we have access to the very different stories different persons often tell about "the same events." We can tell stories about it, reflect on the stories we have told, notice the very different stories that different individuals often construct from the "same events," practice using our stories as themes from which to construct new variations, through reflection-in-action, in new teaching situations. We can see ourselves as builders of repertoire rather than accumulators of procedures and methods.

All of this can become part of a coaching process in which teachers are helped to use their own teaching practice as a source of material for research aimed at the development of their further practice.

Combatting Normal Cynicism

Reflective teaching and reflective coaching, alike, are always undertaken within an institutional context: the classroom, the bureaucracy of the school, the interorganizational field that includes superintendants and principals, parents' groups, school systems, teachers' unions, and the larger social system of the region in which a school is located.

Reflective teaching works uphill against the epistemology built into the bureaucracy of the school, with its lesson plans oriented to the "coverage" of standardized units of privileged school knowledge, its standard divisions of time and space, its routines for testing and promoting students and teachers, its powerful system of incentives—all geared to a view of knowledge, learning and teaching built around "right answers" that teachers should be "covering" and students should be learning to reproduce. In such a context, it is extraordinarily difficult to take the time to listen to a kid, register surprise, become curious, and do the detective work that may lead to insight. For any such activity is likely to seem out of place in relation to the demands of the lesson plan—indeed, may call for at least temporary abandonment of the lesson plan in order to follow the puzzles, difficulties, and possibilities suggested by the spontaneous responses of a child.

Similarly, a faculty member of a school of education can practice reflective coaching only by working uphill against the institutional system and culture of that school. For there, given the epistemology and status system built into the modern research university, practice is likely to be considered a second-class activity and prevailing models of acceptable research veer away from it. The curriculum of the school of education tends to match, on the one hand, the epistemology of the schools and, on the other, the disciplines to which the school of education turns for increased legitimacy within the university—and in both respects incentives work strongly against reflective coaching.

Yet, even within these actual contexts there are zones of discretionary freedom available to individuals, within which they can—and sometimes do—practice reflective teaching or reflective coaching or both. And these zones are expandable, as individuals are more willing to take what they see as risks within their institutions. And there is, for many, a pervasive sense of dissatisfaction and uneasiness in their current work that might presage institutional reform in the direction of reflective teaching and coaching.

Yet there is also an insidious cast of mind that tends to keep individuals—teachers in the schools and faculty members in the schools of education—from taking action either to expand their own zones of discretionary freedom or to participate in institutional reform. This *normal cynicism* causes individuals to believe that their institutions are hopelessly enmired in bureaucracy and petty politics, or in the cordial separation of spheres, the ritual and the banter with which academics camouflage their uneasiness over fundamental issues. Examples of normal cynicism include the following:

— Our culture makes it impossible to pay real attention to teaching; but that's built in—there's no hope of changing it.
— In our department, the norms and incentives work against collaboration; there's no hope of doing anything *new* with anybody else.
— Our leadership doesn't see the need, or doesn't have the guts, to really work at changing this place. So we'll just have to wait for the changing of the guard.

In all such examples, it is striking that the speaker is blind to his contribution to the very things he finds most distressful in the environment around him: the lack of initiative, risk-taking, leadership, or willingness to name and publicly discuss the institutional issues that cause him greatest uneasiness.

For example, a teacher may not see that her distancing from the institution—her disposition to see the problem as exclusively *theirs*—is contagious: it helps to convince others that she could not be counted on to work at the problems of the place. Or a faculty member may not see that the prevailing pattern of mystery and mastery he experiences and deplores in the behavior of others around him, he also mirrors in his disposition to keep the sources of his anger and frustration private (or confined to corridor conversations) while he sanitizes his public utterances, except for a tone of irony that hints at what lies beneath them. Or he may be blind to the fact that his way of expressing his integrity—through advocacy, without inquiry— communicates to others around him, as their expressions communicate to him, a clear and present danger of polarization and, therefore, the hopelessness of any attempt to engage in public debate on the fundamental strategies, assumptions, and missions of the school.

The impact of normal cynicism, and its attendant blindness, is amplified when it is the faculty of a school of education who display these patterns. For how are *they* to help teachers and administrators in the schools overcome their own normal cynicism, or become aware of their own contributions to it?

Reflection on reflection-in-action can challenge normal cynicism when it helps an individual focus attention on his own contributions to the creation of an institutional world in which he does not want to live—that is, when it helps an individual see how the embedded strategies and assumptions of his own theory-in-use mirror and reinforce the features of his organizational world that make him cynical; when it helps him imagine and try out interventions aimed at making his organizational world more vigorous, substantive, and desirable; and most of all, when it helps him see *this* task as something to reflect on, inquire into, and become increasingly competent to do.

This is the kind of reflection that Chris Argyris and I have worked, for many years now, to promote and facilitate through what we call the theory of action perspective.

Conclusion

In these three types of reflective teaching and coaching, there is an underlying view of educational research and its relation to educational practice. Using the language of reflection on reflection-in-action, I have been describing a kind of research that has the following features:

— It builds on the research that reflective teachers and administrators already do—namely, their reflection on their own practice. It is meant to enhance practitioners' capability for this sort of reflection. Hence, it is research that both demonstrates and complements the kinds of research already built into reflective teaching and administration.

— It is research aimed at producing understandings useful to practitioners, hence its products must consist of descriptions understandable by practitioners, useful to practitioners' efforts to carry out their own further research.

— Its ultimate warrant, the primary source of validity in the propositions produced as results, must lie not in their validity as statistical generalizations or "covering laws," but in the extent to which practitioners who reflect-in-action in the light of them are able to use them to design effective interventions, confirm action-oriented hypotheses, or gain new insights into the phenomena of practice. Generalization takes the form of the process I have described as reflective transformation.

— It is inherently collaborative, depending for its essential qualities on the involvement of participants who are both subjects of research and coresearchers.
— It is undertaken in two distinct, though closely interconnected modes. One mode of research is with practitioners. This is the mode in which the researcher is also a coach or consultant who engages the practitioner in reflection on her own teaching, in an action-present where it is still possible for reflection to make a difference. It is illustrated, though by no means exhaustively, in the types of examples I have described above.

There is a second mode of research activity, undertaken in tranquility, off-line, which Hannah Arendt has called a "stop-and-think." It is undertaken, however, in support of on-line research, which is the principal focus of its testing and justification. It includes descriptions of events and interventions that may become elements of repertoire; development of tools of analysis or information-gathering usable in situations of action; construction of theories that provide sources of perspectives or metaphors for reflection-in-action.

This view of educational research has powerful antecedents—indeed, a powerful intellectual tradition—in the work of thinkers like Tolstoy, Dewey, Vygotsky, Piaget, Wittgenstein, Kurt Lewin, Fritz Rothelesberger, Geoffrey Vickers, and David Hawkins, among many others. On this view, research should be based on and oriented to practice. Instructional supervision should be seen, on this view, as a research activity. Both the reflective teacher and the reflective coach are researchers in and on practice whose work depends on their collaboration with each other. It is the nurturing of groups of researchers of this sort, at the core of the schools of education, that I believe holds greatest promise for healing the breach between educational research and practice, revitalizing the schools of education, and mobilizing their resources in support of reflective teaching in the schools.

2

THE DANGERS OF DICHOTOMOUS THINKING IN EDUCATION

Lee S. Shulman
Stanford University

I will reflect on Schön's ideas, by discussing the contributions of his work in the traditions of educational philosophy and the social sciences. Although he does not frequently relate his writings to those areas, his work is quite consistent with both thinking and action in those fields. I will direct special attention to the distinctions around which his work pivots—particularly the distinction between technical rationality and reflection-in-action—and raise questions about both the virtues and dangers inherent in those distinctions. Schön's delightful image of "giving reason" to students will provide an examination of parallel notions of giving reasons to teachers, to professionals in general, and even to the organizations and institutions that prepare professionals of which we are all generally critical.

Connections to Other Traditions

Schön (1988) observes that his work derives from a "venerable tradition shaped by the writings of Tolstoy, Dewey, Schutz, Vygotsky, Lewin, Piaget, Wittgenstein and Hawkins, among many others." This is an important observation, because so many of the ideas that Schön espouses have long commanded, and continue to attract the attention of leading educational scholars. I would certainly add to his list the writings of Herbart (1898) during the latter part of the 19th century, who urged that we understand the "apperceptive mass," what students already understand, know, and expect which strongly influences whatever they can subsequently grasp. Similarly, psychologists like F.C. Bartlett (1958) and David Ausubel (1958, 1967) in their work on cognitive schemata for remembering and thinking, and on the role of advanced organizers in learning, laid the groundwork for much of contemporary schema theory, in which cognitive scientists are studying the effects of preconceptions and misconceptions on student's learning science, mathematics, and other disciplines.

I make these observations because I think one of our obligations as a scholarly community is, if we find Schön's (1983, 1987) work meaningful (and

31

I do), to insist that it not remain isolated. At every opportunity we must connect it with other research traditions and activities with which we are familiar. The goal is not to rob this work of its claimed uniqueness but, in fact, to enhance the richness with which it can interact with the other bodies of work in which we engage. This has been one of the problems encountered by many of us who read his work. Neither we nor Schön have done enough to specify the links between his ideas and those of many other theorists and practitioners in education and related areas.

Reforms in Professional Education

In the field of reform in professional education, which Schön attacks for so slavishly adhering to the tenets of technical rationality, there are several traditions that echo (or prefigure) his emphases. For example, no writings have had more influence on the rethinking of American teacher education than those of Oxford University's Harry Judge. In a slim volume that nearly single-handedly led to the formation of the Holmes Group, Judge (1982) pointed out how schools of education in America's research universities have systematically distanced themselves from the study of curriculum, teaching, and teacher education, those domains of practice that are unique to the theory and practice of education. Instead, they engaged in scholarship that was nearly indistinguishable from that of the social sciences. Schön describes how professional schools operate under "a Veblenian bargain: from the higher schools, their knowledge; from the lower, their problems." Judge observed that even the problems of education often found difficulty wedging their ways into the scholarly consciousness of our graduate schools of education in research universities.

In another field with which I have been associated for some twenty years, medical education, we find another tradition that clearly prefigures Schön's thinking. There is a tradition of reform and innovation in modern medical education that has its source at least thirty-five years ago in the curriculum reforms at Western Reserve University's School of Medicine. They attempted, (and, I think, largely succeeded) to break down the disciplinary boundaries among portions of the basic science curriculum in medicine. They replaced a discipline-based curriculum with an organ-systems model, thereby eroding a major feature of the twentieth-century medical curriculum stimulated by the educator Abraham Flexner (1925). More recently, within the last twenty years, innovative medical schools like Michigan State, McMaster and Southern Illinois in North America, and Maastricht and Ben Gurion in the Netherlands and Israel respectively, moved beyond disciplinary integration to variations on problem-based curricula taught in small problem-solving seminars. The variations in those innovative programs fit very nicely with Schön's exciting conception of a practicum at the heart of a professional curriculum. But, in a significant way, they are more than a practicum; they are also a *theoreticum*. They bridge between practice and theory, between art and science, between the reflective and the technical. In so doing, they raise questions about the usefulness of the distinctions themselves, but about that more later.

Tacit Knowledge

There is great importance in Schön's reminding us of the importance of tacit knowledge, of that which cannot be spoken, of that which cannot be articulated, lying close to the heart of many kinds of artistic expertise and even professional judgment. But I am not sanguine about the sufficiency of tacit knowledge when we speak of educating the professional educator.

Philosophers of education have distinguished between training and educating in part by pointing out the differences between teaching without reasons and teaching with explanations and understanding. To educate is to teach in a way that includes an account of why you do as you do. While tacit knowledge may be characteristic of many things that teachers do, our obligation as teacher educators must be to make the tacit explicit. Teachers will become better educators when they can begin to have explicit answers to the questions, "How do I know what I know? How do I know the reasons for what I do? Why do I ask my students to perform or think in particular ways?" The capacity to answer such questions not only lies at the heart of what we mean by becoming skilled as a teacher; it also requires a combining of reflection on practical experience and reflection on theoretical understanding.

Distinctions and the Dangers of Dichotomies

I was educated by Joe Schwab to think like a Deweyan, and as a Deweyan I have developed a strong immune-response to dichotomies. (I will try to avoid the plague of the Deweyan enemy of dichotomies who begins his talks by saying, "There are basically two kinds of dichotomy . . . ") Schön delights in and perpetuates dichotomies. He offers the dichotomy between school knowledge and reflection-in-action, between teaching and coaching, between technical rationality and artistry, between the determinate and the indeterminate. I worry that his divided worlds are too neat, too clean—and quite misleading.

The dichotomy is a wonderful rhetorical device. It captures our attention and sharpens the lines of our arguments. That is why Dewey always began his own analyses with magnificent dichotomies which he built up layer by layer until one felt obligated to choose one side or the other. He then dealt with the discomfort so created by helping his reader to see that there was virtue on both sides of the divide, and that there was a deeper set of principles through which the dichotomy could be resolved. I therefore await with impatience the publication of Schön's third book on reflective practice in which he will go beyond these dichotomies to help us to understand why there is, in fact, an insufficient portrayal of the ways the world of practice is organized.

At times I find that "technical rationality" is uttered with the same emotional tone that "secular humanism" holds for fundamentalists. We are told that the perspectives of school knowledge or technical rationality "leave no room" for certain more reflective, artistic, or responsive processes. In practice, such assertions will simply not hold up. While the extreme form of routinized teacher can surely be contrasted sharply with a responsive and sensitive progressive educator, most of the teaching world does not parse so readily into extreme groups. Indeed, most teachers are capable of teaching in a manner that combines the technical and the reflective, the theoretical and practical, the universal and the concrete that Schön so eloquently seeks. Schön's important contribution has been to render this often obscured aspect of teaching more apparent. In doing so, he has helped all of us to understand more clearly what we are striving to accomplish as professional educators.

Dichotomy and the Notion of Giving Reason

One of the ideas lying at the heart of Schön's thinking is the notion of giving the learner reason, of somehow treating the learner's own thoughts and judgments as worthy of serious consideration and examination. Our first obligation as educators, as I once heard mathematician Max Bieberman argue, is to ask how we can construe the error we just heard a pupil make as intrinsically reasonable. What must be going on in the mind of the learner to make the apparent error we have just observed seem reasonable to that learner? We give the child reason when we treat his responses with that kind of respect.

We must understand, however—and this is the essential problem with the sharp dichotomy between technical rationality and artistry—that teachers cannot simply discharge their pedagogical responsibilities by giving the child or the professional student reason. It is not enough merely to celebrate the reasons for the student's judgments or actions. Our obligations are not discharged until what is reasoned has been married to what is *reasonable*. What a learner finds reasons for doing are not always what we as teachers or teachers of teachers would wish to encourage as reasonable.

We find a classic example from mathematics teaching, the case study of Benny conducted and published by Erlwanger and Byers (1984). Benny holds all kinds of reasons for claiming all kinds of idiosyncratic and often bizarre rules for arithmetic computation. The researchers interview Benny well enough to elicit both his views of mathematics and his reasons for believing so. We can, through reading and analyzing the case study, give Benny   reason. But if we are his teachers, we have an obligation to make his mathematics reasonable. In this example, the traditions of technical rationality and reflection-in-action must come together. They are not competing principles, not irresolvable dichotomies. The challenge, as Schön stresses in his descriptions of the reflective practicum, is to accomplish a merger of the two perspectives. We must find ways to bring Benny's reasoning to the surface, to challenge it, and eventually to inform it.

Schön places great emphasis on the importance of surprise and of discerning the indeterminate. But surprise presupposes knowing or expecting something in the first place. One needs determinate understandings to comprehend that what one is confronting is not simply chaotic but indeterminate, thus falling outside the boundaries where algorithms or rules of thumb can be employed. Without a base of technical rationality, therefore, surprise of certain kinds may well be impossible.

I remember Robert Merton (1980) writing about W.I. Thomas' famous sociological "law" that asserts, "situations defined as real are real in their consequences." This was Thomas' way of stating that, as a sociologist, his job was first to discover how people defined situations with themselves. Only then could he explain why they acted as they did. He was arguing, more than fifty years ago, for the importance of giving the person reason. But Merton added a corollary to Thomas' law, that nicely captures the distinction between what is reasoned and what is reasonable. "Real situations not defined as real are still real in their consequences." In other words, our interactions with the world are not all instances of phenomenology. There exists a world out there that does behave according to some principles whether or not a given individual or group chooses to believe in them. As before, we need a continuous interplay between the two principles of technical rationality and reflection-in-action.

Giving Reason to Institutions

Schön argues for the creation of institutions that would be organized to foster the development of reflection-in-action. This is a worthy goal and one which I applaud. How one goes about creating such institutions, however, is a fascinating problem. When I was on the faculty of Michigan State University during the late 1960s and early 1970s, we were inventing a medical school curriculum that was problem based and we faced a real dilemma (Elstein, Shulman & Sprafka, 1978). We wanted to create a problem-based curriculum that would dissolve disciplinary and subspecialty boundaries but would instead use clinical cases and problems as the centerpieces of the program. We valued such a curriculum because even then we understood how some of the problems Schön delineates in architecture and other professional schools inhibit effective professional education. Our dilemma was that the more we attempted to integrate the curriculum, the more we had to rationalize the curricular and programmatic organization in which that curriculum was embedded. That is, a program that values integration and reflection must be more highly organized and coordinated than one in which the disciplines are permitted to hold sway.

One of the virtues of the insane way in which universities are currently organized is that they are loosely coupled systems. It is not necessary for all members of a university faculty to share a coherent, internally consistent view of ideal education in order for the university to function effectively. Loosely coupled systems are particularly resilient and adaptive to the unpredictable qualities of an educational system. The kind of education that bridges theory and practice, technique and reason, which both Schön and I would advocate, creates a difficult problem for educational planners. It is much more difficult to maintain flexibility in a program for the individuals undertaking it if everything must be integrated with everything else. This is what I call the institutional or macro-level problem of blending the technical with the reflective or artistic.

We encounter the micro-level problem of blending when we observe a teacher attempting to integrate the universal with the particular, the general with the specific, in the context of a particular classroom. I insist on calling what this individual does ''teaching'' rather than ''coaching,'' which seems to be Schön's favored term when he describes instructing of a kind that remains close to the concrete reality and constantly plays off theory and practice. I will not tolerate a definition of teaching that excludes from it everything that is truly educative, reserving the word ''coaching'' for that more lofty and virtuous endeavor. Yet, if I am educating teachers, how do I manage to focus my students' attention dialectically between general principles and concrete problems?

Case Methods

For this purpose, I have been very much taken with the need to develop and elaborate case methods and case literature for the education of teachers. When done well, the approach begins to resemble the kind of atmosphere you observe in the best business schools, as well as in the most innovative schools of medicine. Teacher education desperately needs its own kind of momentum around the development of case methods.

I hope that by using cases as ways of forging interactions between theory and practice, they can become a powerful vehicle for education. A case is not merely a well-written anecdote; cases extend opportunities for reflection precisely because they take the learner beyond the limits of individual experience and permit opportunities for reflecting on the experiences of others. This is a particularly powerful experience when working with a group. Cases are selected and organized because they are practical occasions for dealing with theoretically interesting problems.

I argued several years ago that learning to teach involved a continuing dialectic between the learning of principles and the experience of cases. The challenge of learning lay in the fact that principles were typically inconsistent even among themselves when tested in the crucible of real cases. Reflection on the problems so created, a process I called strategic reasoning, both deepened one's grasp of the principles and extended one's capacity to wrestle with the messy problems of practice. I find Schön's formulation of reflection-in-action adding to my conviction that this is a fruitful way of thinking about learning in a profession.

What is particularly encouraging is that neither Schön is nor I am alone in conducting research or formulating theory of this sort. Within the philosophy of education, Fenstermacher's (1986) critique of research on teaching and his framing of teaching in terms of practical arguments has helped many of us see how both research results and rules of thumb, both intuitions and concrete experiences, can all interact jointly as premises in the same practical argument. That is, the teacher does not sort through his premises and divide them into the technical and the artistic; he uses whatever he can whenever it is needed. Moreover, Fenstermacher follows Tom Green in observing that being educated as a teacher entails transforming the premises of your practical arguments from primarily subjective to more objective grounds. I find this is a particularly enlightening perspective on the difference between the reason and the reasonable.

Robert Yinger's (1987a, 1987b) emerging work on improvisation in teaching draws from Schön's analyses of reflection-in-action while also moving well beyond it in applications to teaching. Having spent ten years studying the planning process in teaching, Yinger's current analyses help us see the interplay between the intended and the improvised, and the sources of each.

Finally, it is somewhat ironic that in the same forum where we examine Schön's work as an instance of a radical departure from conventional wisdom in education and educational scholarship, we are blessed with Lauren Resnick's (1987) AERA presidential address, "Learning in school and out." In her address, Resnick brings together a variety of research traditions in cognitive psychology, educational ethnology, and instructional psychology—

products of technical rationality all. Her conclusions, however, resonate remarkably well with Schön's. We have come to understand that knowledge in use is situated knowledge, shaped and made meaningful by the contexts in which it is acquired and used. Learning and problem solving go best when individuals can work together cooperatively and share knowledge that would otherwise be insufficient when working alone. Schools, she concludes, must become much more powerful occasions for groups working together to reason about specific, situated problems.

Just as Schön does not cite much of the work of cognitive psychologists in his writings, they are unlikely to cite Schön. Yet the two streams of work have a compatibility that would enrich both were they to acknowledge both the existence and the relevance of the other.

Concluding Note

Schön's recent work has become an important source of stimulation and insight to educators everywhere. Conceiving of teachers as reflective practitioners helps those who educate teachers reformulate both their goals and the strategies needed to reach those goals. It is least helpful, however, to divide the world of practice and theory into two distinctive camps—technical rationality and reflection-in-action—and then assign virtue to only one of the sides. This strategy can only yield the circumstances Dewey (1958) bemoaned in *Experience and Nature* where progressive educators defined their missions by a process of rejection, denying the value of any approaches to teaching that could be defined as traditional. Either-or thinking may be rhetorically effective, but in practice it is limiting and provincial.

For those of us concerned with the education of teachers, it is particularly necessary to connect Schön's work with the other scholarly traditions in education with which it is consistent and compatible. By seeing the ways in which Schön's perspective is related to the work of scholars as diverse as Fenstermacher, Cole, Yinger, Resnick, and Judge—to name but a few—we dramatically increase the value that can be derived from these promising ideas.

REFERENCES

Ausubel, D.P. (1958). *Theory and problems of child development.* New York: Grune & Stratton.

Ausubel, D.P. (1967). *Learning theory and classroom practice.* Toronto: Ontario Institute for Studies in Education. Bulletin No. 1.

Bartlett, F.C. (1958). *Thinking: An experimental and social study.* London: Allen & Unwin.

Dewey, J. (1958). *Experience and nature.* New York: Dover Publications.

Elstein, A.S., Shulman L.S., & Sprafka, S.A. (1978). *Medical problem solving: An analysis of clinical reasoning.* Cambridge, Mass.: Harvard University Press.

Erlwanger, S. & Byers, V. (1984). Content and form in mathematics. *Educational Studies in Mathematics*, 15,(3), pp. 259-275.

Fenstermacher, G.D. (1986). Philosophy of research on teaching: Three aspects. In M.C. Wittrock (Ed.), *Handbook of research on teaching*. (3rd ed.) (pp. 37-49). New York: MacMillan.

Flexner, A. (1925). *Medical education: A comparative study.* New York. Macmillan Co.

Herbart, J.F. (1898). *Letters and lectures on education.* Translated by Henry & Emmie Felkin. London: S. Sonnenschein.

Judge, H.G. (1982). *American graduate schools of education: A view from abroad: A report to the Ford Foundation.* New York, N.Y.: The Foundation.

Merton, R.K. (1980). *Sociological traditions from generation to generation: Glimpses of the American experience.* Norwood N.J.: Ablex Pub. Corp.

Resnick, L. (1987). *Learning in school and out.* Presidential address presented at the annual meeting of the American Educational Research Association, Washington, D.C.

Schön, D.A. (1983). *The reflective practitioner: How professionals think in action.* New York: Basic Books.

Schön, D.A. (1987). *Educating the reflective practitioner: Toward a new design for teaching and learning in the professions.* San Francisco: Jossey-Bass.

Schön, D. A. (1988). Chapter 1: Coaching reflective teaching. In P. P. Grimmett & G. L. Erickson, (Eds.). *Reflection in teacher education.*

Yinger, R.J. (1987a). *By the seat of your pants: An inquiry into improvisation and teaching.* Paper presented at annual meeting of the American Educational Research Association, Washington, D.C.

Yinger, R.J. (1987b). *The conversation of practice.* Paper presented at the working conference on reflective teaching, held at the University of Houston, TEX.

3

THE PLACE OF SCIENCE AND EPISTEMOLOGY IN SCHÖN'S CONCEPTION OF REFLECTIVE PRACTICE?

Gary D. Fenstermacher
University of Arizona

I would like to make two kinds of remarks about Schön's opening chapter in this book and the frame upon which it is based. One kind of comment is very supportive and filled with praise. Another kind is rooted in puzzlement and concern. Before proceeding further, let me say that I consider this chapter to be an instantiation of a very large set of ideas contained in *The Reflective Practitioner* (1983) and in *Educating the Reflective Practitioner* (1987). So I shall pull away somewhat from the chapter on instructional supervision and discuss what seems to me to be the larger context of Schön's conceptions of practice.

The first item of praise is for providing us with a new rhetoric. Reflection-in-action, indeterminate zones, rigor versus relevance, and artistry are all wonderful ways to talk about the practical activity of teaching. The second is for initiating a critical discussion of what it means to be a professional. It is disturbing to me that many persons engaged in the discussion of professionalizing teaching want teachers to be like physicians and lawyers. I find physicians and lawyers much too distant from their clients, and much too arrogant in the knowledge they hold of their activities. Those of you who read to the end of *The Reflective Practitioner,* will find statements like this one:

> As the professional moves towards new competencies, he gives up some familiar sources of satisfaction and opens himself to new ones. He gives up the rewards of unquestioned authority, the freedom to practice without challenge to his competence, the comfort of relative invulnerability, the gratification of deference. The new satisfactions open to him are largely those of discovery about the meanings of his advice to clients, about his knowledge and practice, and about himself. (p. 299)

This conception of a professional is far more consistent with my ideal of what teaching is than the traditional concepts of a professional.

A final appreciative comment concerns Schön's endeavor to address a number of important issues dealing with instructional supervision in the opening of this book. Having recently explored some of the literature in clinical supervision, it is increasingly clear to me how much of a contribution the work on reflective practice can make to the literature in clinical supervision. Moreover, the field of clinical supervision may be especially valuable for Schön as a source of interesting perspectives and case studies.

Some Concerns Over Schön's Account of the World of Practice

Now let me turn to matters that were an occasion of surprise and puzzlement for me as I read *The Reflective Practitioner, Educating the Reflective Practitioner,* and the chapter in this book. First, a matter of concern. Two very important concepts are quite loosely used by Schön. The first is the concept of epistemology. Schön talks often about the epistemology of practice, which he calls "technical rationality," contrasting it to a new or alternative epistemology of practice which is called "reflective practice." This use of the term "epistemology" is quite puzzling to me. Perhaps it's because I was bred as a philosopher, and I understand the word "epistemology" to be the examination of knowledge, evidence, belief, the credibility of our claims, etc., all of which I take to be much the opposite of what Schön is trying to talk about when he discusses reflective practice.

The second term used more loosely than I wish were the case is "research." I wonder, as I note Schön's use of the term, whether he and I are thinking of the same thing. I do not consider myself a positivist or a strict experimentalist. But I would not call any form of systematic thinking "research." There are canons of inquiry and methodology that control research endeavors. These canons do not appear to be applicable in the cases Schön uses to illustrate his argument that reflective practice is a fruitful area for practitioner-based research. Thus to call the product of this work "research" endangers it. It may deceive people who might think they are doing research, then submit it to their academic colleagues in the expectation of salary reward and promotion, only to find that our peers do not count what we are doing as research.

A second concern is what I perceive to be Schön's ambivalence in *describing* the world of reflection and practice as he sees it and when he is *prescribing* a course of action for the reader. Philosophers use the term "normative" in this context, when one is being "prescriptive." It is difficult to determine where in his writing the descriptive Schön stops and the normative or prescriptive Schön begins. This difference is important because, if one were to test his claims, we would want to hold him accountable only for his descriptive claims, his claims about what is there in the world as he sees it. If we were to examine the prescriptive claims, different kinds of questions would be in order. I find it difficult to determine which kinds of questions to bring to bear at which times.

Finally, after all the discussion about technical rationality and reflective practice, I finish his works still not knowing the place of science in reflective action or even in reflection on reflective practice. Consider this quotation from John Dewey in his 1899 Presidential address to the American Psychological Association:

> The decisive matter is the extent to which the ideas of the theorist actually project

themselves through the kind offices of the middleman into the consciousness of the practitioner. It is the participation by the practical man in theory through the agency of linking science that determines at once the effectiveness of the work done and the moral freedom and personal development of the one engaged in it. (1965, p. 301)

Dewey is referring here to the idea that, if we keep the practitioner divorced from the science and theory, the practitioner is thereby enslaved. He thought that was as true of the physician as it is of the factory workman. One reason physicians have gained their freedom is that they have seized their science, and one of the reasons that the working persons remain enslaved is that they remain separated from their science. As I reflect on Schön's argument, I wonder about its consequences for keeping us separated from our social science (the social and behavioral sciences). Thus the possibility that, as appealing as the notion of reflective practice appears, to embrace it is to risk a kind of enslavement. And so it remains a matter of considerable question and concern to me how science finds its way into the thinking and practice of teachers. For I think it must, and the route that I have been examining over the last several years is that of practical arguments.

Teachers' Practical Arguments[1]

After searching for a plausible account of how the findings of educational research might relate to practice, I recently argued (Fenstermacher, 1986, 1987) that Green's (1976) notion of a practical argument might present a reasonable solution to this seeming dilemma. By practical argument is meant a reasonably coherent chain of reasoning leading from the expression of some desired end state, through various types of premises to an intention to act in a particular way. Among the types of premises intervening between the expression of an end state and an intention to act are those that are empirical, and those that are primarily situational in character. While there may be other types of premises, these two types are sufficient to explain the notion of practical arguments.

The situational premises describe the specific circumstances at hand; e.g., what is the situation of this teacher, in this setting, at this time. The situational premises are context-dependent and are required in order to complete the chain of reasoning from desired end state to intention to act. The empirical premises express testable claims the teacher makes about the way students learn, what students may be capable of learning, how to diagnose and remediate difficulties, how to teach certain content to certain children, and a host of other conceptions the teacher has that could be or have already been

---

[1]This section and the section following this section are adapted, with slight revisions, from Fenstermacher, G.D. (1987). A Reply to My Critics. *Educational Theory, 37*(4), pp. 413-421. The granting of permission to reprint these sections by the Office of Patents and Copyright of the University of Illinois and the editorial office of *Educational Theory* is gratefully acknowledged.

submitted to some sort of formal empirical scrutiny.

The empirical premises, then, are the link between the findings of educational research and the practices of the teacher. They also make it possible to say with some clarity and precision how research connects to practice. Research connects to practice when research is used to alter the truth value of existing empirical premises, when it is used to complete or to modify empirical premises, or when it serves to introduce new empirical premises into the practical arguments in the minds of teachers.

The concept of practical argument is an attractive approach to the problem of how research links to practice because (1) it permits a wide range of scientific research programs to impact on teaching practice; (2) it evokes a conception of the practitioner as a thinking, complex agent, rather than as an automaton who simply puts the findings of research into practice; and (3) it permits conceptions of teaching and teacher education that make use of normative theories of education, such as those described by Maxine Greene (1986).

By invoking practical arguments as a way of understanding the connection between research and practice, research undertaken from a wide variety of methodological perspectives may prove useful to the advancement of teaching. Some theorists argue that, if social and behavioral science research is to acknowledge and account for what is essential to being a person, then its theory and suppositions must be rooted in an epistemology and philosophy of mind which incorporate an adequate conception of purpose, free will, intention, and so forth. As appealing as this reasoning may be, it does not, in my view, account for how we make use of knowledge in action.

Research that is rooted in some proper conception of human agency (whatever that is) may be truly fascinating and exciting, but it is hardly required in order for us to make use of formal social and behavioral research in humanistic ways. Human beings are capable of analyzing, interpreting, adapting, and placing research in an action context, and thereby bringing to it the needed normative dimensions for action. Given this capability, research programs in education may be broader in theory and method than some have argued (though not so broad as to amount to the anarchy of which Feyerabend (1975) wrote). This methodological pluralism has the advantage of offering a large supply of evidence which teachers may use to appraise the empirical premises in their practical arguments. It also permits educational researchers to undertake research absent of certain highly prescriptive epistemic and axiological conditions imposed by some of the more recent versions of philosophy of social science and philosophy of mind.

The second value of practical arguments is that they represent the teacher as a purposive, thinking agent in the classroom. The notion of practical arguments does much to strengthen the claims of those who contend that teaching is a complex, intentional endeavor, requiring a great range and depth of professional judgment (Shulman, 1986, 1987). This complexity and need for judgment are easily overlooked by policymakers and educational administrators in need of improved student achievement results, and thus ready to embrace almost any program that claims to rest on scientific research. As research results are released showing that certain practices are correlated with student achievements, the temptation of some decision makers is to insist that these practices be implemented in the classroom. Pointing out that research results do not easily generalize to specific classroom contexts, that they do not account for intentionality, or that current methods of doing research are seldom adequate to yield findings trustworthy enough to mandate in different school settings does not usually diminish the zeal of the regulators. What may forestall instrusive mandates, however, is to acknowledge that the teacher's ability to effect gains in achievement (along with other critical outcomes of education) is dependent upon that teacher's skills and expertise in determining how the circumstances of this particular classroom are best handled, given the knowledge and understanding available to the profession.

The third reason for employing the notion of practical arguments is that they offer a way of introducing normative considerations into what may otherwise be conceptions of teaching driven only by behavioral research, experience, or both. Few of us are satisfied with conceptions of teaching that rest on the metaphor of transporting the content of text, film, museum, or workbook to the mind of the learner. Nor does the teacher as producer of learning gains on standardized tests of achievement hold appeal for many philosophers. Though unhappy with such simple-minded views of teaching, we have not made much progress on finding alternatives that are grounded in defensible normative theories of education and are efficacious in the setting of modern school classrooms. Practical arguments offer a way to join normative theory of education with empirical descriptions of effective teaching.

Practical arguments begin with the expression of desired end states. These end states describe the larger aims and goals of education, such as seeking to develop a sense of honesty, fairmindedness, and mutual regard in the learner. Subsequent premises describe the teacher's beliefs about how these end states are attained, the circumstances under which one is likely to attain them, and the situation that is at hand in this instance. This format requires bringing together means and ends, goals, the means for realizing these goals, the knowledge and techniques that bear on the successful attainment of the goals, and how the context of teacher and learner sustains or shatters the pedagogical relationship.

Thus, practical arguments may serve as a kind of analytical device for understanding how teachers think about what they do, for helping teachers gain a sense of the basis for their actions, and for helping teachers use defensible theory and good research to advance their pedagogical competence. This happens when, for example, an inquirer in the classroom observes the teacher at length, trying to account for what the teacher does. From observations of and conversations with the teacher, the initial premises are developed. The teacher is encouraged to analyze them, in discussion with the inquirer, until a reasonably complete and coherent account of the teacher's thinking about the observed activity is in hand. Then the inquirer might raise questions with the teacher about the completeness of the argument, about its overarching moral goals, about the accuracy and soundness of its empirical claims, or about the teacher's description of the present situation. Such questions are intended to alert the teacher to possible reinterpretations, to different ways of perceiving the situation, to new evidence that might bear on the goals, or to value conflicts in the aspirations the teacher holds for the students.

The exchange between inquirer and teacher over the practical argument is the occasion for considering the bearing of normative theory on the thought and action of the teacher. Indeed, one of the general benefits of the notion of practical argument is that it provides a way to see how what is generated or produced outside the classroom can be brought into the thought and action of the teacher in ways that regard the teacher as a rational, moral agent. The next section examines this point in greater detail.

Knowledge Production and Knowledge Use

There is value, I believe, in making a clear distinction between research and practice. Maintaining such a distinction does not in any way prevent research from being done on practice, nor does it prohibit practitioners from doing research. To do science is to undertake a specific kind of controlled inquiry, subject to publicly defensible canons of epistemic adequacy. I would describe the researcher as one who employs scientific canons to produce dependable scientific knowledge, while the practitioner is one who applies or uses this knowledge in practice.

Schön and others have pointed out that a practitioner can produce knowledge in the course of practice. Normally, however, I would not regard that knowledge as scientific knowledge. When a person is teaching, he or she may be using research results or insights, though not generating new scientific knowledge. Of course, a teacher conversant with research methods may do research as well as teach. I wish only to maintain that the two activities are quite different, and that we are advantaged by keeping them separate.

Wherein lies the advantage? Perhaps the best way to present the argument for maintaining a distinction is to look at a passage by Schön on professional practice:

> In the varied topography of professional practice, there is a high, hard ground where practitioners can make effective use of research-based theory and technique, and there is a swampy lowland where situations are confusing "messes" incapable of technical solution. (Schön, 1983, p. 42)

Schön delights in the distinction between the high ground, where the situation and goals are clear, and the swampy lowlands where "complexity, uncertainty, instability, uniqueness, and value conflict" (p. 39) abound. He calls the swampy lowlands the "indeterminate zones" of practice, and talks about them as places where scientific knowledge does not help. Rather, what is required in the indeterminate zones is a knowledge-in-action. Such knowledge is clarified, validated, and extended by an activity called reflective practice.

If one accepts Schön's analysis, then my own account of the research-practice relationship seems to be in trouble. Schön might argue that my thesis, which he would likely label as "Technical Rationality," would not work down in the swampy lowlands; it is simply too inadequately conceived to grapple with life in the indeterminate zones. If that is so, then my contention that there is a bridge between "the high, hard ground" and the "swampy lowland" appears very much in error.

I disagree. I believe that Schön has offered us an either-or description of a situation that is actually a both-and. I can detect no bifurcation between science (even, to an extent, positivist science) and practice, such that the two are incapable of contributing productively to one another. The results of scientific inquiry can be and have been of great help in the indeterminate zones of practice. Furthermore, the logic, methods, and design criteria of scientific inquiry are valuable in addressing the complexity, uniqueness, and uncertainty of practice. Having said this, we can then agree that there are zones of practice where science has not penetrated and may not penetrate (whether because it is conceptually impossible to do so or because no researcher cares to work there is not a matter to resolve here). Hence, it seems a more accurate description of the science-practice relationship to say that scientific research can and does bear on practice, including those aspects of practice that are in the swampy lowlands. We may also say that there are aspects of practice where science cannot be found, or, if it is there, it may be of little help at the present time.

As I noted earlier, I am unable to make much headway in understanding what it means to argue, as Schön does, that there is a separate epistemology of practice. An epistemology of science makes a tad more sense, but only because science and epistemology share a common interest in such concepts as evidence, belief, validity, and reliable knowledge. In contrast, I have no idea what the critical concepts of an epistemology of practice are. Are they, like in the epistemology of science, evidence, belief, validity, and so forth? If so, do these terms have different meanings in the epistemology of practice? If yes, what are they? If not, why distinguish the two epistemologies?

For me, Schön misses a successful analysis of professional practice on two counts. First, he sets up a kind of Good vs. Evil polarization of science and practice, with Evil having the name Technical Rationality, and Good, the name Reflective Practice. This bifurcation deflects from the obvious point that science can and does have an impact on practice, and that this impact can be salutary, illuminative, and extraordinarily helpful in such swampy lowland activities as problem setting. Second, Schön would have us believe that practice demands its own epistemology, yet we are not given much help in ascertaining how the epistemology of practice is related to any other epistemology with which we might be familiar.

Where Schön adds much to my understanding, and serves as an important correction to my own thinking, is in arguing that there is a knowledge-in-action, and that this is an important form of knowledge in the arena of professional practice. I regard this knowledge-in-action somewhat differently from Schön, inasmuch as I see it as sometimes informed by scientific knowledge, sometimes not. It is not a matter of having either the knowledge that Technical Rationality produces or the knowledge that Reflective Practice produces, but more a case of having both forms of knowledge, each informing the other.

Not only do I regard practical arguments as a way of bridging research and practice, but I believe they are also an excellent analytic device for helping teachers become more reflective practitioners. On Schön's view, it seems that any instrument that has connections with a positivist or other standard scientific epistemology cannot be of much use in advancing reflective practice. Yet, as I understand the spirit of what he regards as reflective practice, practical arguments appear as good a device for encouraging reflective practice in teaching as anything else I have encountered to date.

REFERENCES

Dewey, J. (1899, 1965). Psychology and social practice. In J. Ratner, (Ed.), *John Dewey: Philosophy, psychology and social practice* (pp. 295-315). New York: Capricorn Books.

Fenstermacher, G.D. (1986). Philosophy of research on teaching: Three aspects. In M.C. Wittrock (Ed.), *Handbook of research on teaching.* (3rd ed.) (pp. 37-49). New York: MacMillan.

Fenstermacher, G.D. (1987). A reply to my critics. *Educational Theory, 37,* 413-421.

Feyerabend, P. (1975). *Against method.* Thetford, Norfolk, Great Britain: Thetford Press.

Green, T.F. (1976). Teacher competence as practical rationality. *Educational Theory, 26,* 249-258.

Greene, M. (1986). Philosophy and teaching. In M.C. Wittrock (Ed.), *Handbook of research on teaching* (3rd ed.) (pp. 479-501). New York: Macmillan.

Schön, D.A. (1983). *The reflective practitioner: How professionals think in action.* New York: Basic Books.

Schön, D.A. (1987). *Educating the reflective practitioner: Toward a new design for teaching and learning in the professions.* San Francisco: Jossey-Bass.

Shulman, L.S. (1986). Paradigms and research programs in the study of teaching: A contemporary perspective. In M.C. Wittrock (Ed.). *Handbook of research on teaching.* (3rd ed.) (pp. 3-36). New York: Macmillan.

Shulman, L.S. (1987). Knowledge and teaching: Foundations of the new reform. *Harvard Educational Review, 57,* 1-22.

4

SCHÖN'S REFLECTIVE PRACTITIONER: A MODEL FOR TEACHERS?

Geraldine Gilliss
Canadian Teachers' Federation

Donald Schön is one of a number of individuals who have recently advanced the view that professional practice could be improved if practitioners were encouraged to reflect more upon their actions, rather than simply rely on the knowledge that is gained in their professional studies. Some of these individuals propose a form of reflective teaching which is based in recent research-generated knowledge about the nature of good teaching; see, for example, Cruickshank (1987), Wildman and Niles (1987). Schön, however, goes one step further. In effect, he abandons research knowledge and insists that reflection, which he believes to be the artistry of the competent practitioner, be preferred over increased technical knowledge as a means of improving professional practice.

Schön (1983, 1987) argues that it is the capacity of successful practitioners to "reflect-in-action" which enables them to deal with unique, uncertain, and conflicting cases, which cannot readily be resolved, if at all, by reference to knowledge developed in the technical/rational tradition. These "artists" of professional practice are able to reflect upon actions which are in progress, let the situations "talk back to them," and invent solutions to be implemented before the action is complete—that is to say, when they may still affect the outcome of the action. They do not simply solve problems; they reframe problems. As they reflect and act, they actually carry out a sort of research.

Schön argues that artistry, in this sense, has been neglected in the preparation of professionals, although it may be as much needed as technical knowledge. In fact, without this artistry, practitioners may improperly restrict themselves within the confines of their disciplines and, as a consequence, fail to offer appropriate solutions in difficult cases.

Casting about for a model of the kind of preparation that would encourage the development of artistry, Schön turns to the schools of design and music, which are deliberately planned to develop artists. These schools, he suggests, are grounded in practice rather than theory, and frequently involve a form of coaching which itself exemplifies "reflection-in-action." After developing and examining several case studies of teachers and students in these schools, Schön concludes that professional preparation should generally include a reflective practicum.

There are certain aspects of Schön's presentation which are quite attractive. It is hard to argue with the general thesis that professional practitioners should reflect upon their actions, or that there should be a place for creativity and invention in the solution of professional problems. Moreover, there is a natural appeal to many in the proposal that the best professional practice has a certain mystique, an artistry which is more than the sum of technical skills and knowledge. (This distinction, in fact, is not limited to the professions but is commonly used in art and music as a dividing line between performers of great distinction and others who are merely competent.) There is also considerable charm in the idea of extended practicums in which the masters of the profession coach the neophytes in a one-to-one relationship.

Before accepting or advocating Schön's model as appropriate to the further development of professional education, it is, however, necessary to raise some critical questions, as follows:

1. Is Schön's analysis of the shortcomings of professional practice and preparation accurate and, in particular, is it applicable to the profession of teaching?
2. Is reflection-in-action the solution to the problem of professional practice?
3. Do schools of design and music offer prototypes for the development of faculties of education?
4. Is it either appropriate to recommend or feasible to apply Schön's particular version of reflective practice to the preparation and practices of teachers?

Difficulties in Professional Practice

Schön argues that all professions are under criticism for failing to deliver competent service in the face of the increasingly difficult problems they meet in every day practice. Engineers can build good roads, but cannot anticipate the social consequences of building roads. Teachers, one supposes, can develop good lesson plans, but cannot control the circumstances which govern how well students learn the lessons. Schön attributes these failures to over-reliance on specialized technical knowledge as the solution to human problems.

There seems to be no doubt that the professions are under pressure and are being called to account for their perceived failures. Teachers, in particular, are criticized for failing to ensure that *all* children achieve acceptable levels of competence in basic skills of reading, writing and arithmetic.

While one may agree that the criticisms and pressures are present, it is another matter to argue that the fault lies with the specialized technical knowledge that has been imparted to professionals. Rather, the problem seems to lie with the difficulty experienced by society in coordinating activities within various specialties. For example, the failure of certain students to learn has been exhaustively studied and found to be attributable to such factors as malnutrition, poverty, parental attitudes, and family status—in other words to a host of factors which are largely outside the control of the individual teacher. Problems of this type no doubt face all professionals.

It may, of course, be true that technical rationality plays a stronger role in the difficulties experienced by certain professions. Where teachers are concerned, however, this can hardly be the case. Teachers are typically trained in institutions which neither conduct nor teach about research. It is only very recently that faculties have begun to include research knowledge in their programs. Moreover, it is well known that teachers do not tend to consult research findings when they encounter dilemmas in their professional practice, preferring instead to consult their colleagues or to invent solutions themselves. Schön in fact seems to recognize that his criticism of the professions is less accurate in the case of teaching by his reference to the minor professions which are "least equipped with a secure foundation of systematic professional knowledge" (Schön, 1987, Introduction, p. 9).

If technical rationality is to be found in education, it is more likely to be found in the hands of administrators, bureaucrats, and politicians. It would not be inaccurate to suggest that, over the past ten years, governments in both Canada and the United States have sought to impose on teachers the model of professionalism which Schön's argument rejects. Governments have decided that they will define the problem in education as lack of student achievement and that they will solve it through the use of objective tests, through intensive evaluation of teachers, and by imposing on teachers knowledge which is drawn from the technical rational tradition.

One might conclude that it is in the realms of politics and bureaucracy that more reflection is needed, rather than in teaching *per se*.

Reflection-in-Action as a Solution

If the difficulties faced by professionals arise chiefly from sources outside the purview or control of the particular profession, it is hard to see how reflection-in-action will serve as a solution. Reflection on the learning difficulties of certain children will not, of itself, nourish or warm them if they are hungry and cold. It is true that teachers may invent solutions to these problems, but to do so they must leave the realm of pedagogy and move instead into the worlds of social welfare and political action.

Even where the problem is more intrinsic to the professional specialty one may well question the merits of reflection-in-action as an over-riding approach. In this respect reflection-in-action seems to bear a strong relationship to discovery learning. That is to say, it makes of the professional a gifted amateur, constantly seeking to discover, and no doubt rediscover, particular solutions to arising problems. Schön's description of his own experience in building a gate fails to convince one otherwise (Schön, 1987, Chapter 1, pp. 7-8). It was no doubt pleasurable for Schön to discover that he could solve the problem of stabilizing the gate. However, a professional gate-builder would already have known how to carry out this task and would have completed the job while Schön was reflecting. Moreover, a novice gate-builder might equally well have found a solution by consulting a book on the subject or seeking help from a more experienced colleague. It is also worth noting that Schön was able to solve his problem, not simply through reflection, but by drawing forth some half-remembered technical information about diagonals.[2]

---

[2]See also Selman's critique of this gate-building experience in Chapter 11 of this volume.

To put the matter another way, there is a danger in the reflection-in-action approach of creating wholly idiosyncratic practitioners whose primary way of operating is to invent unique solutions to problems that (to them at least) are unique. Uniqueness, carried to extremes, is a barrier to the development and sharing of knowledge. Of course, it may be true that every event and every action is in some sense unique. However, knowledge and professional practices must rest on a foundation of similarities rather than differences.

This is not to say that there is no place for invention or reaction to unusual events. In fact, teachers are natural inventors. As Good (1983) put it in an address to AERA several years ago, every day teachers unconsciously carry out thousands of field experiments in their classrooms. However, without the development and sharing of a solid knowledge base for teaching, teachers will be doomed to continue repeating the experiments of their predecessors rather than to move forward toward the solution of problems which truly are unique.

Schools of Design and Music as Models for Faculties of Education

In proposing that professional schools model their efforts on the practices of schools of design, music, or similar endeavors, Schön chooses to employ a curious logic. He suggests that the best practitioners are in some sense "artistic." Therefore, if one is to have artistic practitioners, one should consider emulating the training of artists. This reasoning does not seem to follow, since it implies that all graduates of design and music schools are artistic in the sense of being successful, competent performers, whereas they may only be artistic in the sense that they are engaged in artistic types of activities.

Leaving aside this ambiguity, however, it may nevertheless be appropriate to consider whether schools of design or music should, as advocated by Schön, serve as models for other professional schools. In one respect Schön seems to be on firm ground; that is, in pointing out that these schools emphasize learning by doing. Teachers have certainly long emphasized the need for lengthy practicums within the professional program as well as for guided internships in the initial years of teaching. It is not apparent, however, that the demand for these experiences arises from a need to develop more opportunities to reflect on teaching or to engage in problem solving. It seems, rather, to indicate a need to become comfortable with the many skills demanded of the beginning teacher. When recent graduates criticize their faculties of education, they usually suggest that there was too much emphasis on the theoretical foundations of education and not enough emphasis on skills actually needed in teaching. Neglected areas, in the view of former students, include classroom management, interpersonal skills, motivation, how to deal with children with learning problems, use of audio-visual and teaching materials, and evaluation of pupils (Lang and Schaller, 1986, p. 77).

Schools of music and design differ considerably from faculties of education when it comes to offering practical experiences to their students. Unlike typical entrants to teacher education faculties, music students, for example, are already highly competent in their disciplines. One may guess that a music student will have devoted thousands of hours to the practice of basic skills, theory, and performance before entering an advanced school of music.

Moreover, entrance may have been competitive, through an audition specific to the discipline. Music students are ready, it may be said, to aim for the heights of their profession and are sufficiently familiar with the basics of their discipline to be in a position to experiment with various solutions to unique problems of performance.

The situation is quite different for teachers. Although entrance is competitive, it is mainly based on academic performance in disciplines other than teaching. As well, the entrants are unlikely to have had any prior instruction or practice in teaching. As a consequence, they are simply not ready to reflect upon unique aspects of teaching practice. They will be sufficiently occupied in grasping the rudiments of the professional skills and knowledge which form the basis of their profession.

Another point to consider is that in schools of music, and perhaps elsewhere, there is a considerable element of mutual selection. That is to say, students are always seeking the best coaches, and exercise their powers of selection by applying for places. Highly regarded coaches, being in short supply, may pick and choose from among the students who apply. The system works well enough, because there is no specific number of performers needed at any one time. It is difficult, however, to see a system of selection of this type at work in teaching, where the state always requires that an adequate supply of trained individuals be available to the educational system. As well, there seems to be no mechanism for identifying the foremost coaches.

Given that there are rather fundamental differences between both the mission and the students of schools of music and design and schools of education, it is difficult to agree that one should serve as a model for the other. If there is a place for a reflective practicum in education, it would appear to be at a later stage of the teacher's career, not during the preservice program.

Reflective Practice in Teaching and Teacher Education

As noted in the preceding pages, advanced schools of music and design are not particularly appropriate as models for educational practices in other professions. If one wishes to take music, for example, *seriously* as a model for preparing teachers, one must back off to the point where the beginner is spending many hours acquiring basic skills and knowledge—rhythm, speed, flexibility, note-reading, history of music. It is only as these skills develop that the capacity to reflect and to vary interpretations (but always within an acceptable range) emerges. Study of other artistic disciplines, for example, art or writing, would probably indicate that practice of basic skills and imitation of the masters virtually always precedes invention.

Carried into the preparation of teachers it would seem more appropriate to advocate strong emphasis on the practice, and indeed overlearning, of basic teaching skills, such as clear presentation of new concepts, than to substitute amateurish reflection on single classroom events encountered during a practicum setting. Students have some right to expect direct guidance from their teachers and an indication of appropriate behavior. The more subtle discussion of whether or not a particular behavior *is* appropriate must come later.

There is also the question of who the coaches are to be. It appears that

Schön intends the role of coach to be filled by faculty members of the professional school. However, in the case of teacher education, student teachers are usually assigned to schools in different areas and are only visited from time to time by faculty members. In this context, the natural candidates would be the associate or cooperating teachers. That, in turn, raises the question of how the coaches are to be trained and who is to coach them. Faculty members already find it difficult to provide associate teachers with adequate preparation or to determine what sorts of experiences students are actually having during their practicums.

In any case, even if teachers in preparation are offered a reflective practicum, it seems unlikely that they will engage throughout their careers in any lengthy reflection of the type described by Schön. Classroom teaching is, by definition, neither tutoring nor coaching. Teachers caught up in the hurly-burly of instructing twenty or thirty active children are not in a position to reflect upon any large number of unique occurrences. They simply have neither the time nor energy to give prolonged consideration to each child's responses. One has only to note that if a teacher spends 300 minutes a day with thirty children, only ten minutes per child is available. If any reflection is to take place, it must either be lightening fast, or the frequency of unusual events is much lower than Schön suggests.

It may be suggested that reflection-in-action might be promoted within a supervisory setting based on the clinical supervision model. While this might indeed be the most appropriate place for this activity to occur, it seems unlikely to occur with much frequency. The reason again relates to time. Administrators do not normally want to spend a lot of time with individual teachers in a mutual exploration of the intricacies of teaching. While they may be sympathetic and encouraging to teacher innovations, their normal tendency is to carry out their supervisory function in such a manner as to confirm in as quickly as possible that matters are proceeding in an acceptable fashion in the teacher's classroom. Administrators would seem to be unlikely candidates for coaching roles in the sense used by Schön.

As pointed out earlier, teachers and administrators do sometimes reflect, reframe problems, and invent solutions. However, they are not in a position to make these occasions their normal *modus operandi*. Much of what happens must simply follow general routines. Life is too short to allow reflection on every occurrence. Neither the school nor the world can be totally devoted to inquiry.

Reflection-in-action, then, as a guide to professional teachers, must apparently await some more enlightened future, when there is time as well as intention. It will, however, still be to little effect if it does not rest on a firm technical foundation.

REFERENCES

Cruickshank, D. R. (1987). *Reflective teaching: The preparation of students of teaching.* Reston, Virginia: Association of Teacher Educators.

Good, T.L. (1983). *A decade of research on teaching.* Paper presented at the annual meeting of the American Educational Research Association, Montreal, Canada.

Lang, H.R., and Schaller, J. (1986). Secondary education, University of Regina: Responding to the call for reform. *Teacher Education, 28*, 72-98.

Schön, D.A. (1983). *The reflective practitioner: How professionals think in action.* New York: Basic Books.

Schön, D.A. (1987). *Educating the reflective practitioner: Toward a new design for teaching and learning in the professions.* San Francisco: Jossey-Bass.

Wildman, T. M., and Niles, J. A. (1987). Reflective teachers: Tensions between abstractions and realities. *Journal of Teacher Education, 38*(4), 25-31.

SECTION II:

REFLECTION IN SUPERVISION AND TEACHING

This section reports conceptual and empirical research in supervision and teaching.

Glickman's chapter grapples with how instructional supervisors handle puzzles, surprises, and uncertainties in their practice. Recalling his own days as a principal, Glickman identifies with the need of practitioners to act decisively, in a manner that conveys a degree of certainty. At the same time, however, the world of schools defies and denies such certainty. Instructional supervisors, therefore, need to have more knowledge to cope with the pressing demands of such a dynamic world. Glickman's argument is that practicing supervisors can search for knowledge in order to be informed in the complexities they face or they can act with certainty; but they cannot have knowledge *and* certainty.

The chapter by Russell, Munby, Spafford, and Johnston reports a series of studies conducted at Queen's University on how teachers learn the practical, professional knowledge of teaching. Using Schön's account of reflection as their theoretical framework, the researchers are particularly interested in the occurrence and significance of metaphors in teachers' accounts of their practical knowledge. They also report on the changes that occur in teachers' perspectives on their work, over time, during, and as a result of events of practice. The metaphors they discover are ontological in nature, leading them to conclude that the image teachers hold of the theory-practice relationship significantly influences their understanding and development of professional knowledge of teaching.

Kilbourn's chapter also reports research based on Schön's conception of reflection-in-action. He reports a project in which he has attempted to enhance teachers' reflection-in-action through reading or listening to stories about practice. Stories are seen as providing practitioners with vicarious experiences which represent a variant of a practitioner's reflection on the practice of another. The project he reports consists of teachers reflecting on several vignettes of practice in a manner that exemplifies the need in classroom teaching to "give reasons" to pupil actions. Kilbourn sees reason giving on the part of teacher and students as central to the concept of teaching. Reflecting on vignettes not only pays respect to the process of giving reason but also helps inform practitioners' reflection-in-action.

MacKinnon and Erickson's chapter is a further example of research using Schön's conception as a guiding theoretical framework. Their focus is on the practicum in teacher education, specifically on how "a reflective practicum" can be integrated into the educating of prospective teachers of secondary school science. The project explores the extent to which Schön's (1987) three coaching models are applicable and appropriate for illuminating a practicum steeped in a constructivist perspective of science teaching. MacKinnon and Erickson set out to wrestle with the conceptualization of a reflective practicum in teacher education and to identify some of the elements and conditions which seem to provide for its occurrence. They conclude from their data that two primary conditions need to be present if student teachers are to be nurtured to reflect during the practicum: first, the supervisor (or coach) has to be able to articulate and demonstrate a coherent perspective of teaching practice; and second, a climate of trust and a nondefensive posture on the part of both the supervisor and student teacher have to be established.

In three of the four chapters of this section, there appears to be some repetition of Schön's ideas. This has happened because those researchers who use Schön's account of professional knowledge and reflection-in-action as their theoretical framework need to lay out how they understand Schön's conception and are using it in their particular study. The editors considered making changes so that this repetition could be avoided, but decided to go with the text as it stands so that the reader could be familiarized with the specific interpretation of Schön used by each researcher.

5

KNOWLEDGE AND CERTAINTY IN THE SUPERVISION OF INSTRUCTION

Carl D. Glickman
University of Georgia

Return with me to more than a decade ago. As a school principal I was having concerns with the school custodian. The fellow was an older man, kind at heart on the inside, but gruff in manners on the outside; a former sailor spending his retirement working in our school. The problem was, in large part, that he assumed the role of hall disciplinarian which often resulted in verbal eruptions of anger and mild profanity directed at students. His anger would cause younger children to whimper and older students to smolder. Student resentment could be found by "accidental" walks through a recently mopped area, litter thrown on the ground, and defiant slow down walks towards classrooms. Most teachers were afraid to speak to the custodian and would come to me with their complaints. Occasionally, I would happen upon an outburst in the hall and attempt to calm both custodian and student. Later, I would remind the custodian to allow me and the staff to handle discipline. He would nod but mutter to me how difficult the students were making his job and that the teachers didn't have the backbone or strength to get the students to mind. The custodian's behavior would lessen for a day or two but soon return in full force.   I was stumped. The custodian was an excellent worker, he took pride in keeping the school in sparkling condition. He was a well-established member in our working class community. He truly enjoyed his job, did it well, felt warmly to most students, and would never touch or physically harm a child, yet he had this explosive temper. What was I to do? Which decision would work? I didn't know.

One late Friday afternoon while opening my third class mail that had been stacking up for the week, I came across a publisher's brochure extolling a new book for school principals entitled, *A principal's guide to solving the 101 most common school problems*. Intrigued by the title, I turned to the inside of the brochure to review the printed table of contents. Behold, I found an entire chapter on problems with auxiliary staff including a section on the school custodian. Believing in divine providence, I immediately sent the enclosed order form to receive the book.

Within a week, the book arrived. I told my secretary to hold all calls, then I closed my office door, and eagerly sat down. I hurried to the section on the custodian and read to find the solution to my problem. The description of the problem was right on! "Oh boy," I thought, "this author knows what's going on, now what will he tell me to do?" As I read the solutions, my heart sank. Solutions were listed as alternatives such as (1) have a private discussion with the custodian and confront him with your concerns, (2) invite a small group of teachers and the custodian to meet with you to exchange their respective concerns and see how they could help each other out, (3) spend parts of a day walking the rounds with the custodian to determine what he was doing and determine how students and teachers were aiding or interfering with his work, (4) plan with staff how to work the custodian into a positive school-wide discipline program by rewarding students of good behavior by allowing them to help the custodian with certain tasks, and (5) develop with all staff clear job descriptions that include expectations with reference to discipline so that the custodian would know when he should act and when he should refer actions to others. The list of solutions went on and on.

My reaction after putting the book down was "what a rip-off." I thought, "This author doesn't know what will work any more than I do and I just spent twenty-five dollars to find out what he doesn't know." Riding home from school that night, my immediate displeasure with the book was replaced by reflective curiosity. I began mentally to review the book's alternatives and I started to think, "Well, I did talk to the custodian, but I didn't really follow through with my concerns or tell him what I expected nor do we have an overall framework of discipline that speaks to custodians (let alone teacher aides, parent volunteers, or lunchroom workers)." I forgot my disappointment with the book. Instead, I was thinking about what were some possibilities to consider and I began to organize a plan of action. The outcome, with regard to the custodian, was an individual conference, followed up with a faculty meeting, followed with a comprehensive plan for involving the custodian in rewarding behavior of students, and with teachers and students helping to make the custodian's job easier rather than more difficult. A complete success story? No, but temper outbursts to students subsided, occasional grumblings continued, but closer relationships among particular students, teachers, and custodian ensued.

More importantly, I learned a lesson from this experience that I continue to relearn. Most recently, I relearned this lesson in the domain of supervision of instruction. After having conducted research studies, written articles, and authored books on supervision, I have become increasingly aware of the difference between the concept of *knowledge* and the concept of *certainty*. The lesson that I have relearned is that any solution attempting to improve the ways that people work together is never certain in its outcomes and a solution to improve instruction in a school is equally uncertain. We have knowledge but not certainty. No book, no expert, no research, has a correct answer to our concerns. Instead as Dewey (1929) wrote, at best such books, experts and research ". . . are sources to be used through the mediums of minds of educators to make educational functions more intelligent" (pp. 32-33). What we often believe is a truism about improving instruction is, on closer inspection, merely one alternative source of information to consider with other sources before making our own decisions. The decision that we finally make to proceed in a certain way will still have consequences unknown to us. In effect, each supervisory decision that we make *explores rather than controls the unknown.*

The Physical and Human Coast

Let me provide two examples about the lack of certainty in answers—one drawn from the "hard" sciences of mathematics and geometry, and one drawn from the "soft" science of education. Hardison (1986) cites a book by the geometrist Benoit Mandelbrot, *The Fractal Geometry of Nature*, which contains a chapter entitled, "How Long is the Coast of Britain." The argument put forward by Mandelbrot is that, given all that we know about mathematics and geometry, we do not have an exact answer.

> Mandelbrot points out that if you look at a map made at a scale of one hundred miles to an inch, the coast is obviously not smooth. It goes in and out in bays and promontories, estuaries and capes. You include these when you measure it. If you use a map drawn at a scale of ten miles to an inch, new bays suddenly open up and new promontories jut out from the sides of bays. When you measure these and add them to your first total, the coast gets longer. It gets longer still at a mile to an inch—and so on until you are crawling around on your hands and knees measuring the distances around small rocks. If you decide to use a microscope, you will find yourself measuring the irregularities on the surface of each rock . . . (Hardison, 1986, p. 398)

And then what happens when you begin to measure the incoming tide, and a wave moves the coast in by a few inches and the next wave a few more inches. At every moment in time we will have more or less coast to measure than when we started.

> . . . is the problem serious or absurd? It is certainly playful . . . It also has serious implications. Mandelbrot compares the lengths of the border between Spain and Portugal in different atlases. The Portuguese atlas shows the border as twenty percent longer than the Spanish atlas. Should Spain break off diplomatic relations with Portugal? No. Both atlases are correct. The Spanish surveyors based their measurements on a larger unit of distance (and at a different moment in time) than the Portuguese and, therefore, measured fewer "squiggles." (Hardison, 1986 p. 398, parenthesis added)

So how do we know exactly the length of the coast of Britain? We don't. We only can know by agreeing among ourselves as to the purpose behind our measurement, the distance from which we will observe the coast, the unit we will use for measurement, and the time at which we will observe the coast. In other words, geometrists do not know the exact distance of a coast because a coast has no exact distance outside of the purpose, stance, measure, and time agreed to by humans. Geometrists create mathematical models that generate approximations or fictions of nature in order for humans to find a representation that works for them.

If such is the case in mathematics and geometry, what do we actually "know" about a social field that deals not only with physical properties but the psychological properties of how, when, and why people interact with each other? How can we predict with great accuracy what will work with humans to improve education in the future? We have to agree on the distance, unit of measure, time, and purpose of the instructional coast as well as the psychological variables of the persons involved in the change, in order to make a decision. Even then, we are confronted with predicament management rather than problem solving. The eminent cognitive psychologist, Bruner (1983), said years ago that decisions made in social fields are decisions about predicaments, not problems. Problems are clear and stable and there is an answer to them, i.e., a correct answer. On the other hand, predicaments are neither clear, stable, nor simple, and each decision upon a predicament creates competing consequences or further predicaments. In virtually all decisions about human endeavors, we experience both positive and negative consequences of our actions and many of those consequences are unknown to us until after the action has been taken. Therefore, Bruner tells us to think of decision making in education as managing a stream of predicaments rather than finding a correct answer to a problem. Our work in supervision of instruction is to manage predicaments of instructional improvement so as to be moving more forward than backward towards our long-term purpose.

Easy to Answer Questions?

The chapter to this point might appear as a soliloquy of nihilism, rejection, and despair about the uncertainty of not knowing what to do. On the contrary, I would argue that understanding the difference between knowledge and certainty in our work becomes power inducing rather than defeating. It opens us to possibilities, to risks, and ultimately to responsibilities. We have knowledge to inform our decisions, but understanding the lack of certainty in the results of our decisions allows us to use the unanticipated consequences as a further knowledge base for the next decision.   To establish my point that knowledge is quite different from certainty, I would like to dwell on four questions that, on first appearance, seem to have a popular correct answer. On close inspection, the answers to these questions begin to unravel, much in the manner as the answer to the length of the coast of Britain unravels and we are, in the final analysis, left with a human judgment to make.

Question No. 1: **How do school districts change in order to improve instruction for students?**
In a recent study of three improving school systems (measured according to reading and mathematics achievement at both the elementary and middle school levels), we found no common change approach (Glickman, 1987). System A took a "top-down" approach with decisions about curriculum, time allocations, and lesson planning emanating out of the central office and directed through school principals to teachers. System B took a "democracy in action" approach by enjoining representative groups of teachers from every school to assess the needs of students in the district and to decide upon changes. The central office played a facilitative role of coordinating meetings, expediting clerical matters, and arranging schedules. System C took a "top down, bottom up" decentralizing approach whereby the central office made clear the three general goals of school improvement (i.e., achievement,

climate, and community involvement) and asked each school to set its own objectives and strategies. The central office then provided different resources for each school to help it reach its own goals.

After finishing this study, we researchers scratched our heads as to how three improving school districts could have gone about change so differently. Assuredly the consequences of the selected approaches have been different in such terms as teacher long-term acceptance, feelings of pressure and stress, and efficiency of time use. Yet, what we uncovered was not an answer to the problem of change but instead alternatives with competing and varied consequences for those who desire the similar outcomes.

Question No. 2: **How do schools become effective or successful?**

The research is consistent in regard to general characteristics of successful schools or, for that matter, successful organizations. However, our certainty breaks down when we attempt to define both the specifics of success and explain how a school becomes that way. What we tend to agree on is that all successful schools have clear goals that are understood and held in common by those who work in the school and that these goals transcend any individual teacher's or administrator's self-interest. This social belief in the past has been characterized as "a cause beyond oneself" (Glickman, 1985, p. 19). Not only is this true of schools but perhaps, all successful institutions. The norms and values of such organizations create a culture that works foremost for the interest of students (or a company's product) rather than in the interest of maintaining the organization or aggregating self-interest. The lesson appears so simple but the uncertainty or predicament is how to create such a culture?

The philosopher William James knew of this predicament in 1912 when, as a Quaker and Pacifist, he lamented human involvement in war, but on the other hand, admired the qualities of community, courage, and support that war engendered among humans. He saw their bond as a special one, one that transcended self-interest. He stated that the problem of our times is to find causes that unite people to work together, that such causes should be ". . . the *moral* equivalent of war" (Stone, 1986, p. 54). Since his pleas, we have found schools and other organizations that possess such unification *but* (and here is where the length around the coast breaks down) we do not have an agreed upon purpose, distance, measure, and time to know the length and breadth of instructional improvement. For example: Do we agree upon what the criteria of a good and/or effective school should be? Do higher S.A.T. scores warrant calling a school "successful" if the price is an increase in the dropout rate? Should a school unite under a goal of higher scores in reading and mathematics if students gain them at the expense of time in science, social studies, art, or music? Is a gain of eight points in reading scores worth the increased allocation of time and resources to direct reading instruction? Is that gain more desirable than maintaining the present reading achievement levels and providing more time to a whole language approach emphasizing creative writing or critical thinking? Effective schools research does not answer these questions of what goals should unite a school. Instead, we need to explore with our faculty what we mean by instructional improvement so that we can establish a common purpose by which to frame our decisions and gauge our success.

Question No. 3: **Who is the key actor in instructional improvement?**

A dramatic portrayal of the school principal as the shining knight of successful schools has emerged (Burlingame, 1987). Is that depiction really true? In our study of fifteen elementary and middle schools, we found that there was little observable information to suggest that the principal was the sole or prime instructional leader in terms of direct assistance to teachers, curriculum development, staff development, and action research. These instructional tasks were more often delivered by teachers, lead teachers, department heads, assistant principals, and central office supervisors. Most often the principal was seen as an encourager, supporter, and distributor of instructional leadership to others rather than the all-knowing, ever-present instructional expert that we read about in the literature. The definition of the principal as gatekeeper of instructional improvement was more apt than the principal as "doing" instructional improvement (Little, 1982).

Hallinger and Murphy (1987) have noted that, in some very successful schools, the principal does the bulk of the noninstructional matters of paperwork, public relations, and parent contact so as to free other people to observe and give feedback in classrooms, confer with teachers, and lead action research groups. The important question is not who is the instructional leader in regard to school improvement; rather, the question is, "Is instructional leadership occurring?" This is the concept of leadership as a distributed function versus leadership as held by any one person or position. In today's age of reform, we need this additional concept of distributed leadership to augment our knowledge about who to vest with time, education, and resources in order to bring about instructional improvement. The answer is that it might be the principal, it might be teachers themselves, it might be department heads, or central office, or it might be some combination. (In one extreme, I know of a substitute teacher who was the initiator and implementor of a major school reform.) We do not know who it should be without understanding the context and the people, and even then, when we make a decision as to who it should be, we explore the unknown consequences and prepare to modify roles, training and resource allocation according to our goal of improved instruction.

Question No. 4: **What is effective instruction?**

After the past ten years of studying teachers and spending millions of dollars in the development of validated observation instruments, surely we know with certainty what an effective teacher does with instruction? Sorry but we do not. We know *much more* about what the majority of teachers, in particular studies, do that correlate with certain student outcomes but such knowledge does not give us prescriptions to control future instructional outcomes. One of the key developers of a popular teacher performance instrument confided in me recently that the practices and sequence of teaching basic skills appear to be very different from the practices and sequences of teaching critical thinking. Madeline Hunter has railed against the manner in which her work on effective teaching is being applied by saying:

> Teaching . . . is a relativistic, situational profession where *there are no absolutes* . . . We *do not* create absolutes of "thou shalt" on indices of the "effective teacher" . . . We do not check the presence or absence of any behavior . . . In short, we do not submit to the "tyranny of the short right answer." (1986, pp. 70-72) (italics in text)

Last spring Barak Rosenshine, the grand synthesizer of effective teaching, was asked to critique a teaching episode and he said, ". . . it is difficult to apply any of the major elements from the teaching of skills to the teaching of content" (Rosenshine, 1986, p. 14). He found that his research on skill acquisition was inappropriate to generalize to teaching outcomes involving content understanding in which this particular teacher was engaged.

David Berliner, the pioneer of "time on task" research, found in a new study that outstanding science teachers were completely off task for large periods of time. His response:

> All our correlations are based on the notion of stability of teacher characteristics— but every time we do reliability checks we know we're in trouble, because we keep finding the behavior of these expert teachers unstable from day to day and year to year. Why? These are able, experienced people. There is something they are responding to that makes them change a routine that has worked perfectly 30 days in a row. They know something we don't. (Brandt, 1986, p. 9)

I agree with Berliner that we don't know how they are successful. However, I disagree with Berliner in that I believe that these teachers themselves did not know for certain what was going to work until they made a decision and explored the consequences.

So What Do We Do With Knowledge Without Certainty?

The argument thus far is that we have knowledge but not certainty in regard to four supervision of instruction questions; namely, what is the correct change strategy? what is a successful school? who is the instructional leader? and what is effective instruction? Given this state of affairs, it seems to me that, if we are conscious of our uncertainty, it should liberate and assure us to make our own informed decisions. My colleague Ed Pajak is writing an impressive book on the role of central office supervisors. He has found a common trait among successful supervisors to be that they consciously utilize ambiguities, fragmentation, and inconsistencies in their work as a strength rather than a weakness. With such paradoxes, they see themselves free of restrictions or dogma about the right way to proceed and instead see themselves as in control of making decisions with others as they progress towards a district-wide goal of instructional improvement (Pajak, 1988, in press).

Christa McAuliffe's husband, along with family members of the other six astronauts killed in the Challenger explosion, has warned us not to view the tragedy as a reason for not taking risks. Rather in life we should attempt to know all that we can about a particular situation, determine what our priorities are and where we aim to go, attempt to avoid known hazards, and then act with confidence and competence. There are no guarantees that what we attempt to do will work, but we can guarantee that inaction due to fear of uncertainty cannot lead to any greater good. We should be neither anti-intellectual, anti-rational, nor anti-research, for we must have the best of current knowledge to assist us in exploring the unknown. Being intellectual, rational, and research oriented, however, will not take away risks or give us a predictable course of action. To put it simply, we cannot unhook ourselves from our own decision making.

In effect, we have to accept that informed human judgment is the ultimate basis for making decisions. When we accept the unknown, then we turn to others to help us decide. If we were to explore an unknown cave, we would gather all the knowledge that we could about exploring caves, we would read and talk to others who were involved in similar expeditions, and we would review our own previous experiences. Before entering, we would use our knowledge to equip ourselves, to rope ourselves together, and to share carrying the load. Now with confidence and competence, we would duck our heads and step into the dark. As we moved, we would make decisions based on the expertise, experience, and confidence that we have in one another. The consequences of each decision along the route into the unknown would give us further information to be used for the next decision. The same is true when we step into the cave of instructional improvement. No one else has been in this particular cave so we acquire all the knowledge that we can about similar caves and journeys, and act. If we make a poor decision in schools, we find out quickly enough and, rather than stopping us from proceeding, it should provide us with more of the needed information for the next decision. It is when we believe that someone else can decide for us, or that we can control what will happen, that we stick to a plan that overrides human judgment and we lose the capacity to receive information, to educate and correct ourselves.

After a series of decisions have worked and goals have been accomplished, we might look back on how smart we must appear to others. A highly regarded superintendent of an exemplary school district told me "after we showed success, people from outside the district thought that we really knew what we were doing. To tell you the truth, when we started the school-based innovations we had no idea what was going to happen. Decisions seem so linear in retrospect when in reality it was constantly branching and returning. Our decisions were so all over the place."

This superintendent and school district maneuvered through the cave successfully and now can tell others how they did it. Others who listen to their story can use the information for their own journey, but because their cave is different, the uncertainty still remains. (Incidentally the cave analogy to instructional improvement disintegrates when we talk about exiting into the sunshine. In schools, the journey is never at an end. Just when we think that we are near the light, we find that the light is really a weak reflection and there is more to travel.)

In a study that was already mentioned on improving school districts (Glickman, 1987), we did a content analysis of references to decision making in those districts that had been successful for a three-year period of time. Basically what we surmised from ninety interviews is that people knew they had an instructional goal. They simply kept monitoring it to see if they were getting any closer, but how to get to the goal was constantly evolving. From the beginning, there was no three-year precise plan with exact timelines and identifiable activities.

Conclusion

Allow me in conclusion to give a final example of supervision of instruction as exploring the unknown. I was called in as a consultant to a school (in the

West) which was in the midst of intense, adversarial, teacher union and administration relations. My assignment was to help create a shared decision-making process for the school so that it could work together to improve school-wide instruction. After exhausting my initial plan of gaining support by consulting with each teacher and administrator, holding orientation sessions, and mediating between principal and teachers over previous conflicts, I came to a dead end. The teachers were having no part of a shared decision-making process. They did not believe me or the intent behind the process. They saw me as an administrative "set up" aimed at undermining teacher union prerogatives. The last evening of my visit, having resigned myself to the next day's faculty meeting where they would vote down my plan, I was having dinner at a local restaurant. Walking to the salad bar, I bumped into the school's teacher union representative who happened to be dining with her husband. We exchanged pleasantries and asked each other innocuous questions about where we had lived. In short order, we found that our parents had been raised in adjacent towns in Massachusetts. Shortly, we were chatting away, holding up the salad line. The next day, the teachers overwhelmingly approved the plan and two years later the school has made progress.

Explain to me how this case can be written into a textbook example of how to proceed in supervision for instructional improvement. It is a partial success story that came about by gaining trust through an unexpected occurrence. Perhaps I should write a new book entitled *Salad Line Supervision* and provide the three steps to certain edible and pedagogical success. The point is that we can have knowledge, but we cannot have certainty. We often do not learn about what to do until we are in the act of doing it.

That is both the beauty and frustration of education. There is no end, it is always a quest. Many of you are familiar with "writing as a process of discovery" as explained by Murray, Grave, and others. Just as John Updike states "writing and rewriting are a constant search for what one is saying" (Murray, 1982, p. 1), and as Edward Albee says, "I write to find out what I'm thinking" (Murray, 1982, p. 10), I submit that instructional improvement is a constant cycle of decisions, discoveries, and further decisions of exploring the unknown. It is in accepting uncertainty that we find the creation of meaning in our work.

REFERENCES

Brandt, R.S. (1986). On the expert teacher: A conversation with David Berliner. *Educational Leadership 44* (2), 4-9.

Bruner, J. (1983). *In search of mind.* New York: Harper and Row.

Burlingame, M. (1987). Images of leadership in effective schools literature. In Greenfield, W. *Instructional leadership: concepts, issues, and controversies* (pp. 3-16). Newton, MA: Allyn & Bacon.

Dewey, J. (1929). *The sources of a science of education.* New York: Horace Liveright.

Glickman, C.D. (1987). *Concepts of change in improving school districts.* Paper presented at the annual meeting of the American Educational Research Association, Washington, D.C.

Glickman, C.D. (1985). *Supervision of instruction: A developmental approach.* Newton, MA: Allyn & Bacon.

Hallinger, P. & Murphy, J. (1987). Instructional Leadership in the School Context. In Greenfield, W. *Instructional leadership: concepts, issues, and controversies (pp. 179-203).* Newton, MA: Allyn & Bacon.

Hardison, Jr., O.B. (1986). A tree, a streamlined fish, and a self-squared dragon: Science as a form of culture. *The Georgia Review XL* (2), 369-403.

Hunter, M. (1986). To be or not to be—Hunterized. *Tennessee Educational Leadership 12* (2), 70-73.

Little, J.W. (1982). Norms of collegiality and experimentation: Workplace conditions of school success. *American Educational Research Journal, 19(3),* 325-40.

Murray, D.M. (1982). *Learning by teaching.* Montclair, N.J.: Boynton/Cook Publishers.

Pajak, E. (1988, in press). *Central office supervisors.* Newton, MA: Allyn & Bacon.

Rosenshine, B. (1986). *Unsolved issues in teaching content: A critique of a lesson on Federalist paper No. 10.* Paper presented at the annual meeting of the American Educational Research Association, San Francisco.

Stone, R. (1986). A higher horror of the whiteness. *Harper's 273* (1639).

6

LEARNING THE PROFESSIONAL KNOWLEDGE OF TEACHING: METAPHORS, PUZZLES, AND THE THEORY-PRACTICE RELATIONSHIP

Thomas Russell, Hugh Munby, Charlotte Spafford & Phyllis Johnston[3]
Queen's University

This chapter reports data from a program of research at Queen's University in which we are studying how teachers learn the practical, professional knowledge of teaching. Data collection presently focusses on interviews with teachers immediately following a period of classroom observation; typically, interviews are spaced at monthly intervals. The participants include three preservice teachers, four teachers in their first year of teaching, two teachers in their early years of teaching, and four teachers with a number of years of experience.

Our study of teachers' professional knowledge proceeds from assumptions that (1) professional knowledge consists of more than that which can be told or written on paper and (2) professional learning is something more than a process of using "rules" to make decisions about how to behave in a classroom situation. We are particularly interested in the concept of "seeing as" applied to teachers' views of their work: the process of perception is regarded not as observation followed by selection and interpretation, but as a unified process in which observation *is* interpretive. Individuals vary in their ways of interpreting classroom events and in their awareness of possible alternative interpretations. Thus we are interested in the occurrence and significance of metaphors in teachers' accounts of their practical knowledge (Munby, 1985, 1986a). We are also interested in the changes that occur in teachers' perspectives on their work, over time, during, and as a result of events of practice. The theoretical framework for the research is drawn from Schön's (1983) *The Reflective Practitioner*. His account of "reflection-in-action" as a process in which professionals reframe practical problems in

---

[3]The Research reported here is one element of a study of "Metaphor, Reflection, and Teachers' Professional Knowledge" funded by the Social Sciences and Humanities Research Council in Canada.

response to puzzles and surprises has proven to be very powerful in studying the experiences of student teachers and beginning teachers (Russell, 1986).

The metaphors found in the data all fell within the category of ontological metaphors, as defined by Lakoff and Johnson (1980): ideas, attention, behavior, mind, and curriculum content are often presented as if these terms referred to objects. Some examples of grades and attention are helpful: "trying to get attention," "they really can't pay attention," "catch all their attention," "he did get a mark," "I would give them points," and "they want to keep that A." There are two interesting points to note in these examples. First, they may not strike us as being unusual for we are accustomed to speaking in these ways. Second, we may not notice that the metaphors being used treat the terms as if we are talking about commodities that can be given, taken, traded, and so forth. This is true not only of talk about grades and attention, but also of time: "given the right amount of time," "they wasted some time," and "spend more time working on class participation."

Some ontological metaphors in the data have an orientation associated with them. Again, we may not be surprised by these examples until they are highlighted: "*good* grades, *top* students," "I was right *on top* of them," "they get riled *up,*" "*keeping the class under* control," and "he doesn't flare *up* very often." The language here, as with much language about schooling, represents achievement and order or control as existing on a vertical dimension, with the conditions that are prized above those that are not. Lakoff and Johnson (1980) draw attention to such examples as *high* repute and *low* morals to show how approbation is generally represented linguistically by an orientational metaphor.

A second study (Munby, 1986b) highlighted four metaphors of particular interest concerning lessons, information, mind, and subject matter. The data contain so many instances of language depicting motion that one is virtually compelled to suggest that lessons are constructed as moving objects. Examples of this figure in the speech of one teacher, Alice,[4] and their analysis are cited here. "I just went ahead," "they're always a step ahead of the other classes because everything goes so smoothly," "we move along faster," "we'll probably even back up a little bit," "these kids need a push in every direction," "in that particular class, uh, we go very slow," "if he's lost . . . he's just going to get further behind," "they like to get off of the subject on to different topics," "we didn't get to that," "we didn't even get past those ten sentences today," "I get carried away sometimes," "if I go right back to the basics," "I hate going over that two and three times ," "I might move on," "it was time to move on very quickly," "I'm pushing and backing up as far as I can," "I thought the class went fairly slow," "I just start from scratch," "he's kind of a slow starter," "we went through it real quick," "she was slowly plowing through it," "I finally got to the point," and "they get behind."

The common element of movement in these fragments is taken to represent the metaphorical figure "Lesson as a Moving Object." It is as if Alice views her professional reality as continually in flux. But the figure is complex because everything and everyone seems to be caught up in the movement: Alice

---

[4]All names of teachers used in the chapter are fictitious.

moves, the children move, and the content moves. This complexity suggests Alice uses a movement figure to think of many aspects of her work: children are ahead, behind, or lost, for example. The fragment, "I was losing some of them and I wanted to go all the way back," shows how Alice uses a compilation of related movement terms to explain the function and conduct of review. Pace is caught up here, then, just as what is "covered" signals that the metaphorical figure has a spatial character, the coverage being the subject matter involved.

On its own, there is nothing particularly remarkable about viewing a lesson as a moving object. Common parlance suggests in various ways that courses and lessons run through time. Yet it is remarkable that the language of the movement figure is extended into so many of the commonplaces of classrooms (Munby, 1986b, pp. 5-6).

Ways in which information and ideas are presented are interesting because they coincide with Reddy's (1979) analysis of the conduit metaphor. This metaphor, a special case of the commodity metaphor, represents communication as a simple matter of transferring information from one place to another along a conduit. In the data, information is got out, given, missed, picked up, kept, thrown in. Some examples are: "get it out more clear to the kids," "it just comes out that way," "I'll give him a serious answer," "I give them the word," "give him an abstract concept," "I have given my viewpoint," "they took it as it came," "I give them an anecdote," "he'll give me a wrong answer," and "I will give them both sides."

In one important aspect, the conduit metaphor for depicting information is coherent with how the mind and learning are represented in the data. Often, the mind is a container ("things come into my mind") into which transferred information is placed. For one teacher the mind has a top, front, back, and surface: "what was foremost in his mind," "that was uppermost in their minds," "in the back of my mind," and "whatever's on their minds." Learning is sometimes a matter of catching, picking up, and taking in information, suggesting a consistency with the conduit metaphor.

There are two interesting metaphors about subject matter. Ed, for example, speaks of subject matter as something that is *covered:* "a chapter that he's already covered," "I needed to cover latitude and longitude," "what we expect to cover in that year's time," "I just covered modern Texas through a couple of filmstrips," "they cover a lot of material in a short length of time," and "you're so intent on covering *so* much."

When Chad talks of the subject he teaches, mathematics, he uses language suggestive of a sequence of steps: "we try to build on the theory," "we've been dealing with formulas," "they could arrive at the products in a short method," "we're going at this step," "how well you follow those procedures . . . and steps." The idea of mathematics as a series of progressive but discrete skills is also evident in Mike's data.

> People do math in big chunks . . . If they are having trouble, I will advise them to try the basic level . . . I always say, "Go on to the next bunch of questions" . . . If they do want to get ahead, they can because there still is that structure of the course . . . About four or five students that have dropped down have resurfaced . . . I am modulating

the course; it is going to be a cycle and people can enter the cycle at any time and just pick up and work on that section and then go on to the next unit . . . If the student wants to get ahead of the "course" cycle, they can.

Puzzles Raised by the Data

It might be simple to discount the metaphors given above by suggesting that they represent little more than habitualized speech, and then to suggest that there is no reason to expect a relationship between the metaphorical language teachers use, and how they plan and execute their work. For the present, we find this line of argument to be unsatisfactory because, even making allowances for some flexibility and uncertainty in what we count as a metaphor, it is hard to avoid noting that these patterns exist. Accordingly, it is equally hard to disregard the two puzzles that these linguistic phenomena present.

The first puzzle concerns how such metaphors become part of a teacher's ordinary speech. Clearly, many reflect our conventional ways of speaking and thinking—we tend to think of achievement as placed on a dimension from higher to lower. Some metaphors might be assimilated into language repertories from the "in-college" component of preservice programs. Other metaphors might be adopted from the *linga franca* of the staff room. Still others may well emerge during practice teaching and the early part of a professional career, as the beginner develops personally fruitful ways to talk about his or her perceptions.

The second puzzle is related to the first, and is founded on the assumption that there is purpose to the selection and use of language. The puzzle may be posed as two questions: "What roles do these metaphors play?" "What metaphors seem to be significant for a specific teaching situation?" The presence of the metaphors challenges us to consider if they play a part in practical professional knowledge.

Schön's (1983) concept of reflection-in-action provides an organizing framework for examining teachers' knowledge. Reflection-in-action is seen as the process in which a professional, responding to puzzles and surprises in the context of practice, reframes a problem in a way that suggests new lines of action. The results of the new moves, which in this instance are new teaching behaviors, indicate whether the new way of thinking about the problem is both productive and free of unintended consequences. If the process of reframing involves putting language to phenomena in novel ways, we might expect to witness language patterns, particularly metaphors, changing over the course of a beginning teacher's early experience. This line of thinking offers several interesting questions:

1. How do metaphors evolve as beginning teachers acquire experience and consolidate their knowledge-in-action?
2. How do dominant professional metaphors influence the contribution of reflection-in-action in the development of a teacher's practical knowledge?

The major questions about linguistic patterns became framed for the study as questions about metaphors, especially about the relationship between the metaphors used by teachers and our attempts to understand their professional knowledge. The significant questions are:

1. What metaphors characterize the thinking of preservice teachers?
2. Do these metaphors change over the course of a semester of student teaching and what might influence these changes?
3. How are these metaphors different from those of experienced teachers?
4. When the metaphors of student teachers and supervising teachers coincide, what are the characteristics of the student teaching experience?
5. If the metaphors conflict, are conflicts evident in supervision and evaluation of student teaching?
6. What metaphors characterize the thinking of experienced teachers?
7. Are these metaphors related to subject matter or to other features of the teaching context?
8. Are the metaphors generative (Schön, 1979), providing truly useful perspectives for teachers, or are they inert, reflecting no more than a form of casual professional "shorthand"?
9. To what extent are the metaphors influenced by contextual and cultural conditions? (Time, for example, is a major preoccupation for those in schools.)
10. Is it possible to discover the purposes behind metaphoric speech within casual conversation, and thus to unpack its meaning?

Early Analyses from the Current Study

The present two-year study, begun in September 1986, was designed to obtain data that might help resolve these questions, or at least clarify them. In addition, the study's data were to forward our understanding of the development of reflection-in-action. Five brief extracts from developing cases are illustrative of the puzzles that appear when one focusses on linguistic patterns in the interviews.

Ernie
Although Ernie has taught before, his experiences were quite different from those he encountered in his current position. Previously he taught in the penitentiary system, an environment that stresses individual programming and attention. In the third week of the fall semester, Ernie was appointed as a teacher to a "street" secondary school. Here, he was faced with classes for which he was the third teacher in as many weeks, with responsibility for teaching Science, a subject with which he was not too comfortable, to Grade 9 and 10 classes. The classes themselves were the last to be assigned a teacher, and the data support the idea that these were considered "difficult." Despite his apprehension about being involved in the project, Ernie agreed to participate, provided that the interviewer did not insist on observing the teaching at least for the first semester. Interviewing Ernie is challenging because he speaks rapidly and the topics he introduces change quickly. Yet, the effort is worthwhile for there is sufficient information in the four interviews conducted thus far to allow us to note some linguistic patterns, and to venture

questions about these. One pattern concerns his use of the word "problem."

Even the briefest sketch of Ernie's professional circumstance allows one to see that it offers a potential plethora of problems. A particularly salient feature of Ernie's speech is that it affords no differentiation of the severity of these problems. The following reveal the variety of phenomena (whose nature is given in parentheses) that he calls "problems": "Their problem is behavior," "and that discipline is part of the problem," "he had a problem in understanding the assignment ," " a student has emotional problems at home . . . social problems," "he seems to care but I think he's got this problem attitude ," "he realizes that there is a problem not completing assignments ," "let's get the problem of a mark dropping out of the way." The language suggests that Ernie distinguishes problems from phenomena that are not problems, but that he does not linguistically differentiate problems by their persistence, salience, and severity.

This is a tentative analysis based on limited data. Yet, the lack of linguistic differentiation in the discourse raises questions for the research team about how Ernie presently views classroom phenomena, and about how these views might change. We are interested, then, in seeing if Ernie's continuing experiences in some way encourage him to see the need to differentiate among problems. We might expect this to happen as he becomes more accustomed to teaching at the secondary school level. It will be especially interesting to note the language that he invokes to characterize the differentiations that he makes. Possibly, the language will be familiar to all who work with teachers and who frequent staff rooms. If this is so, we might be able to comment on the extent to which Ernie appears to be assimilating the *lingua franca* of teachers. On the other hand, the language might be somewhat novel and employ unusual metaphors, in which case we would want to consider the unique potential that such terms offer Ernie's increasingly sophisticated knowledge-in-action.

We have already conceded that the above analysis is tentative and that it needs to be weighed against incoming data. Yet, the analysis is strengthened when it is considered in light of other linguistic patterns in the interviews. For the research team, the most significant of these is how Ernie describes his feelings. The point is quickly evident if we attach the label "house of horrors" to the following examples: "Then they get someone like me who's new and nervous," " 'taping my class' is part of the nervousness," "first day was a scary situation," " 'with no course outline' I was very scared," "kind of a scary situation," "never having taught it before is a really scary business," "going through it the first time, it's scary." Similar language is used to describe the feelings of the students: Their lighting a bunsen burner for the first time was "a scary situation," "he was afraid to come in and admit that he had a problem; he was afraid to approach me," and "I tried being aggressive 'with one student' and it didn't scare him." The emotion most frequently mentioned in the data concerns fear, and it is frequently presented as "scary," suggesting that the intensity of the phenomena are not differentiated.

The lack of differentiation in Ernie's speech about emotions parallels the analysis of his linguistic representation of problems and so fortifies the analysis of the latter. Accordingly, the research team is interested in seeing how Ernie's descriptions of emotions alter over the course of his first year as a secondary school teacher. Here we will be watching for signals that suggest changes in how he constructs his emotional responses, and we will be interested in the nature of the language used, just as we will attempt to understand the origin and moment of the language he employs. As the case progresses, other emerging patterns in Ernie's speech are being studied for possible interrelationships of the sort discussed.

Carol

Carol completed her Bachelor of Education degree in May 1986, and was hired early in the following September to teach a Grade 2/3 class in a school in southern Ontario. The school where she works offers an individualized program at the K-3 level. As a result, Carol has been thrown into a program quite unlike her previous student teaching experience.

While Carol seems to have quite definite ideas about how she views teaching and learning, there is a sense of potential growth and change in her discussions of the *kind* of learning she would like to foster in her classroom. As the extracts are read, it may be helpful to observe the metaphor of "learning is an action activity" found in much of the text. Words and phrases such as "working" and "doing" and "going through" seem to dominate Carol's discussion of how she teaches and the kinds of learning she observes. The extracts are presented in chronological order so that the reader may observe the unfolding of Carol's professional development. The following statements are from the November, January, and February interviews.

> It's hard to set up an individualized program where kids can work ahead . . . There are problems with the individualized program though. One of the things being, getting on top of a kid who just doesn't get things done . . . The alternative to doing stuff like this individualized instruction and to giving kids activities to do is to hand them out a ditto . . . The individualized program means having more stuff available for them to do. Really, it amounts to showing them how to do something . . . I think you can get kids doing pretty sophisticated things without necessarily understanding them.

This last sentence indicates the beginning of a shift towards a new action metaphor of "showing" or "providing" learning rather than having students "doing" or "getting things done." Carol's discussions begin to focus on her role in creating a learning environment where students are exposed to materials and experiences that will foster their learning. The development towards this view of learning as "providing experiences" is indicated in the following data collected from the March and April interviews.

> I think the Primary years should be more exposing them to things. A lot of hands-on things so that they have the experience with things so that when they have the cognitive skills to be able to put this all together . . . I do have definite ideas about providing experience, and which things are important but I've changed my mind lots of times about things. Maybe not fundamental things, but there's lots of things that I've tried and found weren't the most effective things to do. I think experimentation is important, and you have to be flexible, because not all of your ideas work.

A final example from the data illustrates Carol's concern that teaching should not be a matter of pouring "stuff" into children's heads. She summarized her own journey towards "finding out" how best to meet the needs of her students. The linguistic shift in how she speaks about learning is noticeable here as she explains that one child who has had a particularly troubled history of learning is no longer prepared to "come into" learning with a fresh and open-minded approach, and that knowing how to learn by "finding things out" is the most important knowledge of all. This statement was part of the April interview.

> Some schools seem to say, "It's better to get the kids *doing things* faster." And I don't really agree with that. A lot of private schools seem to measure their success in terms of what the kids can do at what age. I don't think they're ready for that. He (the child) did have stuff poured into his head! He remembers bits and pieces of facts, fragments of stuff, but his understanding, in a way, has been hindered by having the abstract things thrown at him so soon. He doesn't come into things fresh and open-minded . . . The important thing is, if you don't know something, you know how to find it out! So, that's what I tell them.

Diane

Diane has ten years of teaching experience, in Grades 7 and 8, in Kindergarten, and presently at the Grade 1 level; her school is located in a semi-rural area near one of the larger cities in eastern Ontario. The metaphor of "easy learning" dominates Diane's data and is central to her discussions of theory and practice presented later in the chapter. In the following excerpts of interviews from September to December 1986, it is interesting to note the use of "hard" and "easy." She feels that learning is hard for students and her job is to make the task easier for them by discovering their learning paths, and by providing them with the atmosphere and activities to make the process easier.

> It's hard this writing; they have to know so much . . . and then they have to be willing to make the effort . . . They try to please, do what they can, but it's an effort . . . It was a force, "You have to write" . . . That's what I find the hardest is to get the balance of activity that they're comfortable with . . . I might spend a little more time with it, now that I know it was hard . . . I don't like being really hard on kids . . . It eases them into the risk . . . I think it's a more humane way of building up the time . . . It allows them freedom and to work at their own level. It's very relaxing and the children need the quiet time . . . Sometimes it's nice to just sit and do something that's really easy for a minute . . . If you can just find what suits the kids best, at what point in the day, you've found something that's really important.

In later interviews, January to March 1987, Diane's view of finding the students' paths and easing them into learning has shifted. She now talks about "pushing" students in order to get them on to the next stage of learning.

> But they need a little push to write . . . I was being a little strict, "This is business," and everyone of them wrote . . . Maybe I should be pushing a little . . . I don't know sometimes if we push them hard

enough. As long as you're not asking them to do something that's beyond their level . . . A lot of them need, "You tell me what to do and I'll do it!" . . . I seem to want to get the child on to the next stage more.

There may be several reasons for the change in Diane's view of her role as teacher. The children are maturing; parents and Grade 2 teachers have certain expectations of what students should be able to accomplish by the end of Grade 1. Whatever the reasons, the change in Diane's teaching approach is reflected in her use of language.

Nancy

Nancy is a first-year teacher who is working in a suburban school teaching Grade 2. Nancy's concerns this year have covered a broad range of professional puzzles, and she has discussed these in an articulate and positive manner. One of her chief concerns has been what she terms her "professional knowledge," or her knowledge about teaching. The metaphors used to describe this knowledge and the changes present in her language as time passes are of great interest to us for the illumination they shed on the development of practical knowledge and for the focus they provide to her discussions of theory and practice presented later in the chapter.

The following extracts are taken from data collected in October and November of Nancy's first year. The metaphor "nitty-gritty" describes Nancy's notion of the kind of knowledge she feels she needs in order to be successful at her work. This metaphor outlines for us what Nancy considers the practical knowledge of teaching: knowledge of details, managerial considerations, and the logistics of organizing a classroom.

> They "at the Faculty of Education" emphasized things that I don't think needed to be emphasized and instead left out the important nitty-gritty stuff . . . For example, attendance folders, you have to have those ready for the secretaries, collecting the pizza money, all those added little things that can just throw up your whole day. You'll get in trouble from the office if you don't have your things done.

As the year progresses, we see a shift in Nancy's discussions of her knowledge, and changes in her metaphorical allusions. From being concerned with having "nitty-gritty" specific knowledge of practice, Nancy moves to a level where she wants "meatier" knowledge, things to "go away and chew on." This search for larger chunks of knowledge indicates to us that Nancy's professional knowledge is growing and changing along with her way of speaking about it. The following statements are taken from November, March, and April interviews.

> But I don't really know the meaty things that I feel that I should know.
> "The Faculty of Education" taught me kind of an overall philosophy of what was bad and what was good and what you should be steering towards. But it didn't give me any meaty stuff to take away and chew on, it just kind of left me there. It gave me all these things to think about. In Grading and Evaluation, he didn't solve the problem of grading and evaluation for us, and I didn't expect him to. But I expected him to give

us more concrete ideas instead of saying, "Well, this is the way it happens, and this is how evaluation is wrong and this is subjective etc., etc." Well, so what? What do I do when I see a report card?

If I fail Christine, that's a year out of her life that's changed. Can I do that to a child? With all my "professional knowledge" and understanding?

Anne

Anne was involved in Russell's (1986) earlier study and is participating in our current work, so we have interviews with her taken during her first year of teaching in a secondary school agricultural course. The first set of extracts from these interviews concerns Anne's use of "structure" and its association with control. Anne mentions structure eighteen times in the interviews of September 18 and October 16, 1985; the following example is illustrative:

> Things like neat notes and tests keep it fairly structured . . . They've been having such structured classes, the Grade 12's . . . I want that structured feeling because you feel you are more in control to have a really structured feeling . . . I feel like I've got to be in control of every movement that they make or else they're not getting what I want . . . I guess I'm afraid of not having structured classes.
>
> You have to let loose with your idea that everything's going to be structured all the time because it just can't be . . . I must be too worried about not having control at all times . . . I guess I feel that I have to have the control before I can let them loose.

There are very few references to structure in the later interviews of the first year, and even fewer in the second year. On September 30, 1986, she says, "I guess they really like that structure. That's one thing, this year I give a lot more structure." On October 30, 1986, she explains, "I like to see them have enough rules that they're not acting up, and enough to challenge and enough structure to the class."

The earlier uses of structure seem to refer to control more than do the latter, where we see a concern emerging for structure aimed at helping learning: "So I think they almost like to have that sort of structure of note writing where they're writing notes but not really writing." It is as if Anne is seeking a balance between maintaining an orderly class and enhancing learning. The language she uses in describing this presents control as a commodity that can be wielded. Structure is somewhat more complex because it appears as a commodity and it is also used as a qualifier. Certainly it appears to fulfill the idea of order and organization.

A second interesting item in Anne's vocabulary is "attitude." Early uses show that Anne is concerned about changing her own attitude: "In that class I think I'm starting to change my attitude some" (September 18, 1985), and "I think the main change has been just in attitudes towards kids, and changing my idea of what has to be done for work. Like changing this idea that everybody has to be quiet" (October 3, 1985). The remaining uses of "attitudes" are to those of the students': "I just don't think they've got the attitude for it . . . Unless he gets a better attitude about it" (September 18, 1985); "The first day I wasn't all too impressed with her attitude" (January 29, 1986); "Jason's problem was because of a poor attitude . . . it's hard to deal with their attitudes when they're like that" (September 30, 1986). The notion of an attitude being an object that is held and can be changed is evident in these examples. Although the term has not been mentioned in the interviews of the last three months, we will be attentive to how it is used and will begin to discuss with Anne how she views this concept.

Metaphor and Teachers' Knowledge

This brief account, with only a few examples, can hardly reveal the full scope and potential of the current research. However, the above material goes some distance in revealing the complexity of understanding the nature and development of professional knowledge and thought, by pointing to the array of questions that arise when one begins to take note of the linguistic character of the verbal articulations teachers use when speaking of their work. We expect "metaphor" to become a powerful concept in the process of identifying assumptions of which we may be quite unaware. Also, we anticipate that the approach sketched here will assist our attempts to determine which questions about teachers' language are significant to understanding the sources of teachers' professional action. Central to all of this are the two puzzles: how metaphors evolve as teachers gain experience, and how metaphors influence the development of practical knowledge. Although we are unable to resolve these puzzles, we are confident that they will have to be addressed in any coherent and satisfying account of the development of practical professional knowledge.

The second portion of this chapter reports data that speak to teachers' interpretations of the theory-practice relationship as they share personal views of their professional knowledge. As the study moves forward, we are increasingly aware of the extent to which we are involved in trying to document and analyze developments in professional knowledge that have been masked or obscured by the assumptions that dominate existing teacher education programs. These assumptions cover a broad range, from believing that propositional knowledge can be directly applied to practice to believing that theory is more significant than experience. As we listen to teachers speak about these assumptions and how they affect their professional knowledge of teaching, we are beginning to understand the significance of the multiple facets of our research: it is important that teachers be given the opportunity to speak about their work, and it is also important to attend to the language they use to discuss their work. Significant metaphorical shifts in the language of two participants, Nancy and Diane, highlight their views of the theory-practice relationship.

The Theory-practice Relationship in Professional Knowledge

The tension between "theory" and "practice" is familiar in education; it is also poorly understood. During preservice programs, beginning teachers expect substantial amounts of on-campus course work and, at least initially, they can be expected to take it for granted that the content of courses will transfer directly and unproblematically to the inschool practical setting where they begin to act as a teacher. As experience accumulates, particularly in the first years of teaching, the fundamental puzzles of professional education take on more and more meaning as the beginning teacher realizes that much course work seems "irrelevant" from the perspective of practice.

Schön (1983) argues that the tension between on-campus rigor and inpractice relevance is a fundamental characteristic of the present state of education for the professions. This portion of the chapter examines specific features of this tension as it occurs in the professional education of teachers. The tension between theory and practice is examined by considering excerpts from interviews with two teachers, one in her first year of teaching, the second in her tenth year of teaching. Each teacher is presented separately, and then comparisons are drawn between the two cases. Our goal is to call attention to the potential value of assisting beginning and experienced teachers in understanding and coping with the puzzling tension between theory and practice as they work to improve their own practices.

A First-Year Teacher's Views of Theory and Practice

Nancy, the beginning Grade 2 teacher introduced earlier, has been unusually articulate in her discussions of the theory-practice relationship. She is quick to tell us, openly and frankly, that she did not learn the things she needed to learn in her classes at the Faculty of Education last year, during her preservice program. Because of limited classroom space, Nancy and her class spent the first two months of the year in a section of the school library. The move into her own classroom with four walls and a door brought a welcome change in November. But that event did not remove the dilemmas of professional practice for this first-year teacher, and the first quotation makes it apparent that Nancy is a very thoughtful beginning teacher. (Italicized speeches are those of the person interviewing Nancy.) Nancy indicates an awareness of how much she is learning from her practice, and she indicates that what little free time she has would not be spent reading "how to" books. She puzzles about what it means to be "professional" and about the adequacy of her "professional knowledge." She speaks of "theory" as something to have and then apply, and this suggests the familiar perspective that Schön (1983) terms "technical rationality."

> I've been thinking of something else for the past few weeks. I feel that I'm not—my professional knowledge is not good. *Why?* Because, I mean, I'm just learning to cope in the classroom. I'm learning to establish a routine, establish a trust, and all those types of things. And I haven't—that my time is not free—when it is free I certainly don't want to pick up a book on "How to Teach—How Children Learn to Spell." Maybe I'm not being as professional as I could be. But I think in a couple of years, once I get myself feeling that way, maybe then I'll pick up some books on the theory of "why." You see it shouldn't be that way, I should have all that theory and then be able to apply it.

As Nancy continues, she adds detail to her position. What she values, at the level of "practical knowledge," are the techniques suggested at conferences and professional meetings; the contribution of her preservice teacher education program seems to have been minor. She makes first mention of a significant professional puzzle: the tension between "child-centered" and "teacher-centered" approaches. Here, then, is an immediate concern that has consequences at the level of "theory."

> Certainly I know about inventive spelling and I know about things that I learned from the "Reading for the Love of It" conference, and things that I learned from Professional Activity days. And a few minor things from "the Faculty of Education" and the trend in education. But I don't really know the meaty things that I feel that I should know. Over the last few weeks I haven't been doing centers. And that's because I obviously have them more at my fingertips when they're not in centers. And I mean you hear all about being a child-centered rather than a teacher-centered educator. And I'm totally for that and I hope that's the way I run my classroom. However, at first I do want *not* to have control of them. I want them to be responsible to think on their own, but at the same time—I don't think it's a contradiction—but I want to be able to feel like I know where they're at.

It is not surprising to find that Nancy is attentive to what she learns and does not learn from other teachers in her school, and to their comments about her teaching. When one teacher expressed particular surprise that Nancy was "doing centers," Nancy defended her practice to herself by noting that it was the only approach she knew well.

> The other teachers are willing to help me if I go and bang on their door, but as far as coming and saying, "Well look, here's what we're doing. Would you like to do this?" they don't. One of them said to me, "You're doing centers in your first year?" And I felt like saying, "Well, it's the only thing I've ever been taught to do. I wasn't taught to run off dittos!"

Nancy indicates that she is very aware that she is learning more and more about how children think at a particular grade level. What she is learning about individual differences is telling her that there are no absolute rules, and this suggests that no one "theory" can guide a teacher's practices across a group of children. Theoretical positions are here characterized as "traditional" and "modern."

> Like right now I'm learning what a Grade 2—how they think. I don't know how educators can say that you should never sound out words, or that you should never do this or that. You can't. If you're getting children at their individual needs, you have to realize that kids learn differently. I feel there is such a friction between the traditional way of doing things and the modern way. And I think there's a balance between the two. I'm finding with some of these kids that there are some I'd love to give centers to. And they could work independently. But the majority of them can't. And if they don't have the basic skills, I'm not going to give them things independently to do that they are struggling with, that I can't teach a group lesson about.

Nancy is comfortable now with the "theory" of using centers in classrooms at the Grade 2 level, and she has practical experience using centers. The practical difficulties of using centers with the particular group of children she is teaching are generating concerns about the theory she would like to adhere to in her practice. She indicates that she is finding it easier to think about her work, and she could be said to be learning about "theory" in two interactive ways: as she teaches, she comes to understand the full meaning of a particular approach, and she also learns how different children respond to an approach.

> I'm more confident about reflecting on what I've done. I can look now at what the kids are doing and say, "No, I'm going to have to modify that." And I know how I'm going to modify it. I'm getting to know them better.

In one of her first interviews, early in the school year, Nancy spoke of the pressure to set rules and routines and saw herself as "just trying to get through." She also criticized her preservice program because it did not provide specific practices and procedures. These are familiar criticisms: teacher educators often want their clients to understand what they will be doing in classrooms with children, yet those clients yearn for specific practices that will enable them to perform the activities of teaching successfully.

> As a beginning teacher, you're just trying to get through the curriculum. You need to establish your rules, you have to set your routine, things that I think I learned "last year" from talking to teachers . . .
> "At the Faculty of Education" they emphasized things that I don't think needed to be emphasized and instead left out the important nitty-gritty stuff. Yet I look back at the things I did at "the Faculty of Education" and I wonder how much I really am going to use—not a lot. In one course we were given all these questions to ask about evaluating but he "the professor" didn't give us any concrete things about how we should write a report card, and how detailed it should be.

The importance of specific practices and materials to a beginning teacher is very apparent when Nancy is asked what advice she would give to someone in a teacher education program, preparing to begin the first year of teaching. She now admits to herself that the desire to have planned the entire year has given way to the reality of planning one day at a time.

> *Are there any words of wisdom that you could impart to a student teacher, drawing on your experiences so far?*
> Hmmmm. There's lots of things I could tell them. If they got hired early enough, I would tell them to get a hold of their books or get a hold of what is expected of them in Grade 2. And then mentally—do their long-range plans, have a good idea of when they're going to do it. And talk to another teacher and find out what concepts, in Math for example, are harder to grasp. Get busy making games and added things before they get into teaching. Get a good game source for doing Time, Place Value, get all those things done ahead of time. Get your writing folder and your objectives for your writing folder. That's major. Writing folder. Get your aims and objectives. How you're going to set it up. . . Get as many freebies as you can from your Primary-Junior consultant. Take time to relax! Sometimes just leave and forget it and

then come back with your day planned. You're only going to do a day at a time. And as much as you wish to be planned for a year in advance, I don't think there's any way you can do it within your first couple, three or four years unless you're teaching the same grade . . . I would tell them practical things! It wouldn't be like "the Faculty of Education."

As we work to draw a composite sketch of Nancy's views of theory and practice, we see the very strong emphasis on the importance of practical information. She was not "given" enough practical information but she would "give" it to others were she in a position to do so. Both theory and practice are cast as commodities that can be exchanged in classrooms, independent of personal teaching experiences. Nancy is aware of issues at the level of "theory," particularly the issue of modern versus traditional approaches, with the tension between child- and teacher-centered classroom routines.

Although Nancy speaks in the familiar language of "having theory to put into practice," it appears that her real starting point was routines that would enable her to conduct lessons in her first classroom. Routines enable her to acquire teaching experience and thereby to find out whether children can learn what she wants them to learn. Nancy knows that practice and theory relate to each other, but the details of that relationship are not yet clear to her.

An Experienced Teacher's Views of Theory and Practice

Diane, the experienced Grade 1 teacher introduced earlier, adapted very quickly to the process of being interviewed about her work, and most of the quotations that follow are taken from her third interview. Her ability to recall clearly her personal development as a teacher contributes significantly to the richness of her comments about the relationship between theory and practice.

As Diane begins her comments, she recalls a stage very similar to that at which Nancy presently finds herself. The earliest summer courses she attended provided her with techniques of teaching, techniques that she valued considerably but that did not challenge her to think through the "Why?" of her teaching. She suggests that there may be no other way to begin to teach than to accumulate and develop "techniques that work." (Italicized speeches are those of the person interviewing Diane.)

> Instead of taking a "course that ran over" three summers, I took Phys. Ed. one summer, Math the next, something different. So that I tried to grow strong in everything instead of being more narrow. And then when I knew a lot of methods, I felt it was time to consider why I was doing what I was doing.
> *So your first courses were . . . basically methods courses?*
> It's just a quick fix. Monday morning—what do I do Monday morning. Some of them were very good. But they don't get you to think through why you are doing it, what are your objectives. They say, "Here's a package; it'll probably work." That was a really good bag of tricks. For a beginning teacher, maybe that's the only way you can start is to have really sound methods. I don't know.

As Diane continues, she shifts to describing how she began to "feel uncomfortable'' about the teaching techniques she was using.

> Because if you are going to start thinking, "Why am I doing this or why do I feel uncomfortable?" With me, it was usually, "Why do I feel uncomfortable teaching kids this way?"
>
> *And then that's what made you think, "Why am I doing it or how could I do it another way?"*
>
> Most of the things that I felt uncomfortable with were . . . I was imposing things on the children rather than . . . us telling them what they had to learn, how they had to learn, when they had to learn it and I had to use really tough discipline to get them to sit down long enough to do all the things I wanted. And I don't like being really hard on kids. I mean it's nice to have a classroom where they are very quiet and scared to death of you, but I didn't like that. I go uptight teaching that way.

Thus it appears that Diane accumulated and used new techniques across a range of subject areas but found herself becoming increasingly uncomfortable about the fact that she was making all the decisions about the learning process with little or no involvement of her students in those decisions. Enrolling in a Master of Education program provided the avenue Diane needed to make progress in understanding why the techniques she had mastered at the level of practice made her uncomfortable at the level of theory. She indicates in the following statements that she gained support for her discomfort and began to learn of alternative techniques of practice.

> So when I started to . . . into the master's degree, that was the best thing that ever happened because we got to go and look at how children learn how to read, how do they learn how to write. You know, how does one type of instruction not suit certain types of students. And it was really what I was looking for. I knew what we were doing before wasn't right for kids, for a lot of kids.
>
> *But you didn't know why?*
>
> I didn't have anything to replace it with. I didn't have a methodology. Even when they started talking about centers, a lot of people taught centers the same way they taught them when they were in rows. They just moved it to a table. It still wasn't getting at what I needed. I needed to know, really know especially in the primary, really know how they learned how to read so that you could give it to them easy. I didn't like teaching them the phonics and all that. It was too hard for them. They didn't like it. You had to threaten them or they wouldn't learn it and when they did know it, they didn't know what to do with it. So I had to know a lot more about the subject. And then when the center idea came along at the same time, then it all sort of fit in. They could get up and walk around the room, find their own level of reading.

Diane suggests that the development of alternative practices and the development of a coherent framework supporting those practices went hand-in-hand. She is brave enough to admit that she is not certain how much her practices changed, but she found it very important to develop a personal philosophy. Her metaphor of "easy learning" is an intriguing notion.

So I don't know whether I really changed. I just found I felt better about the things I was doing because they suited what I had studied about Reading or Math and they went along with my philosophy of learning, you know, what I call "easy learning": Let the child lead you. And if he's not happy, then you're doing something wrong. You're getting in his way or you're going too fast or something like that. I don't think children are lazy. And they won't fight you if you can just find their path . . . almost all of them. Everything, when it matched my philosophy, the type of instruction I wanted, I kept on with it and I gradually . . . even now I eliminate things that I am not comfortable with.

Diane has concentrated on theories of Reading in her studies, and it is important to her that practices of teaching Reading have theoretical support. At the same time, she continues to attach importance to knowing that her children like the experience of learning to read.

The children look for differences in words. That's what they cue from. And differences in letters. And you start giving them a bunch of stuff that all looks the same, you start making it more difficult. That's one place where the study of Reading has really, I think, helped me a lot to feel, "This is the right way to do it." And even if they don't learn this way, they like it. They all think they are reading. They come eagerly with their books, and they say, "Hey, when's quiet reading time?"

Diane reveals a clear understanding of how difficult it can be for teachers to assess or modify the gaps between their theories and their practices. She also acknowledges that knowing more about theory can stimulate the frustrating process of self-criticism, yet it seems unlikely that she could ever view her practices any other way. She refers to new Math textbooks as "old Math" because of the theory of Mathematics learning on which they are based. Diane also speaks critically of the tendency of some teachers to use a "new" Math program mindlessly. She is very clear about the importance of teaching practices that suit how children learn *and* that can be supported at the level of theory by the teacher.

I remember that one of my objectives one year for "the school board's evaluation process" was to bring my practice closer to my theory. And the vice-principal was so impressed. Yes, he thought that was really worthwhile. But actually I'm always quite serious about these things and that really was what I wanted to do. That's a problem. Every once in a while you think when you're teaching—it is so complex when you start to look at it, if you didn't know the theory, you might be better off. It can get in the way. You see you start to question, you criticize . . . I've got books in my room that are not two years old that are what I call the old Math, where the children learn "two plus one equals three" and there are no counters. Two hundred pages for them to write in. Well, if you didn't have any theory about how children learn Math and you weren't the type of person to question anything at all, you would just hand them the book and they would have to do it. And the parents love it. And the thing is, if you give them a standardized test, they'll do just as well as any other group. That's because the test is wrong. It's made for the book. And it's the same way with *Math Their Way* (Baratta-Lorton, 1976). People take that and they use it as straight gospel, from page one to the end with no thought given to whether they are interested. I mean the lady who wrote that did a tremendous service to the people who were using the old Math because they were looking for a method; they knew they were uncomfortable with the old way.

As Diane continues to comment on the Math program that interests her, she speaks of learning the program "really well" at the level of practice in order to be able to assess it at the level of theory. She reports her personal interest in studying the learning of Math just as she has already studied the process of learning how to read. Diane also admits to a degree of uncertainty about how Math should be taught.

The time isn't there to reflect and say, "What could we do better?" and you need your universities for that. Maybe they have the time to do that. But now we have to learn the *Math Their Way* really well so we can step aside and say, "Hey, where does this fit into the theory?" I don't really think I had much of a theory about Math and that's why it's taken me so long to really inspect the *Math Their Way* approach. I didn't have much to tell me what's right. I know that children need to learn through things that are relevant and that they need a lot of concrete stuff and that they have to be out of their seats and active or active in their seats, whatever, and at the same time you have to have certain objectives for them to reach. They are not going to discover Math on their own. I think that maybe they could more or less discover Reading, but they are not going to discover that "six plus four equals ten." Maybe it would take them five years. They just don't seem to do that. At least they wouldn't get to our objectives. I would like to have some sort of really good theory about Math—or maybe what we're doing with them in *Math Their Way* is good. See I'm not sure.

Earlier in the interview, Diane had given a similar indication that she sees a teacher beginning by mastering a program at the level of practice, then moving from comfort with practice to criticism of practice, using theories acquired by studying how subjects are learned.

I know the units I'm going to do next and I know what's coming in Math. I'm much more comfortable with the Math program. I'm just about ready to start being critical of the Math program. I need to go and study about Math just like I studied about Reading. And then after that Science.

A final quotation from Diane's interviews confirms her strong belief in the role of experience in learning. She seems to indicate that experience is valuable to children even if no "formal" learning results. She also reveals her ability to relate her own learning experiences to those of the children she teaches. Diane begins with a comment about the pitfalls of "direct" application of Piaget's interest in when children understand conservation.

You take Piaget's theory and you try and put that into practice like at the sand center and you are almost telling them. It's something they should discover through years of experience and not in a half hour lesson and yet here we are expecting—sort of teaching, although I never test it and I never check whether they can do it or not. Because, if you started telling parents that they couldn't conserve matter, the parents would say, "Who cares! Is that necessary before Grade 2?" But you set up the experiences for them. They love to play in the sand. It won't hurt them, but to me it's almost an artificial way of getting theory into practice. And we do it at the water center too. We give them these cylinders, one is half as big as the other and we walk around and we say, "Hey, did you notice how many of those it would take to make those?" or "The tall one, how much water does it take to fill it?" I still find that amazing you know. I must have missed that stage in my experience. When the long skinny one would take too much sand I guessed to fill the short fat one, and it was just right. I was as excited as the kids. See that wouldn't stay with them if they hadn't already experienced that.

The overall impression from Diane's interviews is one of an experienced teacher who has thought very carefully about her practices in the classroom. Diane seems very aware of her own mastering of the routines of practice, and readily explains that "comfort" with routines provided both the stimulus to question and the basis from which practice could be criticized in terms of theory.

The Role of Theory and Practice in Learning to Teach

The excerpts from interviews with Nancy and Diane were selected for their potential to reveal how these two teachers, one beginning and one experienced, see "theory" and "practice" in the context of their thoughts about teaching and their experiences of learning how to teach. The picture that emerges in each instance suggests that learning to teach is *not* a two-step process of (1) learning theory and (2) putting theory into practice. Yet, our culture in general and our universities in particular use the phrase "theory into practice" so easily and freely that it would be surprising if those electing programs of teacher education did not *see their own learning as* a two-step process.

Nancy's comments, after several months of experience, indicate that she still feels she should be learning theory before she practices. She seems critical of her own developing professional knowledge *because* she is not learning that way. Nancy accepts the fact that she is learning how to develop and use classroom routines, but she seems to feel "short-changed" by her professional education within a university setting. She is patient about perfecting her practices, but impatient about acquiring the theory that relates to those practices. It is intriguing to note the number of times she uses the term "give" in the context of transferring knowledge (of either techniques and routines or of theory) from one individual to another, regardless of the level of experience. For Nancy, the role of experience in understanding the meaning of theory is not yet clear. Yet she is beginning to deal with the interaction between her teaching routines and the responses of children to those routines, and it is

85

here that she refers to the tension (at the level of theory) between child- and teacher-centered approaches. As Nancy continues to test the value of "using centers" in her classroom, she may come to understand more fully the nature of the tension teachers feel when theories compete in their recommendations for how classrooms should be organized.

Diane displays confidence in her professional knowledge and an acute awareness of how that knowledge developed over time and in relation to experience. If Diane ever did feel that she lacked "theory," she no longer gives any signals to that effect. She presents a striking account of the importance of acquiring routines and mastering their use *as a basis for* moving on to consider theory and ask questions about one's practices. She distinguishes clearly between courses that offer a "bag of tricks" and courses in a Master of Education program that offer theories and questions about the "Why?" of teaching. Diane speaks of becoming comfortable with practice and *then* moving on to theoretical issues associated with questioning and criticism of practice. She admits that theory "can get in the way," yet it is apparent that she cannot stop herself once she begins to ask questions about practice. The cycle that she has completed with respect to the teaching of Reading is one that she now feels ready to begin with Math, and she would like to follow that cycle with a similar analysis of how Science is taught. Diane's awareness of how she began to teach and of how her professional knowledge continues to develop leaves her free from the potential conflict of the "theory into practice" image of learning.

It is neither surprising nor puzzling to hear Nancy criticize her teacher education program for not "giving" her the practical routines that she did gain from teachers and is continuing to gain from conferences and workshops. Teacher educators are not likely to relinquish their interest in having beginning teachers understand the theoretical positions and tensions associated with various teaching practices, nor is it suggested that they should. When the program of professional preparation *ends* at the point that one *begins* to acquire experience on one's own, there is then an inevitable pressure to raise theoretical issues that may seldom arise again. The evidence that teachers will ask questions after becoming comfortable with practice, as Diane does, has not been widely available. Perhaps teacher educators could deal directly and explicitly with the "theory into practice" imagery that made Nancy's university courses frustrating and that continues to concern her as she considers the quality of her professional knowledge. *Is it possible* for teacher educators to deal with theory in a way that conveys to beginning teachers significant details of the process of professional development that awaits them as they develop confidence in their classroom practices? *Is it possible* to shift beginning teachers' unexamined assumption that they are involved in a process of "putting theory into practice"? A colleague has provided one encouraging indication that progress is possible:

> I forget that many of these young people still do not know how to teach when I work with them, and I often share things which I as an experienced teacher *know* they need, but they, lacking the experience, are not receptive because experience has not yet taught them that it is needed. (D. Bull, personal communication, February 27, 1985)

The perspective suggested here and illustrated by Nancy and Diane rejects the view that theory is learned first and then put directly into practice. Research on inservice education of teachers in the last two decades has produced important new insights that have not yet been used as perspectives for recasting the initial professional education of teachers. The data provided by Nancy and Diane encourage us to continue to listen to the preservice candidates whom we teach, to continue to try to reshape directly their assumptions about theory and practice, to continue to heighten their awareness and extend their interpretations of their own experiences of learning to teach. Two assumptions provide one type of summary of the messages in Nancy and Diane's comments about theory and practice:

1. Experience, including one's present teaching practices, *shapes the meaning* that we read into research, theory, and other sources of recommendations for changes in practice.
2. The relationship between theory/research and practice can be one in which the two are alternate phases *of a single activity,* not two independent domains linked by a tenuous act of faith. (Russell, 1987, p. 130)

As our research into teachers' professional knowledge proceeds, we will continue to examine participants' interviews for further insights into their understanding of the relationship between theory and practice. *We are increasingly convinced that the image one holds of the relationship between theory and practice can significantly influence understanding of the personal learning process, at every stage in one's development of the professional knowledge of teaching.*

The puzzle of the role metaphors play in the development of professional knowledge is more readily addressed. It appears that the metaphors some teachers employ in discussing their views of teaching and learning are indicative of their level of experience and professional knowledge. The metaphors used by Diane, an experienced teacher, reflect her theories about learning and guide her selection of activities. Her "easy" learning is mirrored in her classroom. Her gentle manner, her activity-based approach to Reading and Writing, her philosophy of "catching a child doing something right," her thoughtful blending of theory and practice, all contribute to easy learning. The metaphors in her discussions of practice seem to express her theoretical perspectives and to act as guidelines as she works to attune her practice more closely to her theory. For a less experienced teacher such as Nancy, metaphors seem to function more as indications of her level of experience and professional knowledge and less as guides to her practice. Nancy's metaphors shift in concert with her quickly changing experiences and ideas about practice as she moves from discussing the "nitty-gritty" elements of teaching to wanting "meatier" chunks of knowledge, something to go away and "chew on." These metaphors are unique to Nancy, of course, but we believe they indicate the direction of her growth as a beginning teacher.

As we have listened to teachers discuss their knowledge of practice with us, we have been aware of the reflective process many practitioners are engaged in. While reflection may not be a conscious activity, we have seen that, when placed in a situation where reflection and discussion are encouraged and deliberate, most teachers have been enthusiastic about the opportunity this afforded them to think about their work and share concerns with an interested party. As one teacher remarked, "These discussions are just like therapy! Every teacher should have this once a month." As we continue to talk with teachers and explore their understanding of their work, we better understand the role of the reflective process in learning the professional knowledge of teaching. We are also reminded of the value of collaboration. The presence of an interested, nonevaluative colleague appears to stimulate many teachers to reframe their interpretations of classroom events and to become more aware of how they learn from their experiences of teaching.

Our study of how teachers learn the professional knowledge of teaching is yielding thoughtful accounts of teachers' practices, rich in metaphorical language. We see examples of both beginning and experienced teachers who are willing to articulate their puzzles and their reflections as they attempt to make sense of theoretical perspectives on teaching in terms of their own practical experiences. We also see beginning and experienced teachers who seem unable to reflect on their practices, unable to reframe their problems, and unable to interpret their practices in more than one way. The contrast provides scope for further exploration of the development of practical professional knowledge.

REFERENCES

Baratta-Lorton, M. (1976). *Mathematics their way*. Menlo Park, CA: Addison-Wesley.

Lakoff, G., & Johnson, M. (1980). *Metaphors we live by*. Chicago: University of Chicago Press.

Munby, H. (1985). *Teachers' professional knowledge: A study of metaphor*. Paper presented at the annual meeting of the American Educational Research Association, Chicago.

Munby, H. (1986a). Metaphor in the thinking of teachers: An exploratory study. *Journal of Curriculum Studies, 18,* 197-209.

Munby, H. (1986b). *Metaphor in teachers' speech patterns*. Paper presented at the Education Colloquium, University of Redlands, Redlands, CA.

Reddy, M. (1979). The conduit metaphor. In A. Ortony (Ed.) *Metaphor and thought*. Cambridge: Cambridge University Press.

Russell, T.L. (1986). *Beginning teachers' development of knowledge-in-action*. Paper presented at the meeting of the American Educational Research Association, San Francisco, CA. (ERIC Document Reproduction Service No. ED 270 414)

Russell, T.L. (1987). Re-framing the theory-practice relationship in inservice teacher education. In L.J. Newton, M. Fullan, & J. W. MacDonald (Eds.), *Re-thinking teacher education: Exploring the link between research, practice, and policy* (pp. 125-134). Toronto: Joint Council on Education, University of Toronto/OISE.

Schön, D. (1979). Generative metaphor and social policy. In A. Ortony (Ed.), *Metaphor and thought* (pp. 254-283). Cambridge: Cambridge University Press.

Schön, D. (1983). *The reflective practitioner: How professionals think in action.* New York: Basic Books.

7

REFLECTING ON VIGNETTES OF TEACHING

Brent Kilbourn
The Ontario Institute for Studies in Education

Donald Schön's recent work (1983, 1987) has had considerable appeal in the context of professional practice. Reflection-in-action and reflection-on-action are concepts which play a major role in his discussion of a variety of educational contexts such as training in design and psychotherapy. While his work has intuitive relevance to school people, none of his detailed examples come from commonplace educational settings—public schools with teachers and classrooms of thirty or more children. Consequently, those of us concerned with these settings have the task of illustrating the particular ways in which his work has relevance to teachers and their classes. It is within this general context that the present chapter is set. In short, I want to pursue one line of thought as to the connection between his ideas on reflective practice and teachers' work.

Reflection and Vignettes

In *The Reflective Practitioner* (1983)[5] Schön begins the process of articulating an epistemology of practice. The thrust of his work is to give credence to the artistry of practitioners by recognizing that there is such a thing as practitioner knowledge which has its own kind of rigor but which is often intuitive in nature, frequently difficult if not impossible to articulate, and is embedded in the act of doing. Part of his argument is against what he calls Technical Rationality, a view which sustains a relatively clear distinction between theory and practice. Schön's work moves away from the notion that abstract theory is something to be learned and then applied to practical situations.

An entire terminology is developed to carry his argument and explicate specific cases: knowing-in-action, knowledge-in-action, reflecting-in-action, reflecting-on-action, virtual worlds, frame experiments, and so on. Central to

---

[5]Subsequent references to Schön are to *The reflective practitioner (1983)*.

his thesis are the concepts of "knowing-in-action" and "reflection-in-action." As Schön says about the actions of daily life,

> our knowing is ordinarily tacit, implicit in our patterns of action and in our feel for the stuff with which we are dealing. It seems right to say that our knowing is *in* our action. (p. 49)

He points out that this is not a foreign idea and that we even have a crude language for talking about it:

> There is nothing strange about the idea that a kind of knowing is inherent in intelligent action. Common sense admits the category of know-how, and it does not stretch common sense very much to say that the know-how is *in* the action . . . There is nothing in common sense to make us say that know-how consists in rules or plans which we entertain in the mind prior to action. Although we sometimes think before acting, it is also true that in much of the spontaneous behavior of skillful practice we reveal a kind of knowing which does not stem from a prior intellectual operation. (pp. 50-51)

Schön recognizes that often we do think about what it is that we are doing while we are doing it even though the thinking and the doing are fused. He calls this reflection-in-action.

> If common sense recognizes knowing-in-action, it also recognizes that we sometimes think about what we are doing. Phrases like "thinking on your feet," "keeping your wits about you," and "learning by doing" suggest not only that we can think about doing but that we can think about doing something while doing it. Some of the most interesting examples of this process occur in the midst of a performance. (p. 54)
>
> When good jazz musicians improvise together, they also manifest a "feel for" their material and they make on-the-spot adjustments to the sounds they hear. Listening to one another and to themselves, they feel where the music is going and adjust their playing accordingly. (p. 55)

As he says, "it is this entire process of reflection-in-action which is central to the 'art' by which practitioners sometimes deal well with situations of uncertainty, instability, uniqueness, and value conflict" (p. 50).

Schön's articulation of reflection-in-action is descriptive, a more accurate description (than accounts which separate theory and practice) of what it is that practitioners actually do when they go about their work. But there is also a concern about the improvement of practice. It is significant, for instance, that most of Schön's analyzed cases are of practitioners learning to become better practitioners, usually in the context of training (as with the design case involving Quist and Petra). The implicitly prescriptive aspect of his argument seems to be that a facility for improving our own practice will be fostered by a more adequate understanding of the relationship between theory and practice. Among teacher educators, his "fresh," theoretical perspective promises a new avenue for exploring old and tenacious problems of preservice and inservice teacher education.[6] Teachers respond positively because of the dignity that his views bring to their work in terms that are comprehensible. The idea of

---

[6]For a discussion of reflection-on-action in the context of teacher training see: D.A. Roberts and A. Chastko, "Absorption, Refraction, Reflection: Beginning Education Students Think About Science Teaching." Presented at AERA, San Francisco, 1986.

reflection-in-action allows teachers to see themselves as other than trained technicians and agrees with the kind of expertise and experience that they bring to practice. The language seems to fit what they do and experience.[7]

Yet, in spite of the intuitive appeal of Schön's work to standard school settings and the obvious descriptive applicability of his view to classroom practice, it is not entirely clear how a teacher improves practice by reflecting-in-action. More centrally, how does a teacher improve reflection-in-action? The immediacy, pace, and complexity of classroom life with thirty to thirty-five students is such that a teacher is in a constant state of acting and reacting. Given the press of the classroom, if a teacher's concepts (metaphors, images, understandings, constructs, etc.) for reflecting-in-action are narrow or inadequate, where is there a chance for their consideration? Under classroom conditions it is difficult to see how a teacher's reflection-in-action can remain alive, how it can be open to adjustment or change, how it can avoid slipping into a habitual and stale pattern of reflecting-in-action and habitual and stale ways of responding.

One answer to the question comes from Schön's case concerning design. An expert practitioner/observer like Quist can contribute to a practitioner's reflection-in-action by explicitly reflecting on the practitioner's reflection-in-action. Quist comments on Petra's reflection-in-action while Petra is actively engaged in working on a design problem. This kind of on-the-spot commentary contributes to Petra's reflection. In other instances, Petra observes Quist's reflection-in-action which also adds to her repertoire of concepts for reflecting. The comparison with classroom teaching cannot be drawn too far, however. Although Quist and Petra's situation is complex, it lacks the interactional complexity typical of the classroom. In teaching, circumstances are such that it would make little sense for an observer to be beside the teacher in the same way as Quist and Petra. Petra did not have the demands of thirty students and the pace was slow enough that it made sense for Quist to interrupt on-the-spot action.

Of course it does not always take an observer to reflect-on-action. We do it all the time ourselves. Again, commonplace experience suggests that after an event we may think about what we might do differently given a similar situation. As Schön points out,

> practitioners do reflect *on* their knowing-in-practice. Sometime, in the relative tranquility of a postmortem, they think back on a project they have undertaken, a situation they have lived through, and they explore the understandings they have brought to their handling of the case. They may do this in a mood of idle speculation, or in a deliberate effort to prepare themselves for future cases. (p. 61)

Personal reflection on one's own experience seems particularly relevant to public school teaching because of the relative isolation from colleagues which

---

[7]As a teacher in a graduate class remarked on the frustration of working with a student teacher: *She asks so many questions about why I do this or that and the amount of time it takes to explain is so much that I might as well as do it myself.* Such a comment concerns the experience of knowing more than we can say and is nicely encapsulated in the term "knowing-in-action." Schön's language provides a way of talking about familiar experience.

is typical of the life of a teacher. In most schools teachers have very little opportunity to be observed by their colleagues as Quist observed Petra. Consequently, improvement to their reflection-in-action is most likely to come from their own reflection-*on*-action. In this vein Schön notes that self-reflection can be an antidote to "overlearning":

> Through reflection, he can serve as a corrective to overlearning. Through reflection, he can surface and criticize the tacit understandings that have grown up around the repetitive experiences of a specialized practice, and can make new sense of the situations of uncertainty or uniqueness which he may allow himself to experience. (p. 61)

And yet the problem of "overlearning" and a flight to habitualized routine can be as much an issue with reflection *on* one's own experience as it is with reflection-in-action. Reflection-on-action may be of little help in improving reflection-in-action if it too has become routinized and stale. In the following passage Schön is writing in the context of "knowing-in-action" but his comments hold equally well for reflection-on-action:

> And if he learns, as often happens, to be selectively inattentive to phenomena that do not fit the categories of his knowing-in-action, then he may suffer from boredom or "burn-out" and afflict his clients with the consequences of his narrowness and rigidity. (p. 61)

The question is, how do we avoid the merely habitual even when reflecting on our own experience and practice?

> A practitioner might break into a circle of self-limiting reflection by attending to his role frame, his interpersonal theory-in-use, or the organizational learning system in which he functions. Whatever his starting point, however, he is unlikely to get far unless he wants to extend and deepen his reflection-in-action, and unless others help him see what he has worked to avoid seeing. (p. 283)

So long as we stay within the personal, how do we avoid simply looking at our experience in ways that themselves have become habitual? This may not be problematic when reflection-on-action continues to be useful and productive, but sometimes improvement in practice comes from looking at things in a different way.[8]

One other way of enhancing one's skill at reflecting-on-action consists of reading or listening to stories about practice. Stories can give the practitioner vicarious experience. They are a variant of a practitioner's reflection on the practice of another. Stories, vignettes, episodes, cases, narratives, when well

---

[8]The problem of how to look at things differently when it is appropriate to do so is always a difficult one and what works for a practitioner in one set of circumstances may not work in other circumstances. And, clearly, what works varies from practitioner to practitioner. In one of my graduate courses teachers systematically reflect on taperecorded and transcribed instances of their teaching. Part of the explicit agenda is to try new ways of looking at their practice. There is a serious question as to whether a teacher would be able or willing to engage such a process without the impetus and support of a graduate course. In other cases it is apparent that a teacher can learn about his/her own practice by observing and reflecting on the practice of

written or told, can be a potentially powerful means of helping practitioners to reflect-on-action with a view to enhancing reflection-in-action. In the remainder of the chapter I want to provide several vignettes of practice in order to exemplify this point and to indicate an agenda which, while implicitly outlined by Schön in areas like design and psychotherapy, needs attention in the area of classroom teaching.

Vignettes and Reasons

If a story is to be useful for informing us about practice, it must have a point. The development of the point incorporates the writer's reflection on the story itself. The following vignettes, for example, all exemplify a point of view about teaching which takes seriously the place of *reason* in the classroom. This is far from the only view to be taken when reflecting on/in classroom action. The complexity of classroom life would argue for multiple points of view as necessary for its adequate comprehension. However, the role of reasons in the classroom constitutes a fundamental point about teaching and, on those grounds alone, can appropriately serve as an initial instance of a more general suggestion that any point of view needs to be exemplified with particularized vignettes of practice if it is to be helpful to a practitioner for reflecting on practice.

One of Schön's vignettes is a good starting point because it nicely illustrates how a group of teachers came to a different way of reflecting-on-action. Schön (1983) describes a research project in which teachers were asked to discuss their on-the-spot thinking about subject matter which, in a sense, they already knew. "They have allowed themselves to become confused about subjects they are supposed to know ; and as they have tried to work their way out of their confusions, they have also begun to think differently about learning and teaching" (p. 67). He goes on to describe an incident in which teachers were asked to discuss a playback of two boys playing a game.

> The boys sat at a table, separated from one another by an opaque screen. In front of one boy, blocks of various colors, shapes, and sizes were arranged in a pattern. In front of the other, similar blocks were lying on the table in no particular order. The first boy was to tell the second one how to reproduce the pattern. After the first few instructions, however, it became clear that the second boy had gone astray. In fact, the two boys had lost touch with one another, though neither of them knew it.
>
> In their initial reactions to videotape, the teachers spoke of a "communications problem." They said that the instruction giver had "well-developed verbal skills" and that the receiver was "unable to follow directions." Then one of the researchers pointed out that, although the blocks contained no green squares—all

---

colleagues. Again, in the context of a graduate seminar on observation and feedback skills, teachers frequently report that in the process of observing, discussing, and reflecting on another teacher's practice they learn as much about their own teaching as they do that of the person observed. Thinking about how one is reflecting-on-action is a supported process, but supported within the relatively unusual circumstances of a graduate seminar. In more typical school settings, teachers seldom have the luxury of observing their colleagues at work. It is not uncommon that a teacher might go through an entire career having made only a handful of observational sojourns into a colleague's classroom.

squares were orange and only triangles were green—she had heard the first boy tell the second to "take a green square." When the teachers watched the videotape again, they were astonished. That small mistake had set off a chain of false moves. The second boy had put a green thing, a triangle, where the first boy's pattern had an orange square, and from then on all the instructions became problematic. Under the circumstances, the second boy seemed to have displayed considerable ingenuity in his attempts to reconcile the instructions with the pattern before him. (p. 67)

As a result of being redirected and focussed on a salient aspect of the episode, the teachers began to talk in less stereotypical terms about what had happened. While an honest mistake had obviously been made, it also became clear that the second boy had acted intelligently—his *reasoning* had been flawless. He had intuitively compensated for an inconsistency in the data he had been given and did so in a way that might be expected of anyone in a similar situation. (We might imagine someone saying "but there are no green squares," but this perception is highly unlikely unless the notion of a trick is incorporated into the ground rules of the game.) After the intuitive choice had been made (colour superseded shape), he proceeded reasonably and had followed instructions.

> As one teacher put it, they were now "giving him reason." They saw reasons for his behavior; and his errors, which they had previously seen as an inability to follow directions, they now found reasonable.
> Later on in the project, as the teachers increasingly challenged themselves to discover the meanings of a child's puzzling behavior, they often spoke of "giving him reason." (p. 68)

Two thoughts always strike me when I read this vignette. First, in order for the teachers, Schön, and us to come to terms with the heart of the matter, we have had to attend to details. We have had to move away from a generalized, overall reaction to the events ("the boys seemed to enjoy the game," "the game really encourages participation," "you have to be on your toes") and have had to attend to the specifics of what was said and done. The researcher's intervention was a move to get the teachers to attend to detail (in this case, with videotape) and in Schön's reconstructed vignette the detail is highlighted in prose so that we get the point.

In addition, however, for us to see the relevant detail and the relevance of the detail, the whole process has to be slowed down. Schön's teachers saw the videotape a second time and had the luxury of time to discuss the episode. We have the luxury of being able to read Schön's vignette, slowly if we wish, and reread in order to comprehend and savor the substantive issue about *reasons*. Our reflection-on-action not only attends to relevant detail, it often involves a much slower process than the original events themselves. The number, frequency, and pace of these events often means that detail cannot easily be remembered and, when events are reflected on, the terms brought to bear on their understanding may be too generalized to be productive for seeing important issues. The potential of a good vignette, then, is that it can highlight relevant detail and its narrative form allows the pace to be slowed so that we can grasp its substance.

A second thought concerns the substance of Schön's vignette, a concern I shall carry for the remainder of the chapter: the vignette is moral and educational in character. It is moral because it concerns that potential labeling of the second boy as someone who could not do something very well when, in fact, he could. It is educational because, at its heart, the vignette is about reason, the place of reasons in human interaction, and the place of reasons in teaching. The vignette poignantly illustrates that to proceed as though the boy had not reasoned properly would not only be morally unjust, it would simply miss the point of an educational matter. Although the vignette is not about a classroom situation, it reminds us of the importance of reasons in the classroom. Reasons are usually important in educational matters but they assume a greater significance when teaching involves some form of discussion. In any rigorous sense of discussion, reason is the base on which discussion advances. More generally, the whole idea of *understanding* seems to be fundamentally related to the *reasons-for-things*.

Reasons and the Classroom[9]

Schön's vignette alerts us to an important issue in thinking about teaching, but the vignette itself concerns an artificial situation. The relevance of the substance of his vignette to more common classroom situations will be explored in the remaining parts of the chapter with three vignettes chosen to exemplify several points about reasons. Let me begin with a short vignette which echoes Schön.

In the context of the application of mathematics to everyday life, a grade five teacher asked students to measure their neck and waist. Billy proceeded to measure his waist by taking the distance from his left hip bone, across his abdomen, to his right hip bone. He then measured his neck by taking the distance from his lower jaw-line to his shoulder. In other words, rather than measuring the circumference of his neck, he measured how long it was. After seeing his and similar work, the teacher commented to the effect that "some people won't be very good at getting clothes for themselves." This minor incident was buried in the hub-bub of a busy classroom; nevertheless, it upset Billy enough to relate the story at home. He could not understand what was the matter with what he had done and later said, "why didn't [the teacher] tell us to measure *around*?"

This illustrates how even a brief and relatively trivial episode can turn on the issue of reasons. Billy's teacher did not give-him-reason even though his method was not unreasonable. His actions were consistent with the simple direction to measure. We do not know his reason for proceeding as he did. That is, we do not know his personal context that might have made length an

[9]The place of reasons in classroom interaction and "reasons" as a focus for peer observation and feedback has been explored by Kilbourn, Roberts, and MacKinnon in research supported by Grant No. 410-83-1232 from the Social Sciences and Humanities Research Council of Canada. See: Brent Kilbourn, "Oliver: A Case Study of Observation and Feedback." Presented at AERA, Washington, 1987. And: Douglas A. Roberts and Allan M. MacKinnon, "Reasons for Giving Reasons: An Expert-Expert Clinical Analysis of Science Teaching for Non-Academic Students." Presented at CSSE, Hamilton, 1987.

obvious choice (any more than we know why Schön's second boy chose color over shape) and, given the simple direction, an arbitrary choice would not be unreasonable. As far as the educational point of the exercise is concerned, he did know how to measure and did so adequately. The teacher's intent to measure circumference rather than length was not unreasonable however, because it involved a form of measurement commonplace (for adults) for fitting clothes. Pedagogically, it was consistent with the teacher's concern about the use of mathematics in everyday life. So the teacher had reason for proceeding in a certain way as much as Billy had reason for doing what he did. What seems to be missing from the episode is a clear communication from the teacher about why the measurements should be done in a certain way. (It is quite possible, of course, that the teacher did explain why and Billy missed it.) Following that, it points to the need for the teacher to give Billy reason by pursuing with him the thinking implicit in his actions.

This vignette with Billy shows the different, but interrelated, senses in which the term "reason" can be used as a way of looking at aspects of classroom interaction. In Schön's sense we can talk of "giving-Billy-reason," of the need for the teacher to give-Billy-reason. This metaphoric sense of "giving-reason" is a somewhat unique usage but marks out a prominent issue in teaching which this chapter addresses. There are a variety of ways of capturing the meaning of the phrase "giving reason" but it basically means that, as a starting point, the teacher should assume that a child knows what she is doing; that the child has good reason for saying what he says; or that, from her own perspective, the child's actions make sense and are coherent. The meaning can more easily, if somewhat vaguely, be expressed colloquially and in the negative: "don't assume the kid has got it wrong." Interestingly, giving-reason is a common initial assumption in much adult-to-adult interaction but on the whole is less common in adult-children interactions.

Within the metaphoric sense of "giving-reason" there are the various literal and commonplace senses of "giving reasons" (even though the precise word may not be used to convey the meaning). In a typical classroom we may expect to see the teacher ask for reasons and the child give reasons, or conversely in some instances. The argument underlying this chapter is that classroom interaction in which both teachers and students give reasons where appropriate is necessary if the child is to be "given-reason" in the metaphoric sense. For instance, we can imagine Billy's teacher asking "why did you measure that way?" (literally asking for reasons) and Billy responding "Because . . . " (literally giving reasons) and these interchanges, instigated by the teacher, would be in the service of giving-reason (in the metaphoric sense) to Billy. (However, not every instance of a teacher's request for reasons or of a teacher giving reasons would be in the service of giving-the-child-reason.)

However, there is a second metaphoric sense of giving-reason that I wish to address in this chapter and it concerns the observer's (researcher, department head, parent, principal, etc.) obligation to give-the-teacher-reason just as we would have the teacher give the child reason. Here the basic assumption is that the teacher has good reason for doing what he or she does. In the vignette with Billy we can see that the teacher had good reason for "measuring around" even though it was not critical to the act of measuring *per se*. In this particular case we can give the teacher reason while asking that the teacher give the child reason. And, again in this particular case, some of the tension between the two metaphoric senses of giving-reason is released if the teacher either literally gives reason why the measurement should be done in a certain way, or accepts that, for the purpose of the exercise, Billy's way is acceptable.

This vignette is, admittedly, a relatively simple case. It works well to show that the two metaphoric senses of giving-reason (to the teacher and to the student) can be at odds with one another. That is, while both the teacher and the student may have good reasons for their actions, those actions may not be compatible in a dynamic classroom situation. The vignette is not strong, however, for showing the complexity of many teaching situations and for showing why the harder we push on the teacher's moral obligation to give the child reason, the more seriously we must attend to the necessity of giving the teacher reason (and the implications of doing that). The metaphoric senses of giving-reason can be adequately addressed in actual situations only by a persistent question: when is it appropriate for (who) to be giving-reason to (whom) and how should that be done? The remaining two vignettes contain two themes. One, qua teaching, is to remind ourselves of the place of reason(s) in the classroom and the relationship of that to the integrity of the subject matter. The other, qua observation, is to remind ourselves that classroom circumstances are often such that it is difficult at best to give-the-child-reason or to give reasons—this theme emphasizes the necessity of giving-the-teacher-reason. Both of these themes and the vignettes with which they are couched honor aspects of the complexity of classroom life for the teacher and the students.

The above vignettes point to the obligation for the teacher to honor a student's reasoning and reasons when it is appropriate. It sets an expectation that the teacher should take the student seriously, listen to the student carefully—*really attend*. Such an expectation exists within a view of teaching which is more than the transmission of information from teacher to student. There are a variety of ways of expressing this view. Sometimes teachers talk about "interactive" classrooms, or "Socratic" teaching. Sometimes aspects of the view are captured in slogans like teaching "problem solving" or "critical thinking." Sometimes the view is simply expressed by the general term, discussion. Regardless of the specific terms used, the view is that of teachers and students talking about real issues that are of genuine concern; where there seems to be a sincere interchange of ideas; where teacher and students are actually talking with one another; where, even though the teacher may have expertise or experience to share, there is a sense in which issues really are open to question and debate. The view is implicit in these comments by Orpwood (1987):

> The crisis of confidence (in the schools) stems less from what students *know* (or do not know) and more from what they can *do* (or, more often, what they cannot do). Despite decades of curriculum reform, schools are remarkably resistant to change. Students of all ages, but particularly those in the more senior grades, still read predigested information from textbooks, perform repetitive mathematical exercises, copy notes off chalkboards into notebooks, memorize information and regurgitate it with pencil-and-paper tests. These activities are the stuff of students' lives—from 9 to 3:30, from September to June, throughout the most formative and impressionable years of their lives . . .

Businesses require their employees to be creative and innovative, to question rather than accept handed-down opinions, to have strong interpersonal and communications skills and to be highly motivated toward achieving corporate and personal goals.

As futurist John Naisbitt argues in *Reinventing the Corporation,* "thinking, learning and creating" are the new "Three R's" of the information society. However, these skills and attitudes are not being developed in the school system and it's important to understand why not. (p. A7)

Thomas Green's (1968) notion of a "conversation of instruction" helps to give shape to a view of teaching as involving discussion. He distinguishes among terms like "teaching," "instructing," and "training" in the context of classroom work.

This important difference between training and instructing may be viewed in another way. To the extent that instructing necessarily involves a kind of conversation, a giving of reasons, evidence, objections and so on, it is an activity of teaching allied more closely to the quest for understanding. We can train people to do certain things without making any effort to bring them to an understanding of what they *do.* (pp. 32-33)

Green's idea of instruction necessitates teachers using some form of discussion—something that goes beyond the transmission of information from teachers and texts to students. And it clearly indicates that not any old discussion will do.

The point is not, therefore, that instructing necessarily requires communication. The point is rather that it requires a certain *kind* of communication, and that kind is the kind which includes giving reasons, evidence, argument, etc., in order to approach the truth. (p. 33)

Flow, intensity, active participation, and smooth interaction are all important, of course, but central to discussion is that it make sense; that it has an underlying intelligibility; that, in some way, it is suffused with reason—reason giving and giving reason. The vignette with Billy could have moved toward a brief discussion with Billy about the approach he had taken—a conversation of instruction—but the teacher's reflection-in-action moved events in a different direction.

The following vignette is more complex and unfolds in a somewhat different way. A grade 7 class was doing an investigation intended to show that different substances conduct heat at different rates. The handout directed students to:

"Hold what you are testing about 6 cm. from one end and hold that end into the flame of a bunsen burner. Time yourself and see how long you can hold on to it."

A variety of materials were used: chalk, lead strips, glass rods, iron strips, copper strips, slate. In spite of the crudeness of the test it worked relatively well. The "findings" were consistent with what might be expected, given textbook knowledge of heat conduction. For example, a copper strip could be held for a relatively short time, while a strip of wood could be easily held without pain even though it was burning at the opposite end. During the discussion of "Results," a student concluded that metal was a better conductor than some of the other materials:

(1) Teacher: O.K., and looking at your "observation," how did you determine that?

The teacher went beyond (1) merely accepting Peter's answer (2) by asking for the *reasons* underlying his conclusion.

(2) Peter: Well, the aluminium and the copper and the steel conducts heat very fast, but the chalk and the glass tubing and the wood and the rock didn't.

Peter's response (2) seems to reiterate his earlier conclusion that *"metal conducts heat the best"* rather than a very clear set of reasons for the conclusion. Had the teacher wished to pursue Peter's reasoning, he might have redirected him to the data collected or asked him to further explain what happened, and so on. The intent of a variety of potential pedagogical moves would be to insure that the basis of discussion was in terms of appropriate reasons relating to the whole point of the investigation in the first place. Of course, the teacher may have made the most appropriate move given the situation. For example, the teacher's reflection-in-action may have indicated that Peter and the class understood the reasoning behind the conclusion (such information could have been gleaned from the teacher's visiting each group during the investigation), and that to pursue the issue would be redundant. And some of the teacher's reasons for not pursuing the issue with Peter may have concerned other pedagogical concerns. For example, the teacher may have recognized that Peter's contribution was quite significant for Peter and that the interaction should end with this "success"; or the teacher might have recognized that the class was getting restless and, consequently, the pace should be quickened. The central point is to highlight that *among the various considerations that go into a teacher's reflection-in-action are those which relate to the role of reasons in discussion.* In this instance the teacher decided to bring the interaction with Peter to a close; but what followed is rich from the standpoint of reasons and the investigation itself:

(3) Teacher: How many people would agree with the conclusion Peter arrived at? [A number of hands go up]. Good. Does anyone have any other conclusions that you could mention? Matt?

(4) Matt: Different people have different sensitivities to heat.

(5) Teacher: O.K., interesting. [Pause] Could you give me an example of how you arrived at that conclusion?

Matt's offering (4) was unique—"out-of-step" with direction taken by the rest of the class. Again, the teacher accepted the conclusion (5) and asked Matt for his reasoning. As I observed, the teacher's hesitancy suggested that he was not entirely clear where this part of the discussion could lead. As Schön might say, he was (appropriately) "thinking-on-his-feet." Matt attempted to explain more clearly what he meant in (4). The teacher's response was slow and considered:

(6) Teacher: Interesting. [Pause] Does that relate to the purpose of the experiment though?

(7) Matt: No.

(8) Teacher: No; it doesn't. But that's O.K., it's an interesting sideline. It doesn't exactly relate back to the purpose but, as Matt said, obviously some people may be more sensitive than others and perhaps they could feel the heat more quickly.

In an important sense, to ask for reasons as the teacher did in (1) and (5), rather than to just move along, is to take the student seriously and, consequently, is an initial step in giving the child reason. Giving-reason is a matter of degree and appropriateness, of course, and at any juncture the teacher may reflect on a salient interaction and ask if giving-reason had been exploited to the fullest, given the circumstances. It could be asked whether the teacher should have persisted with the student a bit longer, listened a bit more, or perhaps worked with the student to explore and make explicit a line of reasoning that the student only intuitively understood or saw as relevant. For example, if the teacher had wanted to continue giving-reason to Matt, rather than stopping when Matt gave an "incorrect" response, he might have asked why Matt thought the point important to bring up. And he might have had to work with Matt on developing a thoughtful response.

I have used the above vignettes to make a point about the need to give the child reason, and have argued that such a need sits within a broader context which honors the place and potential of reason in the classroom. Giving reason and reason giving on the part of both teacher and student are central to the concept of teaching and, therefore, concern philosophical questions and moral obligations on the part of the teacher. Respect for the role of reasons is also a practical issue because of the potential for advancing genuine discussion. In both of the above vignettes the teacher could have furthered the process of giving the child reason by sincerely asking, "Why did you measure that way?" or "What was your thinking about heat sensitivity?" Yet these possibilities, while real enough, are deceptively simple because, among other things, they do not take into account inner tensions that many teachers face in discussion situations. For example, it is not uncommon that a teacher might value intense discussion while also valuing equal student participation. It is not hard to imagine that Peter and Matt's teacher brought the discussion with them to a close partly because of a wish to have others contribute. When such a move is made, depth of discussion can be sacrificed for equal participation. (The trade-off portrayed here is not the only issue, of course—moving the "discussion" along from one student to another is also a means of controlling a group, for example.)

Similarly, a teacher might value students' expressing their own ideas while, at the same time, not wanting discussion to go off-track or the contribution offered to be erroneous or inconsistent with the nature of the subject matter. A teacher may have a sense of "rightness" about the substance of a discussion which, at times, may be at odds with belief in student participation. What is the teacher to do when he or she works hard to get students to participate and then their participation misses the mark? In Chapter 2 of this book, Lee Shulman notes that giving-reason requires at some point that the student's thinking and doing *be* reasonable. The point broaches issues of the subject matter and provokes recognition of distinctions to be made. Reasons are not only in terms of the student's frame—they are also in terms of the subject matter and the teacher's view of the subject matter.

Reasons and Subject Matter

Matt's teacher "knew" when Matt was off the mark and acted on that knowledge. His action was tactful and well done. More precisely, among a number of plausible reasons for proceeding as he did, the teacher brought the conversation with Matt to a close because Matt's contribution was out of line with the point of the exercise. The teacher said, (8) "It doesn't exactly relate back to the purpose . . . " His reflection-in-action was an implicit judgment that that was not a time to pursue reasons because Matt's response might take the discussion down a path that would be further off-track. In order for the teacher to act as he did, there is some sense in which he had to "know" that Matt was off-track and such knowing rests in part on his understanding of the subject matter. In Schön's terms, a teacher's knowing-in-action, reflection-in-action, and reflection-on-action are also infiltrated, we might say, with an understanding of the subject matter.

But these "knowings" and "reflectings" are not infallible. A teacher's understanding of the place of reasons in the classroom and his understanding of the nature of the subject matter provide opportunities for exploiting and guiding discussions, but they also can limit discussion. Knowing-in-action can be narrow or mistaken, as can reflection-in/on-action. Whether or not Matt's teacher should have exploited the discussion with Matt in the actual situation is open to question. As indicated above, there are any number of good reasons for handling the episode as he did. However, *Matt's contribution was not unrelated to a broader understanding of the purpose of the experiment,* even though his conclusion pried more deeply into the structure of the exercise than his teacher was prepared to go and his classmates appreciated. To whatever extent the teacher made the moves he did because he "knew" that Matt was on a sideline, his reflection-in-action was misguided. Further reflection on the vignette is one way of expanding the horizons of reflection-in-action.

In order for Matt's conduction exercise to *be* an experiment, appropriate "controls" need to be in place. Strictly speaking, only the "experimental variable" should be free from being artificially held constant. In Matt's experiment, the material used (copper strips, glass, chalk, etc.) was the experimental variable and, if the experiment were to function properly, all other aspects of the experiment would have to remain the same; otherwise, so the argument goes, how would you know that differences in heat conduction were due to the differences in the materials used rather than something else? For example, if midway in the experiment a student decided to use insulated gloves to hold the metal strips, we know that the results would be thrown off because we would know that the timed rate of conduction was not only the result of the material used but also the result of the insulated gloves. In this regard, it is significant that the directions to the experiment called for the materials to be held 6 cm. from the flame. Again, to have one's hand closer to the flame with some materials would mean that the heat would have less distance to travel and would confound the results. Holding each material 6 cm. along its length with the tip in the flame "controls" the potential "contaminating variable" of the distance the heat has to travel.

Matt's contribution had considerable relevance to aspects of the subject matter—the notions of controlled experiment and contaminating variables. He addressed one feature of the experiment's underlying epistemology. His idea that different people have different sensitivities to heat focusses on one of the contaminating variables. If, for example, midway in the experiment a person with very calloused fingers were to hold the remaining materials, the results would be contaminated in the same way that they would be if insulated gloves were used. In terms of the potential for discussion it makes little difference that the magnitude of difference in sensitivity among people would be so small that it would be unlikely to distort the results significantly. Nor does it make a difference that Matt may not have appreciated the significance of his observation; indeed, one possibility for teaching would be to collaborate with Matt to help him and his classmates see the significance and relevance of what he has said.

In terms of the potential for discussion, however, it makes considerable difference whether or not, behind the scenes, Matt's teacher understands these aspects of the subject matter. If he does, he has choice. An understanding of these aspects would allow him to continue the discussion with Matt and his classmates in a way that could explore the reasons for the saliency of Matt's observation. The relationship among reasons, subject matter, and discussion as these are incorporated into a teacher's reflection-in-action constitutes a complex and dynamic mix. Any particular piece of subject matter both provides opportunities and sets limits to what can be reasonably done in a discussion setting. What moves the teacher can make, what paths can be exploited as he or she works with students, is shaped by the subject matter. Skillful reflection-in-action involves knowing the subject matter and it involves seeing the potential of the subject matter for teaching.

The intent of discussion can be undermined, however, when questioning is pursued in order to elicit some particular response, one that agrees with the teacher's point of view. The more the teacher's moves are aimed at specific, "correct" responses, the more the teacher drifts from honest discussion to something which is more akin to manipulation. In fact, we sometimes say "he or she manipulated the discussion" to indicate the impropriety of that mode of operation. As Green has said:

> It takes no great powers of insight to see that in proportion as the conversation of instruction is less and less characterized by argument, reasons, objections, explanations, and so forth, in proportion as it is less and less directed toward an apprehension of truth, it more and more closely resembles what we call indoctrination. (p. 33)

Circumstances in which the unavowed intent of "discussion" is to arrive at the teacher's image of an appropriate conclusion presents an environment in which giving-reason to the child becomes problematic and unlikely.

Explanations for phoney classroom discussion frequently involve the institutional context within which it is normally attempted. Some of the features of this context have been alluded to above: pace, class size, control, amount of material to be "covered," to name but a few. Institutional constraints create an environment which almost seems designed to work against a teacher's attempt to have serious and rigorous discussion. These constraints are, moreover, part and parcel of the teacher's knowing-in-action and reflection-in-action and cannot be set aside while the teacher attends to the "real stuff" of discussion. At the same time, considerations about the subject matter also serve as constraints within which the teacher must operate. I have focussed on one explanation for limited discussion by attending to the teacher's understanding of the subject matter and the dilemmas faced when the discussion strays from what the teacher regards as congruous with the subject matter. These dilemmas can be particularly acute when discussion involves matters of interpretation and values. The following vignette shows a kind of complexity well beyond that involving Matt above, and allows us to imagine one kind of teaching dilemma. Again, the function of the sketch is not to prescribe to the episode, but, rather, to address issues of reasons and understanding of subject matter as these shape reflection-*in*-teaching.

A high school English class was asked to read and discuss a short story. A synopsis of this story is as follows:

> A young man, Irving, is lured into a poker game with some sharpsters from his office and loses an entire week's salary. Fearing the anger of his wife for his stupidity, he tears his clothes, roughs himself up, and pretends that a mugger has beaten him up and stolen the money. His wife insists that he call the police to report the robbery. He does, and amazingly enough, the police pick up a young suspect with the exact sum of money which had been reported stolen. Irving is called by the police to see if he can identify his assailant. They ask that he give the youngster a break and not press charges and they will see that the money is returned. Seeing a chance to get back his money and still not "harm" anyone, Irving identifies the youngster as his assailant, has the money returned to him, and drops charges.
>
> The next day Irving is bothered by a guilty conscience and determines that he will call the police and admit the truth about the whole sorry mess. Just as he is about to call, the main recipient of his losses at the poker game enters the office, sporting a black eye and lacerations. After leaving the game he had been mugged by a young man fitting the description of the young man about whom Irving had lied on the previous day. Irving decides not to notify the police.

As will be seen shortly, a number of students take from this story the idea that Irving did the right thing, which at one level is not surprising, given what the story says. The dilemma (we can imagine) for the teacher is how to handle the discussion since the espoused norms of society present a contrary view. The story itself is not a parable—it cannot reasonably be characterized as a "short fictitious narrative from which a moral or spiritual truth is drawn" (Webster's). A parable is usually explicit and clear as to what the moral is and in this case that is unclear. It is more reasonable to suggest that the story presents a moral dilemma. It allows the question "Was Irving right not to notify the police?" to be asked, but it does not answer the question itself. In terms of its potential for teaching, several possibilities can be sketched. The story could be used in a discussion situation to show that there can be a diversity of opinion about moral issues. Or, it could be used to explore the question as to whether the idea that two wrongs make a right is itself right or not. In this case, discussion might contrast the sense of "rightness" to the story's conclusion with the dominant espoused morality of North American, middle-class society (two-wrongs-do-not-make-a-right). Or, the story could be used to make literary rather than moral points. One might be to explore how different kinds of literature are to be read; for example, literally or in other ways. Another could be to show a whole genre of literature and film (e.g., "The Sting," James Bond, etc.) in which evil cancels evil and everything turns out alright, but the actions of the participants are not intended to be models for us to follow in a real world. Yet another would be to discuss the ways in which this kind of story is different from what we might expect in life-like situations.

If one were to argue that the story does reveal a moral truth, its content would seem to be that two-wrongs-make-a-right. In discussion it might be pointed out that no dire consequences befell Irving after his final inaction, for example. It is important to note that such teaching would be contrary to the norms of middle-class society. What does seem quite clear is that there is little potential within the story itself for teaching those middle-class norms. The idea that two-wrongs-*do-not*-make-a-right is simply not embedded in the story.

All of these potentialities and understandings concerning the subject matter provide a backdrop for the teacher to work with the students. Working with students in discussion calls for on the spot judgments and decisions which are played out in a context which is dynamic, messy, and unpredictable. Along with Schön, it seems right to say that the teacher is called upon to reflect-in-action. It also seems right to say that the quality of the teacher's reflection-in-action is influenced by, among other things, the relative sophistication with which the teacher understands the subject matter and its potential for teaching. Such understanding may function as a sixth sense for helping the teacher to think on his or her feet toward ends which preserve the integrity of the subject matter while giving-reason to the student. These kinds of understandings also allow us to reflect-*on*-action with a view to informing ourselves about teaching and for considering potential courses of action in the future.

In the early part of the discussion of the "Poker" story, the teacher worked with students as they tried to answer several written questions given on the previous day. The questions were aimed at provoking an understanding of why Irving did what he did. The concluding question was whether or not his actions were right. Some of the questions were more neutral than others and provided more degrees of freedom for the student to express a personal view. For example, "What indications are revealed in the story of the relationship between Irving and Frances?" allowed for the possibility of a variety of responses, whereas the rhetorical "Would you agree that she appears to be the stronger or more dominant person?" presupposes a particular response. The line of reasoning is preshaped. The teacher frequently brought the students back to the story in order for them to develop reasons underlying their comments. For example, one student suggested that Irving and Frances did not really act like a husband and wife because of *"the way she talked to him and worried about him."* The teacher turned to David:

(1)   Teacher: Anyone in your family act that way, David?

(2)   David: Yah, my mother—always fussing around, being a nuisance, worrying about us.

(3)   Teacher: I think you've hit on it, David. Now, follow it up.

(4)   David: I don't know what you mean.

(5)   Teacher: Does Frances not act more like a mother than a wife? Look again at the story. Find me some examples. Everybody. [Pause, pages turning, some talking] Find any?

(6)   David: Oh yah! She puts a bandaid on his cut.

(7)   Teacher: Good. Any others? Ann?

David was obviously confused by the teacher's request to *"follow it up"* (3) and the teacher responded (5) with the point which was implicit in David's comment in (2). The teacher's actions can be seen as ensuring that the reasoning did not stray too far from what the teacher saw in the story. An alternative path, well within the teacher's apparent goal to give David reason, would have been to ask David as to the thrust of his point in (2) rather than assuming what that thrust was.

The end of the lesson provides a rich basis for reflecting on the moral complexities of some teaching situations and suggests the tensions a teacher might feel if discussion moved in a direction that was either inconsistent with the subject matter or the espoused norms of society. The teacher comments that, *"therefore we have this character who makes up a story to cover himself and then has to keep lying to keep the story going. More people get involved and the thing grows . . . I'm sure you all appreciate the poor fellow's plight . . . "* This hints at the teacher's sense of the story and his moral disposition toward it. He moves to the last question which *"asks for your opinion."* Jim reads the question:

(8)   Jim: "Was Irving justified in not calling the police and keeping the money?" No. I don't think he was. He should've given the money back to Smalley. It was his (Smalley's) money. He won it in a poker game.

(9)   Teacher: Did he win it fairly? And, if he didn't, does that make a difference? Jim?

(10) Jim: No, it wouldn't make a difference.

(11) Teacher: Sharon?

(12) Sharon: It wasn't right for him to keep the money.

(13) Teacher: Why?

(14) Sharon: It wasn't his money.

(It is not clear to whom Sharon is referring in (12) and (14).

(15) Teacher: I suppose that's a good reason. Anyone think he did the right thing? Gary, you do?

Gary says that Irving deserved to keep the money because Smalley had cheated at the poker game. This is the first clear but implicit expression of the moral that two-wrongs-make-a-right. Again, the moral is not generally espoused by the society of which these students are a part. The teacher did not ask Gary or other students to go back to the story itself. Rather, he asked if *"anyone else agrees with Gary? Alex?"*

(16) Alex: Yah, he was right. I wouldn't give it back.

(17) Teacher: Anybody else? One, two, three, six; seven more on that side. Anybody with any better reasons? [Pause]

At this point (17) roughly one third of the class agreed with Gary that Irving's actions were justified. I obviously cannot speak for the teacher's sense of dilemma but I can speak of my own when I try to put myself into the teacher's situation. The tension I imagine is that to let the matter drop at this point would seem to condone the idea that lying and cheating are alright so long as everything ends well. That is fine for a neat story with a twist, but as a teacher I would be upset if I suspected that the story was setting parameters for moral conduct. In that regard, Alex's response (16) is disturbing if he is talking about what he might actually do outside the context of a fantasy. A beginning for one way of dealing with the issue would be to distinguish between the moral potential of the story and its literary potential. One path for discussion would then be to show how a particular genre of narrative can entertain because it preserves a sense of "rightness" yet violates well-known moral codes.

Clarity in discussion was mentioned as an aside after Sharon's comment in (14). It is a more critical issue in the following, especially when we place ourselves in students' position of trying to make sense of the interaction. After the pause in (17) the teacher continued:

(17 cont.)
Teacher: [Pause]. Well, I suppose this is the point of the whole story—the idea that the writer wanted us to think about. There's a saying, or proverb, that might apply here. Anybody know—Brenda? [Pause]

(18) Brenda: Something about two wrongs?

(19) Teacher: Right. Do you know how it goes?

(20) Brian: Two wrongs do not make a right.

The "saying" to which the teacher referred (17 cont.) and Brian articulated (20) cannot be drawn from the story they have read, although its contrary (two-wrongs-do-make-a-right) is more compatible with a literal reading. The teacher left the question open:

(21) Teacher: That's it, Brian. Is that the point the author appears to be making?

Ann then suggested that, *"It's like revenge."* When asked to explain, a brief discussion ensued in which "evening-up-the-score" was put forward as a way an individual might address a wrongdoing. The teacher asked, *"Is that acceptable in our society today?"* Alex said, *"no"* because *"everybody couldn't just go around shooting everybody."* Brenda offered that *"innocent people might get hurt."* Near the end:

(22) Teacher: How does our society handle the whole problem of getting even or revenge? [Pause] No ideas? Why do we have police and lawyers?

(23) Brenda: Oh! That's how.

(24) Teacher: Tell us, Brenda.

(25) Brenda: We're supposed to let the police and law get even for us.

Conclusion

Reflecting-*on*-teaching is to ask hard but not callous questions with a view to informing our own reflection-*in*-action. We need to ask, among other things, about the role of reasons in discussion. What obligation does the teacher have to make his or her own reasoning explicit and to give the child reason? What is the relationship between a teacher's effort to foster discussion and the nature of the subject or the norms of society? What does this relationship have to say about the moves that the teacher might make in working with students? These kinds of questions allow us to ask of the "Poker" vignette, for example, if and where it might have been appropriate for the teacher to make explicit to the students the dilemma he faced as a teacher in this situation. Such a move could make the substantive issues transparent and provide the ground for further discussion.

Implicit in the "Poker" vignette, then, are questions about what might have been done differently and whether those possibilities would have been appropriate. But it is important to keep in mind the broader context within which these reflective questions are asked. The broader context is to recognize that in constructing a vignette we are not prescribing to similar situations, nor are we retrospectively prescribing to the vignette itself. There are a variety of relevant contextual threads into the present, past, and future, the omission of which makes prescription implausible. In the "Poker" vignette, for example, what the teacher does on the following day is critical to the broader pedagogical context of the situation, even though they may leave untouched the points made in the vignette itself. It would be cynical to assume that what followed Brenda's comment (25) made no difference to the quality of these students' lives as learners. We have to assume that in some way it makes a difference if the topic is dropped after Brenda's comment, or something else happens:

(26) Teacher: Something like that. Think about it. We take a lot of things for granted without really thinking about it. That's one of the reasons we

look at stories like this—to help us think. Now, I want you to think and write what you think. But remember some of the things we've already mentioned. Irving behaves in a certain way because of a specific set of circumstances. He really was able to achieve some kind of revenge without any real action on his part. Things worked out, if you want to think they worked out, through dumb blind luck. Now take some of the information here and write a paragraph for me suggesting the actions that you think Irving should have taken. As well, try to account for the reasons that he didn't do them. Is that clear?

In the construction of a vignette, then, some particulars are selected over others because they help to make a point. The point developed is to be taken seriously, but not as a prescription. Even with the construction I have placed on these vignettes, nothing I have said would indicate that the classroom should only be a haven of "reason." Nothing I have said would indicate that there is no place in the classroom for intuition, brainstorming, gut reaction, or shooting-from-the-hip, for both teachers and students. The central question for reflection-*on*-action and reflecting-*in*-action is when is it appropriate to do what.

The quality of a learner's experience ultimately involves (but is not "reduced to") the particulars of what was said and done in context. There are many shapes that can be given the particulars, many issues worthy of attention. Implicit in the shaping of the above vignettes is a point of view which sees teaching as more than transmitting information, which values a "conversation of instruction," which values the integrity of the subject matter, and which values "giving the child reason." The point of view says that, among many considerations, a teacher's moves are and should be informed by (but not "ruled by") an understanding of the relationships among the subject matter, the place of reasons, and the demands of sincere interaction. These understandings contribute to knowing-in-action and reflection-in-action. When we construct a vignette to make a point, we reflect-on-action. We insinuate into the construct our own images of relevant points to be made and appropriate actions to be taken. These are not and cannot be rules to-be-followed. They must be seen as points for discussion and consideration. They provide food for thought, concepts, and ways of looking at issues which can inform subsequent reflection, for ourselves and for others. The function of a vignette is to provide vicarious experience which can be reflected *on* with a view to informing reflection-in-action.

REFERENCES

Green, T. (1968). "A topology of the teaching concept." In C.J.B. MacMillan & T.W. Nelson (Eds.). *Concepts of teaching: philosophical essays.* Chicago: Rand McNally.

Orpwood, G. (1987). "A new approach to what goes on in the classroom." *The Globe and Mail*, Tuesday, November 24, p. A7.

Schön, D.A. (1983). *The reflective practitioner: How professionals think in action*. New York: Basic Books.

Schön, D.A. (1987). *Educating the reflective practitioner: Toward a new design for teaching and learning in the professions*. San Francisco: Jossey-Bass.

8

TAKING SCHÖN'S IDEAS
TO A SCIENCE TEACHING PRACTICUM

Allan M. MacKinnon
University of Toronto
and
Gaalen L. Erickson
University of British Columbia

For years students of education and teacher educators alike have struggled with problems associated with entry into the profession of teaching. Much attention has been focussed on the role of the practicum in the education and socialization of beginning teachers. But while teacher educators agree that student teaching is likely the most influential component of teacher education, researchers who have analyzed the empirical literature have, in many cases, characterized the knowledge base on practicum experiences as weak, ambiguous, and contradictory (Davies & Amershek, 1969; Peck & Tucker, 1973; Zeichner, 1980; Feiman-Nemser, 1983; Griffin et al., 1983). There continues to be a great deal of debate about the role that practicum experiences play in teacher education, about ways of conceptualizing and researching practicum, and about ways of systematically improving it.

Our particular concern in this chapter is with the character of practicum. Focussing on the experiences of student teachers of secondary school science—the lessons that they teach, their dialogue with supervisory teachers, their interaction with pupils—our intent is to examine the utility of an analysis by Donald Schön (1987) on the nature of a "reflective practicum." In his book *Educating the Reflective Practitioner*, Schön has put forth ideas about education in the professional schools that seem to promise fresh understandings about the character of practicum. This chapter, then, explores the extent to which Schön's account of professional education—his three "coaching models" in particular—are applicable and appropriate for illuminating science teaching practica. This exploration will take the form of examining some excerpts from several supervisory dialogues which occurred near the beginning of a four-week practicum in a secondary science class.

Although there are several meanings associated with "reflective teaching" and "reflective thinking" current in educational literature, our work draws principally upon only one: the notion that reflection involves the reconstruction of experience—for instance, when a practitioner assigns new significance to events, or identifies and attends to features of a practice situation that were previously ignored. Further constraints are placed on the notion of reflection developed here by the perspective of science teaching held by the supervisory teacher—one which pays particular attention to how pupils perceive and interpret science classroom events. Since the supervisory teacher embraces this "constructivist perspective" of science teaching (Driver & Oldham, 1986; Erickson, 1987) to guide and interpret his own practice, the analysis is an examination of how a student teacher was initiated into a particular "school" of reflection on practice. It should be clear at the outset that there are other kinds of reflection in addition to the kind that Schön is referring to, and that even within Schön's general account itself, this analysis attends to certain types of reflection and ignores others. While it is necessary to explicate the characteristics of a constructivist perspective on science teaching and learning, the primary focus is on the practicum itself. One of the broad goals of our research agenda, then, is to generate concepts and understandings of a unique form of a science teaching practicum, one that occurs within the boundaries of a constructivist orientation to science teaching. More specifically, the purpose of this chapter is to identify some of the elements and the conditions which seem to promote a "reflective practicum" involving a student teacher working closely with an experienced science teacher.

The Problems of the Practicum

Research reports in the teacher education literature have given rise to a general concern about the knowledge base required to prescribe specific procedures for practicum. In some cases this concern has to do with the "amount" of information about the practicum that is available, and whether, given more information, it would be possible to derive defensible prescriptions for its organization. For example, Samson, Borger, Weinstein, and Walberg (1983) came to the following conclusion in their analysis of thirty-eight studies related to the influence of field experiences on the attitudes of education students:

> Insufficient information is available about aspects of the subjects and settings, the quality and character of the field experience, the field experience location and other important variables to recommend more specific policies than generally providing early teaching and related experiences in the first few years of college. (Samson et al., 1983, p. 11)

A similar concern was raised by Griffin, Barnes, Hughes, O'Neal, Defino, Edwards, and Hukill (1983) in an extensive study of student teaching. They concluded from their literature review that, "The current research derived knowledge base appears to be too limited to direct decisions and practices in clinical experiences for prospective teachers" (p. 4). Empirical work with ninety-three student teachers from two universities led these researchers to the following observation:

Awareness of policies, expectations, purposes and desirable practices was not widespread across participants in the student teaching experience. It was rare that university and school-based teacher educators agreed upon, or could even articulate, the policies and practices which were supposed to guide student teaching. (Griffin et al., 1983, p. 335)

Another type of concern about the knowledge base on practicum experiences can be found in the literature. This concern has more to do with the "type" of information that has been collected than its availability. For instance, Zeichner (1984) presented a comprehensive meta-analysis of research into early field experiences and student teaching, based on Bronfenbrenner's (1976) conception of the "ecology of education." He argued that there was a need for researchers to attend to contextual features of practicum by considering three basic elements of the "ecology of field experiences": (1) the structure and content of a field experience program, (2) the characteristics of placement sites, and (3) the relationships between education students and those with whom they interacted.

. . . the particular quality of a field experience cannot be understood solely by its procedures (e.g., length), its organizational structure or even by the curricular intentions and plans of its designers . . . its influence on teacher development cannot be discerned from the examination of only isolated fragments of its ecology. It is hoped that research on field experiences will give more attention in the future to the complex and multidimensional nature of these experiences and that this ecological approach to the study of field experiences will stimulate discussion and debate over which particular curricular and contextual dimensions of programs will help us more closely realize our goals for teacher development. (Zeichner, 1984, p. 17)

Given the complexity of student teaching experiences, it is not surprising that many research results seem to be ambiguous and conflicting. Popkewitz, Tabachnick and Zeichner (1979), among others, have criticized the widespread use of research methodologies that, they say, ignore the quality of particular contexts. For example, Popkewitz et al, (1979) called for a methodology that views teacher education as a "constellation" of dynamic social events.

The events of professional preparation are not independent or freestanding, but are embedded in a social history and in relation to other contemporaneous events. While that embeddedness gives them some stability, dynamic social events are also characterized by their evanescent characters since they are in the process of continually becoming. (Popkewitz et al., 1979, p. 58)

Another example is provided in a recent review of 102 reports investigating Canadian teacher education, in which Wideen and Holborn (1986) reported that they found a

quantitative flavor in which questionnaires and standardized measures were used to focus on variables isolated from their contexts. The reductionist nature of the research under such paradigms and the focus on variables taken out of context are unlikely to improve our understanding to any great extent or lead to development of the theory we so critically need. Thus a first methodological priority in research into teacher education is a move toward a more liberal methodological approach. (Wideen & Holborn, 1986, p. 577)

115

One of the possibilities that Wideen and Holborn discuss as a viable way of conceptualizing practicum phenomena entails a position presented by Russell (1984), in which he argued for a model of teacher education based on "reflective" action by teachers. Russell's position has at the center of teacher education the development of prospective teachers' reflections on their own teaching. He examined Schön's (1983) perspective in terms of the significant role played by reflection in learning a practice, and considered its implications for teacher education.

> Finally, we have the beginnings of a way out of what I regard as one of the basic dilemmas of teacher education—the relationship between the university, where teachers are "trained" and "retrained," and the schools, where most teachers practice their profession. If the daily work of teachers and student teachers can be removed from its present inferior status, we may find that much of our current work in teacher education can be redirected to exploring the meanings of "reflection-in-action" and, in time, coming to understand the stages through which a teacher moves in learning to reflect-in-action. (Russell, 1984, p. 28)

This present chapter is sympathetic with Russell's position as it is concerned with documenting some aspects of the early stages of the initiation of a student teacher into a way of "reflection" about the practice of science teaching. In order to accomplish this task it is necessary to outline briefly the nature of reflective thinking as conceptualized by Schön and then discuss some strategies that he has proposed to encourage such thinking in a practicum setting.

Educating the Reflective Practitioner

By way of an introduction to Schön's ideas, it will be useful to draw upon an analogy he has used to point to a dilemma that exists in professional education. Schön (1983) refers to this dilemma as one of "rigor or relevance" (p. 42). He imagines the topography of professional practice to consist of a hard, high ground overlooking a swamp. The hard, high ground is comprised of well-formed theoretical problems that can be solved by applying the methods of science. In the swamp below there are the important, but messy and difficult problems of practice—problems that require particular lines of action.

To deal with the dilemma that this topography suggests, Schön has proposed two courses of action. One can remain on the hard, high ground where it is possible to be rigorous in solving problems, but where the problems are relatively unimportant to practice. The other alternative is to descend into the swamp below where the problems are relevant, but where one cannot be rigorous in any way that he or she knows how to describe. At first glance, the problems inherent in dealing rationally with this topography of professional practice seem to be insurmountable.

However, the landscape that Schön has provided warrants close examination. Is he proposing that we cannot be rigorous, or scientific, in thinking about what we do? Is it that we cannot describe what practitioners do in a language that provides clarity and precision? In our judgment, Schön is saying neither. Rather, he has tried to bring to life a set of concepts with which we can discuss professional knowledge, how it might be learned through reflection, and the importance of providing models for students of the professions to emulate. Certainly, it is not the only language with which we can describe professional competence. What seems to be unique about Schön is his insistence that professional education ought to be as much concerned with the problems located in the swamp, as it is with the propositions and theories that appear to have a firmer footing on the high ground, and in particular, with looking at ways of marrying these sources of knowledge about teaching.

To begin the task of developing a language of professional knowledge, Schön points to the kind of knowledge that a competent practitioner displays in action—the nonlogical processes that are manifest in recognition of patterns and making sense of complexity. Here, Schön draws extensively from Polanyi's (1962) notion of tacit knowledge, and he develops the concept of knowing-in-action to refer to the spontaneous, intuitive awareness that practitioners bring to their work. The phenomenon of carrying out a sequence of actions without articulating them is of central importance. One's ability to do so, according to Schön, does not depend on the description of the sequence. Rather, one's ability to recognize patterns in situations of uncertainty and uniqueness, and to act efficaciously in those situations, depends on one's capacity to "frame" problems. In doing so one is drawing upon a repertoire of past experience and ways of apprehending that experience, both of which lead to an ability to "reframe" problems in the light of the information obtained from the practice setting. (Of course, it is just "this" experience that is being provided for the student in the practicum setting.) Schön refers to these processes as "reflection-in-action," that is, where the reframing occurs in the action setting; and "reflection-on-action" where the reframing occurs in retrospect, some time after the problem situation. Reflection-in/on-action, then, is the mechanism he proposes which permits practitioners to continue to develop a rich repertoire of strategies and ways of making sense of experiences that, ultimately, accounts for their competence in dealing with the "messy" problems of practice.

While reflection-in/on-action consists of problem setting and problem solving, a central feature of reflection, that is often ignored in conventional accounts, is problem setting.

> Problems do not present themselves to the practitioner as givens. They must be constructed from the materials or the problematic situations that are puzzling, troubling and uncertain. When we set the problem we select what we will treat as the "things" of the situation, we set the boundaries of our attention to it, and we impose upon it a coherence which allows us to say what is wrong and in what directions the situation needs to be changed. Problem setting is a process in which, interactively, we *name* the things to which we will attend and *frame* the context in which we will attend to them. (Italics in original, Schön, 1983, p. 40)

Following Schön's account, problem setting and problem solving are interdependent; a particular line of action taken to solve a problem that is identified in practice follows from the frame that has been engaged to set the problem.

> . . . the practitioner's effort to solve the reframed problem yields new discoveries which call for new reflection-in-action. The process spirals through stages of appreciation, action and reappreciation. The unique and uncertain

situation comes to be understood through the attempt to change it, and changed through the attempt to understand it. (Schön, 1983, p. 132)

When a practitioner sees a new situation as some element of his repertoire, *he gets a new way of seeing it and a new possibility for action in it, but the adequacy and utility of this new view must still be discovered in action.* (Emphasis added, p. 141)

Having developed this description of professional knowledge and some plausible conjectures about how this knowledge is generated in the practice setting, another constellation of questions and issues emerge when Schön turns his attention to an examination of how one might educate this "reflective practitioner." A central feature of any such endeavor, Schön argues, is the way in which the practicum is conceptualized—the primary concern of this chapter.

The Reflective Practicum

To obtain some insight into the issues of designing appropriate educational experiences for reflective practice in general, Schön (1987) has looked toward what he refers to as the "deviant position" of the arts, and he has drawn upon the architectural design studio and the conservatory of music to develop a model of artistry in professional education. He then asks how we might marry the deviant position of the arts with the legitimate role and function of science derived from universities to assist in rethinking the role of practicum in professional education. To that end, Schön has put forward the notion of a "reflective practicum." Although the model is somewhat sketchy—perhaps necessarily so—Schön's illustrations of professional education for reflective practice are rich in detail and they make his analysis of professional education compelling. But these ideas have yet to be examined in the context of teacher education, a task addressed in this chapter.

One important feature of the practicum setting is that it provides a "virtual world," that is, a world that represents the practice world, but which allows the student "to experiment at lower cost." In the context of teacher education, this notion of lower cost needs to be unpacked. The student teacher's reality in a practicum is becoming part of a school, albeit in a special role. Supervisory dialogue and the student teacher's own internal dialogue may be in a type of virtual world, depending on how we choose to use the term, but, in the end, the student teacher is actually immersed in the practice setting. However, the cost of experimenting in this situation may indeed be costly as the students' self-esteem, their ability to continue with the practicum or even their future job prospects may be "on the line."

The second feature of a reflective practicum has to do with the supervisor, or "coach," to use Schön's term. The practicum situation of learning by doing in the context of science teaching should involve the supervisor as a "helper"—someone who is sensitive to the issues and concerns of becoming a science teacher. Third, the competence to be learned in a practicum is a design-like competence; it is holistic, it involves learning how one reflects-in-action and reflects-on-action by the framing and reframing of indeterminate situations.

Professional competence, according to Schön, is the sort of thing about which one could say either you get is as a whole, or you don't get it at all. The beginning of practicum is likely to be confusing and mysterious since the competence to be learned cannot simply be told to the student in a way that he or she could at that point understand. Even when the coach is very good at describing what he or she knows, the likelihood of the student grasping the meaning that the coach has in mind is very small. Under these circumstances, Schön says, some students discover that they must learn the required competence for themselves; they cannot be taught it directly. Yet, as time passes by, some students and coaches begin to communicate effectively. They begin to finish each other's sentences, or leave sentences unfinished, confident that their essential meanings have been grasped. Of course, some students never do understand what the coach is talking about, and some coaches never get through to their students. Nevertheless, many succeed in crossing an apparently impassable communications gap to achieve some degree of convergence of meaning.

Schön (1987) has proposed three "coaching models" to characterize a reflective practicum: "follow me," "joint experimentation," and "hall of mirrors." These are not mutually exclusive models; rather they point out three analytically distinct features of a reflective practicum that may, in the end, blend together in practice.

> In the dialogue of coach and student, each of these approaches calls for a different sort of improvisation, presents different orders of difficulty, and lends itself to different contextual conditions. (Schön, 1987, p. 295)

It is important to remember that the three approaches to coaching are idealized types. In practice, a coach may shift from one coaching model to another, or the several approaches may be combined.

The "follow me" model is foundational to a reflective practicum, suggesting that the supervisor/student relationship involves two component processes: "telling and listening," and "demonstrating and imitating." The supervisor must at first try to discern what the student understands, what he or she already knows how to do, and where the difficulties are. These things must be discovered in the student's initial performances. In response, the supervisor can show or tell, that is, demonstrate a particular technique that he or she thinks the student needs to learn, or, with questions, advice, criticism, and instructions, describe some feature of practice. The supervisor models actions to be imitated and experiments with communication, testing with each intervention both the diagnosis of the student's understandings and problems, and the effectiveness of his or her own strategies of communication. The student tries to make sense of the supervisor's demonstrations and descriptions, testing the meanings that have been constructed by applying them to further attempts to display skillful practice. In this way, students reveal the sense they have made of what has been seen and heard.

The model of "joint experimentation" takes an exploratory, analytic stance: the coach joins the student in experiment in practice, testing and assessing the student's ways of framing problems and acting in uncertain situations.

In *joint experimentation*, the coach's skill comes first to bear on the task of helping the student formulate the qualities she wants to achieve and then, by demonstration or description, explore different ways of producing them. Leading the student into a search for suitable means of achieving a desired objective, the coach can show her what is necessary according to the laws of the phenomena with which she is dealing . . . From her side, the student's artistry consists in her ability and willingness to step into a situation. She risks declaring what effects she wants to produce and risks experimenting with an unfamiliar kind of experimentation . . . The coach works at creating and sustaining a process of collaborative inquiry . . . [He] puts his superior knowledge to work by generating a variety of solutions to the problem, leaving the student free to choose and produce new possibilities for action. (Emphasis added, Schön, 1987, p. 296)

The "hall of mirrors" model points to how the coach's performance, in the very process of supervising the student, is exemplary of the craft that the student is attempting to acquire.

In the *hall of mirrors*, student and coach continually shift perspective. They see their interaction at one moment as a reenactment of some aspect of the student's practice; at another, as a dialogue about it; and at still another, as a modeling of its redesign. In this process they must continually take a two-tiered view of their interaction, seeing it in its own terms and as a possible mirror of the interaction the student has brought to the practicum for study. In this process there is a premium on the coach's ability to surface his own confusions. To the extent that he can do so authentically, he models for his student a new way of seeing error and 'failure' as opportunities for learning . . . But a hall of mirrors can be created only on the basis of parallelisms between practice and practicum—when coaching resembles the interpersonal practice to be learned, when students recreate in interaction with coach or peers the patterns of their practice world, or when . . . the kind of inquiry established in the practicum resembles the inquiry that students seek to exemplify in their practice. (Emphasis added, Schön, 1987, p. 297)

Some students are more successful than others in joining the supervisor in reflective experimentation. These students seem to be distinguished by three qualities (Schön, 1987, pp. 294-5): they are able to recognize logical inconsistencies when these are pointed out; they dislike inconsistency and incongruity; and they are ready to test their assumptions by appeal to directly observable data. Further, they are

inclined toward cognitive risk taking; more challenged than dismayed by the prospect of learning something radically new, more ready to see their errors as puzzles to be solved than as sources of discouragement. (Schön, 1987, p. 294)

Schön's conception of reflection-in/on-action is particularly useful when considering the nature of the dialogue that occurs between a student teacher and a supervisory teacher. Further, the three coaching models seem to be promising starting points for conceptualizing the character and dynamics of a reflective practicum in teacher education. The supervisory dialogue included in this chapter is intended to illustrate the utility of these ideas and models in the context of a science teaching practicum.

Before proceeding to a discussion of this supervisory dialogue it is necessary to provide a brief overview of the general perspective of science teaching that was embraced by the supervising teacher and hence formed the basis of some aspects of the "appreciative system" that was being communicated to the student teacher. That perspective has been called by some "children's science"; others refer to it as a constructivist approach to science teaching.

Children's Science: A Constructivist Perspective

Over the past decade there has been a great deal of science education research dealing with the ways in which children make intuitive sense of natural phenomena (Driver & Erickson, 1983; Driver, Guesne & Tiberghien, 1985; Erickson, 1979; Gilbert & Watts, 1983; Osborne & Wittrock, 1983). It is generally accepted that children form their own ideas about natural phenomena long before they arrive in the science classroom, and that their ideas are usually quite different from currently accepted scientific views. The term "children's science" is used by some of the researchers who investigate the intuitive ideas that children hold about natural phenomena (Osborne & Freyberg, 1985). Many researchers have observed that children's science often remains uninfluenced, or is influenced in unanticipated ways by science teaching (Erickson, 1983; Erickson & Aguirre, 1985; Gilbert, Osborne & Fensham, 1982; Osborne & Freyberg, 1985; Smith & Anderson, 1984).

Information that has been collected about children's science has been interpreted in terms of a constructivist view of science teaching and learning. Central to this perspective is the premise that individuals construct their own meaning of new information and ideas on the basis of their existing knowledge; learning is not a matter of passively taking up "static" information. A second premise underlying the constructivist view is that learners are "purposive" beings (Magoon, 1977). Thus, the constructivist account of learning is concerned with the "intents, beliefs and emotions of individuals as well as their conceptualizations, and recognizes the influence that prior experience has on the way phenomena are perceived and interpreted" (Driver & Oldham, 1986, p. 106). This perspective has clear implications for the practice of science teaching as Osborne and Wittrock (1983) argue, "Considerable emphasis in research, in curriculum design, and in teaching at all levels needs to be placed on the nature and detail of children's views of the world and meanings for words used in science. Teaching needs to take fully into account pupil perceptions and viewpoints and, where appropriate, to attempt to modify or build on, but certainly not ignore children's ideas" (p. 492). Furthermore, Fensham (1983) has proposed six "new objectives" for science education based on a general constructivist view of knowledge. Among them is, "to make explicit the world views of natural phenomena that students hold and to relate these to world views held now and in the past by scientists" (p. 7).

From a constructivist perspective, much learning in science involves children coming to hold new and more powerful ways of conceiving natural phenomena—ways that are more consistent with our intellectual heritage of scientific inquiry. This view of teaching and learning as "changing one's mind" is actively being pursued by several research groups. For example,

Posner, Strike, Hewson, and Gertzog (1982) drew extensively upon philosophical analyses offered by Toulmin (1972) and Petrie (1981) to postulate a "conceptual change model." The logical implications following from this model have been discussed by Hewson and Hewson (1984, 1986) in the contexts of science teaching and teacher education. Another active research group, which has implemented this perspective through the production of curriculum modules and other support materials, is headed by Rosalind Driver at the University of Leeds (Driver & Bell, 1985; Driver & Oldham, 1986; Driver, 1982). This group consists of several university-based researchers plus a large team of classroom teachers who produce and test the materials in their classrooms.

Our present work, then, draws upon two general perspectives—Schön's account of the development and growth of professional knowledge in practice settings and a particular approach to science instruction referred to as a "constructivist perspective." From this orientation we have derived the following propositions about science instruction: (1) a reflective science teacher will recognize that children are constantly constructing meaning of classroom events, (2) a reflective teacher will have a disposition for attempting to "see" science classroom phenomena from pupils' perspectives (Erickson, 1987; MacKinnon, 1987a, 1987b), and (3) a reflective science teacher will be in a better position to teach children about orthodox science. The next section explores the potential of a conceptual frame, derived from these orientations in making sense of several supervisory dialogues which occurred during a science teaching practicum.

Analysis of Supervisory Dialogue

The analysis that follows is focussed on two discussions that took place between a student teacher, Barry, and his supervisory teacher, Mr. Kelly, during the first two weeks of Barry's second practice teaching assignment. Barry had previously completed a three-week practicum with Mr. Kelly earlier in the year. (The names have been changed to preserve the anonymity of the student teacher and the supervisory teacher.) Mr. Kelly was selected for this study from a research group at the University of British Columbia that has been investigating students' intuitions and science instruction. In addition to being a well-known and highly respected teacher in his school district, Mr. Kelly has used a constructivist perspective as a framework for guiding and interpreting his own science teaching, and he is familiar with the theoretical formulation of reflective practice as put forth by Schön (1983).

The supervisory dialogue is analyzed for recurring patterns that can be seen in the discussion. A pattern of thinking about classroom phenomena from pupils' perspectives is identified in the dialogue, which is referred to as "intellectual empathy" for science pupils. We are suggesting that one type of reflective practicum in science teaching entails the development of intellectual empathy. Hence, we argue that it is necessary to explore the notion of intellectual empathy further; to examine what it might take to evoke in a student teacher intellectual empathy for pupils, and in addition, to consider what it means when a supervisory teacher displays intellectual empathy for a student teacher.

Supervisory discussions between Barry and Mr. Kelly were audio-recorded and transcribed for analysis. A striking feature of this supervisory dialogue involves Mr. Kelly and Barry reflecting on classroom events from pupils' perspectives. Mr. Kelly repeatedly constructs plausible pupil interpretations of Barry's instructions, demonstrations, questions, etcetera. Two excerpts are presented to illustrate the pattern of Mr. Kelly introducing "pupil frames" to Barry. Both cases deal with a physics class in which Barry was teaching about ways of graphically representing motion.

The first excerpt deals with a question that Barry gave requiring pupils to draw a "line-of-best-fit" on a distance-time graph in order to solve for the average speed of a moving body. Mr. Kelly recognized that at least one student, Beth, misinterpreted Barry's instruction to draw a line on the graph such that "half the points are on one side of the line, and half are on the other". ("K" identifies the speaker as Mr. Kelly; "B" as Barry. An ellipse indicates a slight pause, *not* an omission.)

K: Sometimes its useful to exploit a wrong answer. For example, the [average speed] question . . . one of the answers that I expected some people might give would be 24 rather than 21. And what they do is they just use the "m" part in the $Y = mx = b$ . . . they get the slope a bit wrong because they put it like . . . Beth over there . . . what she was doing . . . she had an interesting solution. You see, she said, "Well, you told her to form half of the points on one side and half on the other." Well, what she did was to join the origin to the middle point.

B: Oh, I see.

K: Then above that point, all of them were on one side and below that point all of them were on the other side. So it satisfied the conditions that half were on one side and half were on the other, but they were not randomized.

B: Yeah.

K: So she had misunderstood. But do you see what goes through kids' minds? Well then what you do, of course, then you'll get 24 rather than 21.

B: Oh right.

K: And something to be . . . when you have to think about evaluation, there's the notion of a carried error. For example, if she makes a mistake there and then she gets 24 because she made a mistake before . . . but did everything else from that point, how do you mark that?

B: It's just really the one error, really.

K: Well you have to think about that. It's a difficult . . . I don't think you can mark it all wrong, but you have to conclude yourself how you're going to sort that out. Uh, the other thing that . . . I mean if the wrong answer doesn't come out . . . like 24 . . . you see some kids think that you work out slope by just dividing the "y" by the "x" . . . and what they're assuming is that it goes through the origin and that there is another point there which is zero-zero.

B: Actually, that's a good point.

K: But you can do that because the "y" is really a "delta y" and the "x" is really a "delta x" because you have chosen another point, the origin zero-zero, but you have just not bothered to talk about it.

Intellectual Empathy

The essence of Mr. Kelly's commentary is summed up by his question, "But do you see what goes through kids' minds?" The excerpt illustrates how "what goes through kids' minds" is bound to the particular content at hand—in this case, finding the slope of a line-of-best-fit. Given the content-dependency of pupil perspectives and possible misunderstandings, Mr. Kelly draws extensively from a rich repertoire in making sense of the situation from Beth's position. He has vast knowledge of content and experience with pupils' understandings of content. Further, it was Mr. Kelly who observed Beth working on the problem at her desk, and who had the time before hand to think about her interpretation of Barry's instructions. But what interests us in particular is the way in which pupil perspectives are introduced to Barry; the general pattern of examining classroom events from pupil perspectives seems to be well established.

The next excerpt comes from the discussion that occurred the following day. Again, the focus is on a pupil's interpretation of a distance-time graph. In this case, Mr. Kelly begins by drawing Barry's attention to the interpretation, after which he invites Barry to explain it:

K: There was another point at which one student looked at the rising line on the distance-time graph and said, "Oh, he's accelerating." Why do you think he said that?

B: [10 second pause] Was that Mark who said that?

K: I'm not sure if he did . . . I thought it was somebody over in this corner.

B: They would . . . I guess somehow the idea of constant speed they would be thinking in terms of a constant straight line. So not being on a slant must be doing something other than . . . no, maybe they don't think in those terms. I'm not sure.

K: One of the things that is a standard problem for kids is confusing a distance-time and speed-time graph.

B: Uhm hmm.

K: I wonder if this student was suddenly thinking that because the line was rising that the speed was increasing. And suddenly in his mind, he was interpreting the vertical axis to refer to speed. You see now, the reverse will happen. If you're on a speed-time graph, they'll think, "Oh, the speed is changing."

B: If he'd . . . now, if he's thought that far ahead . . . I can see a confusion. But we haven't even talked about acceleration.

K: But he used the word.

B: Yeah.

K: Well, I think one of the things that might have been done is to say, "Yes, this is a straight line . . . yes, something is increasing, but distance is increasing and we call that speed. Later on, we're going to look at how you represent acceleration."

B: Yeah.

K: And it's easy to get the two confused. Uh . . . you recapitulated, which was good, you said, "Well, what we've covered today was this, this, this and this." I like that. That kind of summarized it at the end.

It is impossible to know with certainty what was going through Barry's head during this interchange. Although he concedes his confusion about the way Mark could have been interpreting the graph, he does give the general explanation of the misinterpretation that Mr. Kelly later constructs. Barry does say, "Somehow the idea of constant speed they [the pupils] would be thinking in terms of a constant straight line. So not being on a slant must be doing something other than . . ." If we interpret Barry's use of "a constant straight line" to mean a horizontal line, then it may be safe to say that he has already explained the pupil's misinterpretation in the way Mr. Kelly goes on to do. This interpretation raises questions about how much of the analysis should be left to Barry. Surely, Barry's confidence in systematically analyzing his teaching performance rests on his developing autonomy as a competent science teacher. Such autonomy, we would argue, is inextricably bound to the way in which Mr. Kelly recognizes and responds to Barry's reflections.

An alternate interpretation of this excerpt is that what we have here is good "teaching" on the part of Mr. Kelly. Putting aside questions about developing autonomy and how much of the analysis should be left to Barry, notice that Mr. Kelly delivers the input that is required by Barry to help make sense of a situation, which, at first, is perplexing. Mr. Kelly knows about the likelihood of students to misinterpret a distance-time graph as representing acceleration. As noted above, this is the kind of knowledge that comes with teaching experience. It is the kind of knowledge that we could not expect Barry to intuit on his own before gaining the required experience; if left to be autonomous in a situation such as this, Barry could well "flounder." In our judgment, the scenario captured by these alternative interpretations of the excerpt presents an intriguing dilemma faced by supervisory teachers: should the student teacher be allowed to develop autonomy at the risk of floundering? This point will be taken up later in the discussion of Schön's "coaching models."

Before proceeding, it will be useful to review the notion of "intellectual empathy" for science pupils. This notion has been derived from an analysis of Mr. Kelly's and Barry's supervisory dialogue; it is manifest in an explicit attempt by Mr. Kelly to get Barry to "see" classroom phenomena from pupils' points of view. Thus far, we have shown how in the supervisory dialogue pupil interpretations are introduced in a rather didactic fashion, much of the intellectual work being done by Mr. Kelly. The next excerpt illustrates an instance where Barry initiates and completes the framing of a plausible pupil interpretation. The discussion is focussed on another physics class, in which Barry introduced a model to explain electrostatic induction:

K: One of the things you can . . . one of the ways to answer a question . . . if you say, "What does a water molecule look like?" and you say it's H-O-H . . . if it was in line here, would it behave any differently than it does? So you see . . . an "if, then" sequence. Say, "What are the implications of your explanation?"

B: There is a question I can anticipate coming out of that. We've been talking about these sticks and objects . . . all kinds of . . . the electrons moving around and they might simply say, "Okay, so your molecule is a straight line, but why don't the electrons all zip over to one side anyway?" Wouldn't those little molecules act like little acetate strips or little . . .

K: All right, that . . . that's . . . you mentioned . . .

B: I don't know if they'll ask that.

K: You're saying that the molecules move?

B: No, I'm saying that a kid might say that . . . here's your molecule . . . why don't the electrons all sort of head over to that direction a little bit?

K: Oh, so they . . .

B: But I don't know if they'll ask that, but . . .

K: So what you're saying is that essentially the atoms are rearranged because of the field they're in . . . is that what you mean?

B: They might say that . . . they won't say that the atoms . . . yes. Yes, the atom itself. The electrons within the molecule might rearrange leaving this little unit. You know, it's as easy for them to think that explanation as it is for them to think of that one.

K: Yeah. I would say at that point, "That's a terrific explanation. That's a very creative . . . and if you were a scientist and didn't know what the water molecule looked like, that's a perfectly legitimate model." And then you say, "Well, do we have any other information?" For example, I would say that there might be things that you could explain with this vee shape that you couldn't explain with the other.

B: Snow crystals and . . .

K: Snow crystals. "Can you explain snow crystals using your model?" And you say, "Well, you might adapt it again." But that's really good teaching, I think. When you take a model that the kid has suggested such as your reorganization of the electrons . . . and say, "Okay, that's a good model. You've come up with something that explains this particular instance. Are there any . . . let's test it." And push it and push it. You don't say, "It's not right."

The above excerpt supports the claim that Barry seems to be developing the disposition for interpreting classroom events from the perspectives of pupils. The discussion carries on with some very interesting dialogue about the nature of scientific models. Notice, though, that while Barry seems to understand the general strategy of negotiating with students about acceptable explanations, he does raise a dilemma concerning his knowledge of content, and his ability to respond in appropriate ways to students' ideas. The problem he faces, of course, may only be resolved with more teaching experience:

B: Yeah, I realize that you don't say it's not right. I have a problem with just having the right things at the forefront of my head to deal with those kinds of questions. I don't think they would be there. I don't know how I would deal with . . . well, I'd kind of get flustered, I think, 'cause I wouldn't have it right there . . . the right explanation for the Grade 10. I would have it there if somebody else explained to me why that model is wrong . . . I'd understand their explanation, but I don't know if I'm far enough along to . . .

K: Well, how do you see your role with respect to a question like that? Do you feel that you always have to know the answer?

B: Uhm, I feel that it's important. It's not that I always have to know the answer, I think that if you do know the answer you're a much better teacher . . . if you can drag that up. So that you can collect all the things that you do know and you can focus them on the issue. That's the point I'm making . . . is that a lot of those questions do come up . . . and I know a lot of stuff, but it's not organized to flow into the answer.

The problem that Barry raises about not having content organized in such a way to "flow into" responses to students' questions is interesting in its own right. Mr. Kelly may ease the tension inherent in Barry's dilemma when he reflects on his own experience in recognizing and responding to the kind of pupil questions and interpretations to which Barry refers:

K: Yes. Well I would think at that point that you don't necessarily have to hold up the whole class and say, "We can't go on until we solve this problem." Uh, I find myself saying . . . when I come across that . . . there are times when a kid asks and doesn't really realize himself how good of a question it really is. There are times when I recognize it as being a good question. Say, "Well, what you're really getting at is this underlying problem . . . and I don't know that, but I'll try to find out and I'll get back to it." Sometimes I miss it. You know, you're just not going to pick up on all of them. But if somebody came up with that sophisticated model that you're describing . . .

At this point in the practicum (approximately two of the four weeks had elapsed) we discussed the notion of intellectual empathy with Mr. Kelly and we explained that we thought there was sufficient evidence in the dialogue to indicate that Barry was beginning to acquire the disposition to examine classroom phenomena from pupils' perspectives. Mr. Kelly agreed that Barry was showing signs of being able to empathize with pupils intellectually, but went on to tell us that Barry was experiencing difficulty relating to pupils on social grounds. Mr. Kelly's report was echoed by another supervising teacher with whom Barry had been working, who contrasted Barry's "content orientation" with another student teacher's "pupil orientation."

Mr. Kelly explained how he made an explicit attempt to model the kind of behavior toward pupils that he felt was lacking in Barry's teaching. At the beginning of one class, Mr. Kelly stood at the door casually talking with pupils as they entered the room. He spoke loudly enough so that Barry could hear the interactions and note the kind of information Mr. Kelly was gathering about the pupils. Later, during the discussion of the lesson, Mr. Kelly described what he was attempting to do and why he was attempting to do it:

K: Okay, there were a couple of things about the physics. They're mostly fairly small. One of the things . . . is that when you circulate with the kids after you've taught the lesson . . . or at the beginning of the period . . . uh, I think it helps to try to get to know the kids. What I mean is . . . I'll give you some examples. Nellie . . . who's sitting right at front . . . she's an interesting case. She's an art student and . . . just talking to her today I found out that she wants to go into the military. She's very interested in physics and she said that she has made a decision that for her purposes physics is going to be the most interesting or useful of the science courses . . . for that purpose. Now that makes her interesting because she's involved in the militia and that gives her a whole background of practical experience exposure to ballistics and whatever . . .

B: So examples you can pull . . .

K: If you know that you can call on that. Now, let's see . . . one thing that was happening today . . . what's that girl's name in the corner . . . Carol . . .

B: Carol, yeah.

K: She is a very proud lady at the moment because her sister has just had a baby. She's very turned on . . . she brought a picture, she was showing it to her friends.

B: Yeah.

K: Now, if you know that personal side to it, you will make a special contact if you just touch base on that.

B: Uhm hmm.

K: Don came in today. He was at outdoor school. If you know that there might be a time when you can tap into that as an example for a question or something.

B: Yeah, that's . . .

K: Now, I'm just trying to . . . these two boys here . . . Stan and . . .

B: Stan and Fred . . .

K: . . . and Fred . . . they're basketball players.

B: Yeah.

K: Every time they come to class with a tie, that's the sign that they have a basketball game that day.

B: Oh, I see.

K: And they have a game that they're thinking of today. I think it's against . . . who is it against? I don't know who it's against, but you could use . . . see, ballistics and basketball go very well together.

B: Oh yeah.

K: Now, you're not going to do ballistics actually, but you can use examples . . . you could ask them to describe what it feels like when a ball is under various conditions.

B: Well, the example with the ticker tape . . . if you were bouncing a ball at a steady rate, how far is it between . . . where it hits the floor if you're going fast or going slow or standing in one place?

K: Beautiful example. As a matter of fact that is such a good example you could almost have a kid come up and demonstrate that.

B: Yeah, that would have been an idea. Well, I could still fit it in.

K: But do you see my point . . . that just tapping into some of these special experiences of the kids will build up a relationship for you . . . but it will also allow you to build on those four examples. I mean that basketball example you just described would have been fantastic.

Barry is rightly commended by Mr. Kelly for the "ticker-tape-basketball" example of "tapping into some of these special experiences of the kids." Further, we think that Mr. Kelly should be commended for his demonstration and description of a feature that he apparently regards as being central to the craft of teaching, albeit difficult to describe. When we return to the discussion in the excerpt below we can notice that, inspite of the rather awkward description of this feature by Mr. Kelly and how it might be accomplished, there is nonetheless some evidence that Barry understands it.

B: I find . . . I have tutored people and things . . . and there I do that. I've often used that. In fact I often thought of starting to explain something was that some how what you've been saying and their understanding has become [separated] . . . it's a matter of going back until you find a place where they're stuck together and then taking them along. What I find difficult with the class, though, is . . . my memorization of names isn't great. But I work on that. But I just get a bit floored by all the other things.

K: There's so many things happening.

B: That's what I find . . . all these examples . . . if I was talking to Stan and I knew he was a basketball player, then that is how I would go about it . . . because I have done that sort of stuff. But as a class I find it . . . and I find all that spark, and that *is* the spark . . . that's lost.

K: I think that we might have the organizational thing in gear well enough that you can begin to go on to something like that. Why don't you try it with your Science 10 tomorrow? Talk to them . . . you know, you don't have to pick out . . . I don't know how exactly you go about doing it . . . I mean, the human being in conversation . . . you know, I . . . just talking to these kids I found out about Nellie when she came in. I don't remember exactly the context . . . we were just talking and then she started telling me about why she was taking physics. And then she was telling me this . . . uh, Carol, she had a picture in front of her, and these kids here . . .

B: Well, Nellie made a comment about . . . "Well, I'm just an art student . . . And I thought well, I want to do something with that comment. And then there were so many other things to do.

K: Well, put it on the back burner.

B: Yeah. Yeah, I can see that there's tremendous power in that.

Mr. Kelly's approach to supervision can be cast in a variety of ways. There are times at which he adopts a "follow me" model, as illustrated in the passage above. At other times, Mr. Kelly and Barry share in "joint-experimentation," an example of which would be the dialogue concerning electrostatic induction. Of course, these models require further elaboration; in terms of their use in understanding various approaches to supervision, as well as their consequences for the student teacher. Before proceeding with that task, though, it will be well to examine one more excerpt from the discussion on the second day.

What makes this next passage interesting is that it occurred on the day after the discussion about "tapping in to some of these special experiences of the kids." Barry had just taught a lesson in which he showed a class of thirty-two pupils a demonstration of electrostatic induction using a van de graaf generator. He wasn't happy with the lesson for several reasons, one of which was that few pupils were able to see the demonstration well enough to become involved in the lesson. Mr. Kelly asked Barry to think about the way he had been grouping pupils; perhaps the class could be split in half, each responsible for its own different activity:

K: Do you think it would have been possible to get one going in one group and the other [demonstration] going in the other group?

B: Yeah, except that one's more exciting than the other.

K: Which is more exciting?

B: Well, that van de graaf generator's intrinsically more exciting. I don't know . . . I guess I could have probably taken somebody like Allan, actually, who's done the electronics and said, "Here . . . show half of them how to do it." That would have worked. That might have worked well.

K: Do you think that the fact that he knows electronics is indicating that he's competent in electrostatics?

B: Uh, not necessarily, but he's very competent anyway. I think, in fact, there were a couple of people that had the induction idea no problem. And I think . . . I suppose there's always the risk they might have explained it all wrong to somebody.

K: I think you can use students to teach each other.

B: Yeah.

K: What are the objectives of the induction with the record? You're trying to teach them the four steps? Did that come out?

We believe that Barry shows that he is learning to do precisely the sort of thing Mr. Kelly meant by "tapping into" pupils' experiences. This suggests that Mr. Kelly has been successful in modelling the pattern of "tapping pupils' experiences," even though at this stage Barry may be doing so out of concern for his ability to handle the content he is teaching, rather than for enhancing the understanding of particular pupils.

This type of analysis of the supervisory dialogue has raised important questions regarding the nature of a reflective practicum in science teaching. In summary, a pattern of reflecting on classroom events from the perspectives of pupils was identified in the dialogue. The notion of "intellectual empathy" is one way of describing the pattern, and excerpts from two supervisory discussions have been presented to illustrate cases of intellectual empathy in the discourse of both Mr. Kelly and Barry. While the analysis has shown that Barry may be developing the disposition to examine classroom events from pupils' perspectives, there is reason to suspect that he does so out of a general concern for his own mastery-of-science content and his survival as a teacher. Nevertheless, Barry does display a tendency to analyze content and teaching strategies from pupils' points of view.

Mr. Kelly's approach to supervision seems to fit most closely with the "follow me" model of coaching (Schön, 1987), although there are times when a "joint-experimentation" model is evident. The analysis of the coaching approach led to important questions concerning what the "joint-experimentation" and "hall of mirrors" models would look like in practice, the conditions around which they might evolve, as well as the different demands they place on the coach and the student in different contexts. Further work is required to conceptualize these coaching models, to illustrate them in practice, and to show their consequences for student teachers.

Coaching In a Reflective Practicum

The illustrative analysis above indicates the presence of a pattern of supervisory dialogue that we argue was evident during much of the four-week practicum period. This pattern consisted of a series of moves by Mr. Kelly to reorient Barry's "frame of reference" for perceiving classroom events to one which included the pupils' cognitive and emotional needs and interests. We described this process of reorienting in terms of encouraging Barry to develop a disposition of "intellectual empathy" toward the pupils.

While our data base would have to be much more extensive to make any strong claims about the sort of coaching models actually employed by Mr. Kelly and the extent to which they were effective, it is sufficient to develop some preliminary conjectures about the utility of Schön's coaching models in a practicum setting and to raise some important questions which clearly will require further scrutiny. The primary type of supervisory move made by Mr. Kelly can be readily described in terms of a "follow-me model." While the excerpts that we examined depicted Mr. Kelly mainly in a "telling" mode, there were were some examples of a "showing" mode as well, particularly when he deliberately modelled for Barry some way in which he might get to know more about the out-of-school interests of pupils. It is not surprising that we captured primarily a strategy that relied on a verbal transmission of information because we only analyzed the supervisory dialogue. However, it was clear both from segments of this dialogue and from discussions with Barry and Mr. Kelly that many of the "showing" moves occurred earlier in the practicum when Brian spent much of his time observing Mr. Kelly teaching.

Because of the limitation of using only the post-instructional supervisory dialogue, it was difficult to identify instances where a "joint-experimentation model" was employed. The instance that we highlighted above, with respect to the "hypothetical discussion" about a plausible student model to account for the electrostatic properties of the water molecule, actually represents a type of thought experiment on the part of Barry and Mr. Kelly. It comes the closest to creating the less risky "virtual world" that Schön discusses where experimentation can indeed take place at a much lower cost. In this excerpt we can see Mr. Kelly inviting Barry to consider the implications of a particular explanation or model for what a "water molecule might look like" and then Barry takes up this invitation by inventing what he thinks might be a common student response. Once this model is clarified for Mr. Kelly, they both explore its pedagogical utility. Yet, as the subsequent dialogue suggests, Barry is very aware that the implementation of these kinds of moves with pupils in a "live" classroom setting is much more complex than their little thought experiment carried out in the privacy of the science preparation room.

The third model outlined by Schön, the "hall of mirrors," entails a recognition both by coach and student of the parallels between the supervisory process and the practice to be learned in the practicum. While there are indications in the dialogue that both Barry and Mr. Kelly are recreating in their own interactions some of the sought after instructional patterns, the most convincing evidence of the presence of this model would require one to look at the holistic character of the interaction between coach and student over the entire production experience—not simply some excerpts from several supervisory conferences. In summary, it does appear as though one can recognize in these brief supervisory conferences instances of at least two of the three coaching models described by Schön. Furthermore, we would argue that these models and the language used by Schön to describe them would seem to have considerable potential in illuminating some of the characteristics and conditions necessary for establishing a reflective practicum. It is these conditions, then, that we turn to in the final section of this chapter.

Conditions for a Reflective Practicum

One of the primary aims of a reflective practicum is to develop a disposition and a capacity to enable a student teacher initially to be able to reflect-on-action and then eventually reflect-in-action. Since we have only focussed upon the supervisory dialogue, the only evidence we have is of Barry's increasing willingness and ability to reflect on his own actions to the point where he is able to engage in a type of joint "thought experiment" with his supervisor. What conditions were present to enhance this apparent development of ability to reflect on his own teaching practice?

We think that the most important condition is to be found in the ability of the supervisor to articulate and demonstrate a coherent perspective of teaching practice. This means that supervisors also must be able and willing to reflect on their own practice as well as that of the student and try to make explicit some of the underlying beliefs and principles of the "appreciative system" that directs their own practice. In the present situation, a significant component in this appreciative system has been described as a "constructivist perspective of science teaching." It provided a conceptual lens through which Barry was encouraged to view pupils as continually constructing meaning from classroom events—drawing upon their previous knowledge and experience to do so. The various supervisory moves that accompanied Barry's initiation into this perspective have been described above in terms of developing an "intellectual empathy" for the pupils. Of course the supervisor must also be able to communicate many other facets of teaching practice in addition to this type of general, substantive framework. For example, basic techniques of lesson organization, presentation modes, management techniques (that is, the so-called "survival skills") must be mastered before a novice teacher is even in a position to begin framing and then reflecting upon classroom events from a pupil's perspective.

A second crucial condition for nurturing reflection in a practicum setting is that of establishing a climate of trust and a nondefensive posture on the part of both the novice teacher and the supervisor. This condition is essential because the novice has to be able to experiment in as risk-free an environment as possible. As indicated earlier, because novice teachers are indeed acting in real classrooms with real consequences, there are inevitably some risks involved, but one of the roles of the supervisor must be that of mediating between the action of the classroom and the way that these events are construed by the novice teacher. In other words the supervisor must provide a climate where experimenting and the inevitable "mistakes" that follow are encouraged, discussed, and viewed as departure points for growth. Such a climate of trust and willingness to reflect upon problematic situations are not easy to establish particularly in view of the situation in most practica whereupon the supervisor is also required, in some official capacity, to also make a summative evaluation on the performance of the novice teacher. Given this type of "evaluative bind" typically experienced by a supervisor, it follows that one of the most important criteria for making this evaluation should be "a willingness" to experiment and then reflect upon the results of that experiment. This criterion tacitly recognizes that the development of an adequate teaching repertoire of specific technical skills, capacities, and dispositions is a long-term developmental project (one might even be tempted to say it should be life long, or at least career long). Hence the best evidence on future teaching performance that we may have available to us at the very beginning stages of a teaching career is this propensity to reflect upon the results of our actions and realistically assess the implications of these actions in terms of further actions. There are many tensions involved in nurturing such a stance towards this type of reflective teaching. One of the most important of these was referred to earlier as the decision about how much autonomy must be given to the novice, "trading off" the potential deleterious effects of floundering. These decisions obviously have no "pat" answers and must be a product of a careful analysis of the particular situation. It does seem clear from our data base that it is important initially to provide the novice teacher with a wide variety of "teaching exemplars" (Erickson, 1987) as early as possible in the practicum through the use of various "follow-me" types of teaching moves.

While Schön describes competent practitioners in terms of their ability to reflect both in-action and on-action, we would submit that the latter type of reflection is most easily accomplished in a practicum setting and, that while the former can indeed be encouraged, it is extremely difficult and threatening (as Barry readily acknowledges) because of the lack of experience and the limited repertoire of most novice teachers.

There are undoubtedly many other conditions for enhancing a reflective practicum that we could add to the two overarching conditions we have described above, but these would take us beyond the scope of this chapter and certainly beyond the data base that was available for illustrating these issues.

In closing, we can only encourage others who "see" the potential utility of Schön's description of competent professional practice to take and extend both our data base and our analysis of how the coaching models might be used to enhance supervisory practice in a teaching practicum.

REFERENCES

Bronfenbrenner, U. (1976). The experimental ecology of education. *Educational Researcher, 5,* (8), 5-15.

Davies, D. & Amershek, K. (1969). Student teaching. In R. Ebel (ed.) *The Encyclopedia of Educational Research*. New York: Macmillan.

Driver, R. (1982). Children's learning in science. *Educational Analysis, 4* (2), 69-79.

Driver, R. & Bell, B. (1986). Students' thinking and the learning of science: A constructivist view. *School Science Review, 67,* (240). 443-456.

Driver, R. & Erickson, G. (1983). Theories in action: Some theoretical and empirical issues in the study of students' conceptual framework in science. *Studies in Science Education, 10,* 37-60.

Driver, R., Guesne E. & Tiberghien, A. (1985). *Children's ideas in science.* Milton Keynes, U.K.: Open University Press.

Driver R. & Oldham, V. (1986). A constructivist approach to curriculum development in science. *Studies in Science Education, 13,* 105-122.

Erickson, G. (1979). Children's conceptions of heat and temperature. *Science Education, 63* (2), 221-230.

Erickson, G. (1983). Student frameworks and classroom instruction. In H. Helm & J. Novak (Eds.) *Proceedings of the International Seminar on Misconceptions in Science and Mathematics.* Ithaca, N.Y.: Cornell University.

Erickson, G. & Aquirre, J. (1985). *Students' intuitions and science instruction: Stability and task context in students' thinking about vector quantities.* Paper presented at the annual meeting of the Canadian Society for the Study of Education, Montreal.

Erickson, G. (1987). *Constructivist epistemology and the professional development of teachers.* Paper presented at the annual meeting of the American Educational Research Association, Washington, D.C.

Feiman-Nemser, S. (1983). Learning to teach. In L. Shulman and G. Sykes (Eds.) *Handbook of Teaching and Policy.* New York: Longman.

Fensham, P.J. (1983). A research base for new objectives of science teaching. *Science Education, 67* (1), 3-12.

Gilbert, J., Osborne, R. & Fensham, P. (1982). Children's science and its consequences for teaching. *Science Education, 66* (4), 623-633.

Gilbert, J.K. & Watts, D.M. (1983). Concepts, misconceptions and alternative conceptions: Changing perspectives in science education. *Studies in Science Education, 10,* 66-98.

Griffin, G., Barnes, S., Hughes, R., O'Neal, S., Defino, M., Edwards, S. & Hukill, H. (1983). *Clinical preservice teacher education: Final report of a descriptive study.* Austin, Tex: University of Texas Research and Development Centre for Teacher Education.

Hewson, P.W., and Hewson, M.G. (1984). The role of conceptual conflict in conceptual change and the design of science instruction. *Instructional Science, 13* (1), 1-13.

Hewson, P.W. and Hewson, M.G. (1986). *Research on student conceptions: Implications for science teacher education.* Paper presented at the annual meeting of the National Science Teacher's Association, San Francisco, California.

MacKinnon, A. (1987a). Detecting reflection-in-action among preservice elementary science teachers. *Teaching and Teacher Education, 3* (2) 135-155.

MacKinnon, A. (1987b). Toward a conceptualization of a reflective practicum in science teaching. In J.D. Novak (Ed.), *Proceedings of the second international seminar on misconceptions and educational strategies in science and mathematics* (pp. 301-315). Ithaca, New York: Cornell University Press.

Magoon, A. J. (1977). Constructivist approaches to educational research. *Review of Education Research, 47* (4), 651-693.

Osborne, R.J. & Freyberg, P. (1985). *Learning in Science: The implications of children's science.* Auckland, New Zealand: Heinemann.

Osborne, R.J. & Wittrock, J.K. (1983). Learning Science: A generative process. *Science Education, 67* (4), 489-508.

Peck R. and Tucker, J. (1973). Research on teacher education. In R. Travers (Ed.) *The Second Handbook on Research on Teaching.* Chicago: Rand McNally.

Petrie, H.G. (1981). *The dilemma of enquiry and learning.* Chicago: The University of Chicago Press.

Polanyi, M. (1962). *Personal knowledge.* Chicago: the University of Chicago Press.

Popkewitz, T., Tabachnick, B.R. & Zeichner, K.M. (1979). Dulling the senses: Research in teacher education. *Journal of Teacher Education, 30* (5), 52-60.

Posner, G.J., Strike, K.A., Hewson, P.W. & Gertzog, W.A. (1982). Accommodation of a scientific conception: toward a theory of conceptual change. *Science Education, 66* (2), 211-227.

Russell, T.L. (1984). The importance and the challenge of reflection-in-action by teachers. In P. Grimmett (Ed.) *Research in teacher education: Current problems and future prospects in Canada.* Vancouver: CSTE/CSCI Publications, The University of British Columbia.

Samson, G., Borger, J., Weinstein, T. & Walberg, H. (1983). *Pre-teaching experiences and attitudes: A quantitative synthesis.* Paper presented at the annual meeting of the Amercian Educational Research Association, Montreal.

Schön, D. (1983). *The reflective practitioner: How professionals think in action.* New York: Basic Books.

Schön, D. (1987). *Educating the reflective practitioner: Toward a new design for teaching and learning in the professions.* San Francisco: Jossey-Bass.

Smith, E.L. & Anderson, C.W. (1984). Plants as producers: A case study of elementary science teaching. *Journal of Research in Science Teaching, 21* (7), 685-689.

Toulmin, S. (1972). *Human understanding.* Vol. 1. Princeton, NJ: Princeton University Press.

Wideen, M.F. & Holborn, P. (1986). Research in Canadian teacher education. *Canadian Journal of Education, 11* (4), 557-583.

Zeichner, K. (1980). Myths and realities: Field-based experiences in preservice teacher education. *Journal of Teacher Education, 31* (6), 45-55.

Zeichner, K. (1984). *The ecology of field experience: Toward an understanding of the role of field experiences in teacher development.* Paper presented at the annual meeting of the Association of Teacher Educators, New Orleans.

SECTION III:

REFLECTIONS ON REFLECTION

This section contains three chapters. All three critiques of Schön's work come out of the interest and debate that his visit to the University of British Columbia stirred. Each critic uses a different frame to look at Schön's ideas, indicating a wide divergence of perspective in the lively debate that has ensued.

Court writes from the perspective of a practitioner and comes to question the extent to which Schön's conception of reflection-in-action can really be operative in teaching. Claiming that Schön's description of what constitutes the "action setting" is neither definitive nor explicit, Court infers that "action" must mean when practitioners are "in the thick of things." Given this inference, Court argues that it becomes controvertible to assert that teachers can reflect in such settings; for, in her view, reflection involves the kind of "time out" and "double vision" that would cause teachers to lose lesson momentum and that sense of professional competence that accompanies the skilled execution of teaching. She ends by suggesting that deliberation is a better term than reflection for the kind of thinking that teachers do when they focus on the solving of immediate practical problems.

Hills and Gibson see Schön's work in serious need of clarification of the linguistic-conceptual system within which the reader can think about not only what Schön's competent practitioners do, but also what Schön himself has attempted to do in writing about them. Such a linguistic-conceptual system, if assembled, would, Hills and Gibson argue, enable the reader to reframe Schön's observations and also clarify the relationship between technical rationality and Schön's view of competent practice. They go on to explain what they mean by a linguistic-conceptual system and suggest that Schön has overstated the case in driving a wedge between the knowledge of technical rationality and the knowing-in-action of professional practice. They view the difference not as one kind of knowing being pitted against another, but rather that the knowing-in-action of professional practice is essentially constituted by an underdeveloped linguistic-conceptual system. It is this lack of a developed linguistic-conceptual system which restricts professional practice to a limited form of technical rationality analogous to Bruner's analytic competence. Having articulated their own understanding of a linguistic-conceptual system, Hills and Gibson go on to use such a framework to reinterpret Schön's (1983) mini-case studies in architecture, psychotherapy, town planning, and management. They conclude that Schön's competent practitioners think analytically but not reflectively. That is, they have developed reasonable levels of analytic competence and are fluent in the use of their specialized linguistic systems but rather than having mastered those languages, Schön's practitioners appear to be bound by them in the sense that there is no suggestion in the mini-case studies of their being able to change at will from one "notation system" to another. Put differently, Hills and Gibson claim that their reinterpretation of Schön's case studies shows that the practitioners in question do not reframe problem settings. This leads to their ultimate claim that, if Schön's practitioners are representative of competent professionals and reflection is positively related to competence, then competent professionals are a good deal less competent than they might be.

Selman's chapter critiques Schön from a very different perspective. Far from comparing Schön's view with that of technical rationality, Selman examines the ideas in relation to the range of competing alternatives to technical rationality that have been proposed in the last forty years or so. In doing so, he addresses the questions of how educational practice and epistemic theory are linked, to what extent Schön's account of an epistemology of practice provides for the resolution of those problematic features of practice which deny the adequacy of technical rationality (i.e., competing values and interests) as objects of reasoned consideration, and whether it is possible (as Schön implies it is) to develop a theory of knowledge which applies usefully to professional practice in general. Noting that Schön bases much of his theorizing on aesthetic exemplars derived from the design studio, Selman suggests that educational strategies found to be effective in a particular aesthetic setting should not be assumed to be effective in other professional settings which are less obviously aesthetic. Put differently, the special case cannot be generalized to other settings in a manner similar to the epistemological assumptions of technical rationality that Schön criticizes so vehemently. As a consequence, Selman finds Schön's alternative epistemology wanting because it only allows for the reasoned consideration of aesthetic values, leaving a range of other value standards to be overlooked or excluded. He illustrates his argument by reinterpreting Schön's own description of building a gate. Selman argues that Schön brings the standards of stability and squareness and knowledge of geometry to the act of gate building, and it is Schön's realization (as distinct from the wobble) that the gate would not meet these standards that created the surprise. Selman's point is that concepts, theories, rules, and standards play an intelligible part in the account of building the gate but that they do not explain the artistry involved. Accordingly, he suggests that we must decide whether teaching is more analagous to carpentry in which concepts and rules are operative or to design-like aesthetic enterprises in which concepts and rules play a significantly reduced role. After examining the concepts of "knowing-in-action," "reflection-in-action," and "tacit knowing" deemed central to Schön's treatise, Selman concludes that the criteria for reflective practice are neither clearly explicated nor ably demonstrated by the examples and nonexamples given. Learning to be competent involves, for Selman, acting according to the normative rules or social constructions which constitute a given practice. These rules, he argues, are not to be confused with scientifically-derived law-like theories which attempt to explain causality; rather, they govern the concepts and standards of practice. In the final analysis, Selman calls for a careful description and reconstruction of practice in specifically focussed settings rather than the global solution of a "new epistemology" offered by Schön.

9

"REFLECTION-IN-ACTION":
SOME DEFINITIONAL PROBLEMS

Deborah Court
University of British Columbia

Donald Schön's 1983 book, *The Reflective Practitioner*, and his later writings on reflection have been influential, and justly so, in the field of education. Schön has made a valuable contribution by stressing that professionals can and do improve their practice by reflecting on what they do and on the knowledge, beliefs, and values that they hold. By illustrating that practitioners can focus on and articulate their knowledge, beliefs, and values, Schön has helped to counteract the tendency among some current writers on teaching to stress too heavily the notion of tacit knowing. When "tacit" becomes an almost magical word for things which cannot be described, mystification of practice, rather than understanding, is the result.

Schön (1983) says that in our daily lives "our knowing is ordinarily tacit, implicit in our patterns of action and in our feel for the stuff with which we are dealing" (p. 49), but he also points out that "on the other hand, both ordinary people and professional practitioners often think about what they are doing, sometimes even while they are doing it . . . They may ask themselves, for example, What features do I notice when I recognize this thing? What are the criteria by which I make this judgment? What procedures am I enacting when I perform this skill? How am I framing this problem that I am trying to solve? " (p. 50). Schön recognizes that the articulated answers to such questions will be inadequate representations, but he does not see this as a hinderance to reflection.

> When practitioners reflect-in-action, they describe their own intuitive understandings . . . It is true, nevertheless, that there is always a gap between such descriptions and the reality to which they refer . . . [but] incompleteness of description is no impediment to reflection . . . Reflection-in-action does not depend on a description of intuitive knowing that is complete or faithful to internal representation. Although some descriptions are more appropriate to reflection-in-action than others, descriptions that are not very good may be good enough to enable an enquirer to criticize and restructure his intuitive understandings so as to produce new actions that improve the situation or trigger a reframing of the problem. (pp. 276-277)

Schön holds, then, that while much of our knowing is tacit as we go about our private and professional lives (he calls this "knowing-in-action), we can, when we choose, think about what we know and about how and why we do what we do.

However, Schön claims that professionals do this focussing and articulating while they are in the midst of professional activity, and problems arise with the way he has argued this claim. In *The Reflective Practitioner* Schön defines and attempts to illustrate his idea of "reflection-in-action," an activity in which he claims that professionals engage. He distinguishes between reflection-on-action, which occurs after the fact and involves looking back on the action using memory and imagination, and reflection-in-action which he claims professionals engage in while they are actually practicing their profession. He says that reflection-in-action is undertaken especially when a practitioner encounters a situation that is puzzling, troubling, or in some way unique. He describes how practitioners compare new situations to ones they have encountered in the past, and how they experiment to find the answers to problems by generating and testing hypotheses. His examples of people doing such "reflection-in-action" are drawn from various professions.

Schön's examples seem to illustrate several rather different kinds of "reflection-in-action" and most, upon examination, appear to involve *removing* oneself from the action in order to reflect. Thus the term "reflection-in-action" may not be appropriate. Also, the following passage, in which Schön attempts to explicate reflection-in-action, does not seem to be illustrative of professionals reflecting while actively engaged in practice:

> There are indeed times when it it dangerous to stop and think. On the firing line, in the midst of traffic, even on the playing field, there is a need for immediate, on-line response, and the failure to deliver it can have serious consequences. But not all practice situations are of this sort. The action-present (the period of time in which we remain in the "same situation") varies greatly from case to case, and in many cases there is time to think what we are doing. Consider, for example, a physician's management of a patient's disease, a lawyer's preparation of a brief, a teacher's handling of a difficult student. In processes such as these, which may extend over weeks, months or years, fast-moving episodes are punctuated by intervals which provide opportunity for reflection. (p. 278)

While it is clear that the physician, lawyer, and teacher described here would be reflecting on their practice as they pondered problems of diseases, briefs, and difficult students, it is not clear that such reflection is occurring "in action." Obviously a definition of "action" is needed, and the definition Schön offers suggest questions about the rightness of his claims. Schön continues.

> A practitioner's reflection-in-action may not be very rapid. It is bounded by the "action-present" the zone of time in which action can still make a difference to the situation. The action-present may stretch over minutes, hours, days, or even weeks or months, depending on the pace of activity and the situational boundaries that are characteristic of the practice. (p. 62)

Reflection-*on*-action, for Schön, would not occur in the "action-present," but after the fact, when action can no longer make a difference to the situation. This definition of the "action-present" is unclear and inadequate. Imagining Schön's example of a teacher working over a period of time (a whole school year would not be unreasonable) with a difficult student, there would be incidents or days on which the teacher would reflect after the fact, when she could no longer make a difference, in that the incident or the day is over. Her relationship with the student is ongoing, however, so she can still make a difference in terms of the larger picture. In Schön's sense this is the "action-present." But reflecting at home on a Saturday night over a cup of tea, or even in conversation with a fellow teacher on the same day as a troublesome incident has occurred does not seem like reflecting-*in*-action, because the action in which the teacher interacted with the student is over. Reflecting-*on*-action seems a more appropriate term. "Still being able to make a difference" is an idea which could be interpreted in many ways. A teacher could reflect on her relationship with a student even after that relationship has ended, benefitting from this reflection so that she can make a difference with another student who may have similar problems. The "action-present" is rather nebulous, and a more precise definition of "action" is needed.

It might seem from the preceding discussion that interacting with clients is the only time when a practitioner is really "practicing." Of course this is not so; professional practice entails many activities and many phases, some more "active" than others. But reflection engaged in during quiet moments over a period of days, weeks, or months when a problem or case is being dealt with does not seem to earn the title "reflection-in-action." "Action" seems to mean times when one is "in the thick of things."

Schön also describes what seems like a rather different activity which occurs when people *are* "in the thick of things" and take a momentary "time out" to reflect on a problem at hand. For instance,

> In the split-second exchanges of a game of tennis, a skilled player learns to give himself a moment to plan the next shot. His game is the better for this momentary hesitation, so long as he gauges the time available for reflection correctly and integrates his reflection into the smooth flow of action. (p. 279)

This might more reasonably be called "reflection-in-action," but it still requires a time out, albeit a brief one, from the action.

Schön also speaks of times when "reflection incongruent with a present course of action may be maintained through double vision. Double vision does not require us to stop and think, but the capacity to keep alive, in the midst of action, a multiplicity of views of the situation" (p. 281). Such "double vision" undoubtedly does exist, but it is questionable whether it can legitimately be called reflection. It might be possible to view the routinization of many of a teacher's tasks in light of this idea of double vision. As a teacher goes about calling the roll, checking homework, and doing other fairly routine tasks, her mind may be free to engage in other thoughts about what is going on in the classroom. When one is engaged in very demanding mental activity, though, the idea of double vision seems less plausible. It would be difficult to maintain two concurrent demanding lines of thought without losing the thrust of one or both.

It may be useful to introduce into the discussion of "reflection-in-action" the notion of deliberation. This is not a term that Schön uses, but deliberation is discussed, in relation to reflection by John Dewey, whose work has influenced Schön. Deliberation and reflection both involve a kind of "thoughtful thinking" and both, I would assert, require at least a momentary "time out" from the action. As well, both are usually directed toward the resolution of doubts or problems. Schön describes "reflection-in-action" as the way practitioners deal with "situations of uncertainty, instability, uniqueness, and value conflict" (p. 50). The difference between deliberation and reflection lies, it seems to me, in deliberation being more focussed on a specific problem, more deliberate, one might say, and less free ranging than reflection can be. One might see "reflecting on" as closer to "meditating on" and "deliberating" as closer to "considering" or "weighing alternatives." This is close to the distinction that Dewey (1932) makes when he says that "reflection when directed to practical matters, to determination of what to do, is called deliberation" (p. 134).

The concept of interactive decision making and the many "stimulated recall" studies of teachers' classroom decisions seem to allow that teachers do decide in action. Deliberation or the weighing of alternatives is usually seen as prerequisite to decision. Many of Schön's examples of "reflection-in-action" are questionable because they do not seem truly to involve action, or "the thick of things." Other examples, such as the tennis player's planning of his next shot, do not seem truly to involve reflection. The concept of "reflection-in-action" would seem to be in question on both counts. However, if we are to allow that teachers can decide (and thus deliberate) in action, it would appear we must also allow that they can reflect-in-action. This is a grudging admission, made on logical grounds and not on the basis of Schön's arguments. Even deliberation, or "careful thought" as it is sometimes defined, is difficult to assign to teachers in the midst of teaching, but if we follow Dewey's distinction, it may be that deliberation is a better term for the thinking that is done in brief "times out" from action, because it is usually directed to the solution of immediate practical problems. Momentary "times out," which could perhaps be called "reflection-in-action," might better be seen as moments of quick deliberation leading to decision.

The reflecting which Schön describes doctors, lawyers, and teachers as doing over days, weeks and months is not, it is submitted here, reflection-*in*-action, but it is reflection-*on*-practice, a worthy endeavor which Schön's work has done much to encourage.

REFERENCES

Dewey, J. (1932). *Theory of the moral life.* New York: Holt, Rinehart and Winston.

Schön, D.A. (1983). *The reflective practitioner: How professionals think in action.* New York: Basic Books.

10

REFLECTIONS ON SCHÖN'S
THE REFLECTIVE PRACTITIONER

Jean Hills and Carol Gibson
University of British Columbia

The intent of this chapter is to: 1) identify a specific question posed by Schön in relation to professions generally; 2) identify a similar question posed in relation to the field of educational administration; 3) identify the basis for Schön's question; 4) identify the basis for the question in relation to educational administration; 5) examine the answer Schön proposes in response to his question; and 6) present a framework within which it may be possible to formulate our own answers, and to reinterpret Schön's answer and his explanations.

Questions

Schön poses a question and provides an explanation as to why it has been difficult to provide an answer to the question. In relation to educational administration, we pose a similar question and offer an explanation concerning the basis for asking the question.

Professions Generally

Schön's question is: "Given the mismatch between the knowledge purveyed by professional schools and the problems of professional practice arising from the complexity, uncertainty, and instability of the practice situation; given the inter-connectedness of problems, the turbulence of environments, the conflicts of values, goals, purposes, and interests; and given competing and conflicting views of professional practice among practitioners, how can we account for the fact that some professionals succeed as well as they do?"

His explanation of the inability to explain the success of some practitioners is simple. The problem, he argues, is that we are bound to an inadequate "epistemology of practice," an inadequate theory of the kind of knowledge on which professional competence is based. Schön terms the historically and currently accepted epistemology of practice, "technical rationality" (1983, p. 21). According to the technically rational view, as presented by Schön, the kind of knowledge on which the competence of practitioners is based, is scientifically validated knowledge of the means best suited to the solution of given problems. Professional practice is viewed as problem solving, and those who engage in it are seen to draw upon the theories and techniques of basic and applied science to identify problems, diagnostically to analyze problems, and to prescribe solutions for them.

However well the technically rational approach may have served the science-based professions, e.g., medicine and engineering, Schön insists that it does not serve them well in dealing with certain kinds of problems, and it does not serve the minor professions (social work, architecture, education, planning, etc.) at all well. The reasons for its inadequacy in the latter case are not far to seek. Technical rationality is applicable only in those situations which exhibit the following characteristics, none of which is found in the practice of the minor professions.[10] First, technically rational performance requires that problems be formulated unambiguously. A profession that cannot identify a set of unambiguous problems common to the experience of practitioners cannot develop the basis for technically rational problem solving.[11]

Second, technically rational problem solving is possible only when problematic situations occur in stable forms. If the problematic situation is unstable, if it will not hold still, one cannot define problems clearly,[12] much less solve them.

Third, if problematic situations are unique, technically rational problem solving is impossible. Actually, given his assumptions, the situation is worse than Schön indicates. If every situation is unique in all respects, one could neither develop theories to explain them nor know whether or not the solutions applied had worked. The development and testing of theories requires the occurrence of multiple instances of the phenomenon in question. And, if every problematic situation is unique, one can never know whether the solution applied succeeded or failed. One cannot establish a generalizable relationship between variables on the basis of a sample of one.

Fourth, there are social requirements for the practice of technically rational problem solving. Even in cases in which the preceding three requirements are

[10]Schön (1983) also argues that they are also absent in the "truly significant problems" in the practice of the science-based professions. See pp. 42-45.

[11]We should note (though Schön does not) that, from our perspective, the identification of a common set of problems is possible only when three conditions are met. Problems may be conceived not as objective states of the phenomenal world on which all competent observers can agree, but as gaps between what is perceived to be the case in that world and what is conceived to be desirable, a gap between the "real" and the "ideal." Given that, the identification of a common set of problems requires: (1) a common cognitive framework within which to perceive the world; (2) a common conception of the desirable (value system) in relation to which to evaluate what is perceived; and (3) the occurrence of similar empirical conditions across the settings of different practitioners. The medical profession's success in the identification of unambiguous, common problems can be attributed to the existence of shared cognitive frameworks within which to perceive aspects of the object of clinical interest (the patient), the existence of a widely shared value system (health), and the fact that patients everywhere are susceptible to the same kinds of departures from the desirable state.

[12]With the exception of instability itself.

met, it is often the case that there is conflict among those who have a legitimate stake in the enterprise over what it is about the situation that is problematic. Where problem solving is a social, as opposed to an individual process, agreement about the end is a condition of rational selection among alternative means.

Finally, Schön (1983) argues that a number of professions, e.g., psychiatry and town planning, are characterized by multiple and conflicting conceptions of professional practice.

> There is contention over multiple ways of framing the practice role, each of which entrains a distinctive approach to problem solving. And when practitioners do resolve conflicting role-frames, it is through a kind of inquiry which falls outside the model of Technical Rationality. (p. 41)

So, why the difficulty in explaining the success of some practitioners? Because, on the one hand, we conceive of professional practice as technically rational problem solving. On the other hand, the state of knowledge and the conditions of practice preclude the application of technically rational problem-solving procedures.

Educational Administration

We pose a question similar to Schön's in relation to the field of educational administration: "What can practitioners of educational administration learn from university programs that is likely to enable them to perform more competently than they would have performed without it?"[13]

Although disputed vigorously by some of our colleagues, we base our question on the following observations which we hold to be empirically defensible:

1. The number of empirically validated solutions to non-routine administrative and organizational problems available for inclusion in university programs is severely limited.[14]
2. The number of firmly validated empirical generalizations that are relevant to the solution of nonroutine administrative and organizational problems, and also directly useful to administrators is similarly limited.[15]

---

[13]We are inquiring here about learning that goes beyond such obvious areas as educational law, budgeting, and finance, and the organization and routine operation of the educational system.

[14]This statement requires qualification because there is a sense in which existing organizational structures and processes constitute a complex of field-tested solutions to routine administrative and organizational problems—problems concerning who is to teach what, to what categories of learners, in what numbers, where, with what facilities, according to what rules, for what purposes, etc. In this sense, a wide variety of field-tested solutions is available. However, when one wishes to know which of several demonstrably workable solutions is most satisfactory in relation to some criterion, or when nonroutine problems, i.e., those not covered by existing arrangements arise, few tested solutions are available.

[15]We consider *directly* useful only those generalizations in which a substantial percentage of the variance of a dependent variable of concern is accounted for by causally related independent variables that are, within acceptable moral, legal, political, and economic limits, subject to manipulation.

3. There are few, if any, well-supported theories that are relevant to the solution of nonroutine problems of administration and organization.
4. Given the same value premises, the theories that are available often have conflicting implications for practice.

Explaining Professional Competence

Professions Generally

On what base does practitioner competence in the nonscience-based professions rest? Schön provides a clue, *to wit*, "And when practitioners do resolve conflicting role frames, it is through a kind of inquiry which falls outside the model of Technical Rationality." Generalize that sentence to include problems of conflicting ends, instability, and uniqueness, and we have Schön's thesis. The kind of inquiry of which Schön writes comprises "reflection-in-action," "problem framing," and "problem setting," all of which are based upon the practitioner's "knowing-in-action."

Knowing-In-Action

By "knowing-in-action," Schön means " . . . the characteristic mode of ordinary practical knowledge" (p. 54). Such "knowing" has the following characteristics:

— There are actions, recognitions, and judgments which we know how to carry out spontaneously; we do not have to think about them prior to or during their performance.
— We are often unaware of having learned to do these things; we simply find ourselves doing them.
— In some cases, we were once aware of the understandings which were subsequently internalized in our feeling for the stuff of action. In other cases, we may never have been aware of them. In both cases, however, we are usually unable to describe the knowing which our action reveals. (p. 54)

Examples are: making judgments for which we cannot state the criteria, or for which the norms are tacit; riding a bicycle; recognizing familiar faces; recognizing the moods of others from facial expressions, and; speaking in conformity with complex linguistic rules that we cannot describe. "Knowing-in-action" occupies a strategic position in Schön's conception of competent professional practice, and justifiably so. Knowing-in-action is the raw material on which reflection-in-action operates.

Reflection-In-Action

Reflection-in-action is thinking about what one does while, or subsequent to, doing it; "surfacing" or raising to the level of consciousness, the implicit knowledge, the patterns of action, the "feel for the stuff of the action," and the implicit norms that are a part of knowing-in-action. Schön provides an exemplar of the concept by citing the Inhelder and Karmiloff-Smith experiment in which children of varying ages were observed while performing the task of balancing wooden blocks, some of which were "loaded" (in the sense that a die may be loaded) on a metal bar. Older children not only succeeded in balancing a number of normal blocks of varying shapes and sizes, but also discovered that they could balance the "loaded" blocks by decentering them on the bar.

> The children now behaved as though they had come to hold a theory-in-action that blocks balance, not at their geometric centers, but at their centers of gravity. (p. 58)

In an aside that is particularly important for our purpose, Schön noted the fact that, as Inhelder and Karmiloff-Smith observed and described the behavior of their subjects, they were " . . . *compelled to invent a language.* They describe theories-in-action which the children themselves cannot describe . . . they convert the child's knowing-in-action to knowledge-in action" (p. 59, emphasis added).

Taken together, the behavior of Inhelder's and Karmiloff-Smith's subjects in abandoning their geometric approach to balancing in favor of a center of gravity approach, and the behavior of Inhelder and Karmiloff-Smith themselves in formulating a theory of the subjects' knowing-in-action, provides Schön with a model of reflection-in-action. Had the subjects, confronted with their failure to balance the loaded blocks, "surfaced" their geometric theory of balancing, criticized it, constructed a new center of gravity theory, and tested it on the spot, they could have been said to have engaged in reflection-in-action.

Thus,

> When the phenomenon at hand eludes the ordinary categories of knowledge-in-practice, presenting itself as unique or unstable, the practitioner may surface and criticize his initial understanding of the phenomenon, construct a new description of it, and test the new description by an on-the-spot experiment. (pp. 62-63)

Among other things, Schön sees reflection-in-action as an antidote to overlearning. Through it, the practitioner can "surface" and criticize tacit understandings internalized in the course of dealing with repetitive cases. "Understandings," like other terms, has a broad meaning for Schön. It includes systems of knowing-in-action (knowing-in-practice), tacit norms, values, theories, strategies, feelings for situations, and roles enacted. All these constitute grist for the reflection-in-action mill.

Summary and Prolegomenon

A convenient way of summarizing Schön's argument is to answer the question, "In view of the contents of Part I, of *The Reflective Practitioner*, what advice might we offer one who wished to become a more reflective practitioner?" The most general answer would seem to be, "As you go about your work responding to phenomena, identifying problems, diagnosing problems, making normative judgments, developing strategies, etc., think about your responses to situations and about what it is in the situation, and in yourself, that leads you to respond that way; think about the theories that underlie your diagnoses and strategies; think about the norms and values on which your judgments are based; think about the manner in which you frame problems, and think about "your conception of your role." "Surface" and criticize your implicit understandings. "Construct and test your own theories."

All this is interesting, but it is not very useful. What is required to make it useful is precisely what Schön took note of in his comments on the Inhelder and Karmiloff-Smith experiment, but failed to pursue, *viz.*, a language—more accurately, a linguistic-conceptual system—within which to think about what competent practitioners do. The question is, within what linguistic-conceptual system can we think more precisely and usefully about what Schön speaks of as "knowing-in-action," "reflecting on phenomena," surfacing prior understandings," and "conducting frame experiments"? What we need is a linguistic-conceptual system within which, to use Schön's terms, *to "reframe" his observations,* within which to answer the question, "What is it that one does when one surfaces implicit understandings?" Should we find it possible to assemble such a system, we should also find it possible to clarify the relationship between the kinds of knowledge that provides the basis for technically rational performance, on the one hand, and the performances of Schön's competent practitioners, on the other. It is to the task of assembling such a system that we now turn.

A Linguistic-Conceptual System

The discussion presented in the present section is complex. It is divided into nine subsections, each of which presents an aspect of the linguistic-conceptual system under development.

Internal Representation

The first component of a possible system was provided by Bruner (1964) in his answer to the question, "How do we benefit from contact with recurrent regularities in the environment?" Bruner postulated the existence of three interdependent systems of information processing and coding, the outputs of which are models or representations, that are internal to the organism. The types of representations corresponding to the three information processing systems are "enactive," "iconic," and "symbolic." Enactive representation refers to "a mode of representing past events through appropriate motor response . . . segments of our environment—bicycle riding, tying knots, aspects of driving—get represented in our muscles, so to speak" (1964, p. 2). In iconic representation, "images stand for perceptual events in the close but conventionalized way that a picture stands for the pictured object" (1964, p. 2). Finally, symbolic representations represent regularities linguistically, using the latter term broadly enough to include such specialized languages as mathematics. Clearly, what Schön treats as "knowing-in-action" may be conceived as different kinds of internal representations.

Perception, Concepts and Meaning

But the question arises, how are environmental irregularities perceived as objects that are represented appropriately by a particular symbol? Following a number of investigators (Kuhn, 1963; Brown, 1977; Bronowski, 1977, 1978; Hanson, 1965; Northrop, 1959; Holzner, 1972; Geertz, 1973) we assume that the human mind has no direct, unmediated access to "reality." Nothing that "exists" or occurs in the world is inherently or automatically meaningful to the human observer. Nothing comes with a label attached revealing what it "is"; a table, a chair, a book, an organization, a social system, a conceptual framework, etc. "Raw" experience would, with few exceptions, consist of " . . . a flow of sensations and percepts in which there is no continuity and stability of objects" (Holzner, 1972, p. 19). However, with learning, the phenomenologically described human experience of the environment

> consists of objects, properties and actions and we are tempted to assume that these exist ready-made in the outside world, and present themselves directly to the senses. But this is a naive simplification of the complex interlocking process by which we are persuaded of the existence and persistence of even so unitary a natural object as a tree or a bird. (Bronowski and Bellugi, 1970, p. 673)

What is it that we learn which enables us to decode the confusion of early phenomenal experience? In a word, "concepts"; the mental categories with which we discriminate objects and events from one another and within which we associate them with similar objects and events. Concepts provide meaning for acts and objects. "Meaning in this sense is location in a context, in a larger interrelated framework . . . " (Bellah, 1970, pp. 260-61). Placing an object in a category confers a meaning upon it, and an act, object, or event that has no context, that fits into no category, has no meaning save meaningless.

Smith and Medin (1981) have provided a partial account of the functions of concepts as follows:

> Without concepts, mental life would be chaotic. If we perceived each entity as unique, we would be overwhelmed by the sheer diversity of what we experience and unable to remember more than a minute fraction of what we encounter. And if each individual entity needed a distinct name, our language would be staggeringly complex and communication virtually impossible. Fortunately, though, we do not perceive, remember, and talk about each object and event as unique, but rather as an instance of a class or concept that we already know something about. When entering a new room, we experience one particular object as a member of the class of chairs, another as an instance of desks, and so on. Concepts thus give our world stability. They capture the notion that many objects or events are alike in some important respects, and hence can be thought about and responded to in ways we have already mastered. (p. 1)

It is important to note that any given object can be placed in a very wide variety of categories, and hence be given a wide variety of meanings. The object to which we give the meaning "cup" can also be classed as a container, as a cylindrical object, as pottery, as white, etc. Put in another way, the categories into which we can place a given object always focus on selected aspects of that object. Categories, concepts, or meanings are always abstract generalizations based on selected, common properties of groups of objects. Thus no category, concept, or meaning ever deals with an object in its entirety; meanings are selective and partial, and every object can be given multiple meanings. The several meanings may be on a comparable level of abstraction, e.g., chair, furniture, artifact. It is also possible to distinguish among several types of meanings.

Categories of Meaning
Meaning is not a unitary category. Within one linguistic-conceptual system, there are four analytically separable subcategories of meaning (Parsons, 1961).

These are the "cognitive," the "expressive," the "moral evaluative," and the "constitutive." They are most easily exemplified by indicating how a single event can be given four types of meaning. Let the event in question be the death of a loved one.

To give such an event meaning and to symbolize it in cognitive terms is, minimally, to categorize it dispassionately as death, with all its factual implications. Beyond that, it is to provide an account of the causes of the event of the sort that a medical examiner might write. Within the expressive mode, however, the meaning and symbolization emphasis is on the emotional impact of the event—often grief, desolation, and anguish. Expressive symbolization involves the clarification, formulation, and expression of the emotional significance of cognizable events. Painting, poetry, music, sculpture, the dance, and rituals are common forms of symbolism giving primacy to expressive meanings. Symbolization of the moral-evaluative meanings of events portrays them in terms of their desirability, their goodness or badness. Quite generally the death of a loved one could be expected to have a negative-evaluative meaning, but there are circumstances under which the opposite could be the case. Finally to give such an event a constitutive meaning is to categorize it in terms of its ultimate meaning, as "a spoke in the wheel of Karma," "the beginning of eternal life," or some form of religious-philosophical interpretation.

Two of the categories of meaning described above relate directly to Schön's discussion. The cognitive encompasses his "Theories and Strategies." The evaluative seems to correspond to his "appreciations."

Symbols, Communication and Calculation

Concepts are represented and conveyed by symbols and rule-governed combinations of symbols—numerals, gestures, movements, music, but most importantly for present purposes, by words. Symbols have no intrinsic relation to either the concepts they represent or the "concrete" objects and events (exemplars) that are given meanings within those concepts. The word "telephone" has no intrinsic relation to the object on my desk, and none to the category of objects to which the particular object is an exemplar.

Symbols both represent and evoke meanings and those who share a more-or-less common symbol-meaning system, or linguistic-conceptual system, can exchange meanings, i.e., they can communicate. "A" can assign meanings to his experiences and inform "B" about those experiences. "B" can experience vicariously what "A" has experienced.

Communication does not exhaust the functions of linguistic-conceptual systems. Given a system of symbols (a vocabulary), a corresponding system of concepts, a system of rules for relating symbols, concepts, and exemplars (semantic rules), and a system of rules for the combination and transformation of symbols (syntactic rules), we can use the system not only to represent and communicate our experience, but also to transform it, i.e., to represent and communicate not only what was actually experienced, but also what might conceivably be experienced. In Bruner's (1964) terms, linguistic-conceptual systems provide

[a] means not only of representing experience, but also of transforming it. As Chomsky (1957) and Miller (1962) have both made clear in the last few years, the

transformational rules of language provide a syntactic means of reworking the "realities" one has encountered. Not only, if you will, did the dog bite the man, but the man was bitten by the dog and perhaps the man was not bitten by the dog or was the man not bitten by the dog. The range of reworking that is made possible by the three transformations of the passive, the negative, and the query is very striking indeed.

Once the child has succeeded in internalizing language as a cognitive instrument, it becomes possible for him to represent and systematically transform the regularities of experience with far greater flexibility and power than before. (p. 4)

But these playful transformations are not the only kinds possible. Again, given an appropriate linguistic-conceptual system, we can calculate:

We can handle the symbols as if they were the things represented (the exemplars). If the symbols as well as the grammar are well chosen, the result of the mental operation of symbols will correspond to the real course of events. The consequences of the images will be images of the consequences . . . (von Bertalanffy, 1966, p. 276)

Thus, if the dog was rabid, and if the dog bit the man, then the probability is high that the man will develop rabies.

Of course what von Bertalanffy says our linguistic-conceptual systems permit us to do is precisely what Schön says practitioners of the minor professions cannot do because of the mismatch between the knowledge (linguistic-conceptual systems) purveyed by the professional schools and the problematic situations encountered in practice. It is for that very reason that he argues that the competent practitioner employs a kind of knowledge different from that purveyed by professional schools.

To foreshadow subsequent discussion, we shall argue that Schön has overstated the case; that the difference is not one of the kind of knowledge, but one of the degree of development of the linguistic-conceptual systems available. We do agree that it is the rare case in which, for the practitioner of a minor profession, "the consequences of the images are images of the consequences."[16] However, we believe that even underdeveloped linguistic-conceptual systems have their practical uses, some of which Schön has labeled "surfacing" and "reframing."

Theories as Specialized Linguistic-Conceptual Systems

Following Bronowski (1961, 1962, 1966, 1977, 1978) we regard it as useful to view each of the disciplines and subdisciplines of the sciences as engaged in the process of developing highly specialized languages, or, as we prefer, linguistic-conceptual systems. Like their natural language counterparts, well-developed scientific languages have their own vocabularies, concepts, semantic rules, and syntactic rules. Since

. . . every language is open, alive and changing; it has to invent new words and to experiment with new usages and thereby discover new meanings in what it can

---

[16]This is due not only to the underdeveloped states of the relevant linguistic-conceptual systems, but also to the fact that the empirical systems of concern are nearly always open, probabilistic systems.

say. When J.J. Thomson discovered the electron in 1897 he added a new word: [and] a new concept in science; a unit of matter smaller than the atom. In showing that what he had found behaved like a particle, he fixed (as it were) the first grammatical rule to govern the use of the new word. (Bronowski, 1966, p. 38)

As in the case of natural languages, the syntactic rules, the grammars of scientific languages

[tell] us how to arrange the concepts [words] in sensible sentences—that atoms can capture neutrons for example, and that heavy atoms when they split will release them. (Bronowski, 1966, p. 38)

There is an exact sense, then, in which scientific progress is a process of linguistic-conceptual development and refinement. As Bronowski (1977) pointed out, seventeenth century apothecaries wrote that the treatment of common salt with oil of vitrol yields spirits of salt and *sal mirable*. A century later, the same sentence was written, "If you mix salt with sulphuric acid, you get Glauber's salts and hydrochloric acid," (1978, p. 53) and still later, it was written "$2NaCl + H_2SO_4 \rightarrow Na_2SO_4 + 2HCl$." According to Bronowski, the latter sentence is the result of breaking down the earlier sentences, and numerous others like them, into the elements of a code and the laws of their arrangement. The laws of their arrangement constitute the grammar of the language. Hence, $2NaCl + H_2SO_4 \rightarrow Na_2SO_4 + 2HCl$ is a grammatical sentence in the language of chemistry. $2NaCl + H_2SO_4 \rightarrow Na_2SO_4 + HCl$ is not. The former is, within the language of chemistry, "true." The latter is "false." From this point of view, the grammar of specialized cognitive linguistic-conceptual systems adds standards of logical and empirical validity to the rules of natural language.

The Utilization of Specialized-Conceptual Systems

Given the conception of theories as linguistic-conceptual systems, what can we say about their utilization? One way of answering that question is to say that we treat observed (or described) empirical phenomena or situations as particular instances (special cases) of a general concept (general case). Consider the following example in which we deal not with a well-developed theory, but with a "conceptual framework" of the sort common in the social-behavioral sciences.

Alfred Kuhn (1963) has argued that all information about our environment comes ultimately through our senses, through processes of communication. Given this premise, we may say that the receipt of sensory information by the human animal is subject to all the conditions and constraints of communication systems. Such systems comprise five basic elements:

1. A source, or transmitter
2. An encoder
3. A medium of transmission
4. A receptor, or detector
5. A decoder, or interpreter.

These elements may be identified in all cases involving the receipt of sensory information:

For example, a large branch breaking from a tree emits a series of creaks, snaps, and groans. While the breaking is in progress, various layers of wood rub against each other or snap off under tension, each movement in the wood creating its own particular pattern of sound [waves]. In this communications system the wood is the *source* and the sound waves are the *coded representations* of the breaking action. The medium receptor, and decoding mechanisms are—the air, ear, and brain. Anyone able to interpret (that is, decode) these sounds receives no less a communication from the tree than if it had uttered the words, "I just dropped a branch." Without further examples it can be stated that all communication involves these five elements, regardless of whether any or all parts of the communication system are animate or mechanical, and regardless of what sense is appealed to (sight, hearing, touch, etc.). (Kuhn, p. 15)

According to Kuhn, normal usage treats detecting and decoding as a single process termed "perception." In his view, it would be more useful to say, for example, not that we heard or perceived a car door slam, but that we sense or detect sound waves which, given our previous experience, we decode, or interpret, as the slamming of a car door. For casual, everyday discourse that would be hopelessly cumbersome, but for analytical and investigative purposes a good case can be made in support of his advice.

Now, what have we done here? We have treated perception as a special case of communication. We have given it a different meaning within the context of a more general framework of concepts. And, since the word "communication" is more than an empty label, since it has associated with it a complex of symbols, concepts and propositions (a specialized linguistic-conceptual system with its own vocabulary, concepts, semantic rules, and grammar), we have said implicitly that, at least tentatively, all the statements that are true of communication generally are true of perception specifically. Having identified perception as a special case of communication, we can use the specialized linguistic-conceptual system of communication to think about perception generally, e.g., in identifying the conditions required for perceptual accuracy, or to diagnose particular cases of misperception. In the latter context we can ask, "In which component(s) of the system did (does) the difficulty lie?"

The Utilization of Linguistic-Conceptual Systems and Information Selection

We have observed that theories and conceptual frameworks may be treated as special cases of specialized linguistic-conceptual systems, and that in applying them we may be said to be treating particular phenomena as special cases of more general cases. But that answer raises another question; "What is it that we do when we do that?" Luhmann (1982) provided one answer.

Luhmann wrote of processes that are capable of becoming reflexive, i.e., of being applied to themselves, or to processes of a similar kind. Examples are thinking, writing, making decisions, conducting research, formulating rules, etc. Clearly one can think about thinking, write about writing, make decisions about decision making, conduct research into the nature of research, formulate rules governing the formulation of rules, etc. Luhmann argued that:

The success of a process is enhanced when it is applied to itself, or to processes of a similar kind, before it fulfills its proper function. Social *processes capable of becoming reflexive in this way are always based on a selective manipulation of information,* and *the success of this selection can be increased once the selective*

157

mechanism is itself preselected through a second mechanism of the same kind. Along with the increase in selectivity is an increase in the complexity of the situations that a mechanism can handle—precisely because it distributes the reduction of this complexity into two or more sequential stages (emphasis added). (p. 100)

Luhmann referred specifically to social processes, but that seems an unnecessary qualification. Psychological processes fit the category equally well.

The immediately relevant implication of the above is that to utilize a concept, even so simple a one as "book" is to *select* information. Recall that concepts are abstract generalizations based on selected common properties of groups of objects or events. They never deal with things in their entirety. Hence, to give an object or event meaning within a given concept is to select certain information and to exclude other information about the object or event. We may say, then, that *concepts and linguistic-conceptual systems are information selection and exclusion mechanisms.* Moreover, to select a concept, or a linguistic-conceptual system for application is to select an information selection mechanism. And, as Luhmann observed, the success of the information selection processes—i.e., success in the application of the concept or linguistic-conceptual system—can be enhanced if the information selection mechanism—the concept or linguistic-conceptual system applied—is preselected through a second mechanism of the same kind—a second, higher-order, concept or linguistic-conceptual system. Thus, to provide a specific case, if the task at hand is to make decisions, then success in the selection of the information on which to base those decisions can be enhanced if the mechanisms (concepts) for the selection of that information are preselected through a prior process of making decisions about how decisions are to be made. Put more generally, if the task at hand is the application of a conceptual framework (which involves the selective manipulation of information), then the success of the information selection process can be enhanced if the selective mechanism (the conceptual framework) is preselected through a second mechanism of the same kind (a higher order conceptual framework).

Other writers have made similar observations. Twenty-five years ago, Vygotsky (1962) wrote:

As long as [one] operates within the decimal system without having become conscious of it as such, he has not mastered it but is, on the contrary, bound to it . . . *When he becomes able to view it as a particular instance of the wider concept of a scale of notation,* he can operate deliberately with this or any other numerical system (emphasis added). (p. 115)

In Luhmann's terms, Vygotsky has said that success in the application of numerical systems can be enhanced if the systems applied are preselected through the application of the concept of scales of notation. On a general level, Bruner's (1964) comment makes the same point.

I suspect that much of growth starts out by our turning around on our own traces and recoding in new forms . . . what we have been doing or seeing, then going on to new forms of organization with the new products that have been formed by these recodings. We say, "I see what I'm doing now," or "so that's what the thing is." The new models are formed in increasingly powerful representation systems. (p. 21)

Clearly, what is involved here is developing the capacity to do wittingly and purposefully that which we do unwittingly all the time, i.e., to make witting, purposeful selections from among available information selection mechanisms (concepts, conceptual frameworks or linguistic-conceptual systems). Following Luhmann, we shall term the witting selection of such mechanisms "reflexive," and the unwitting selection as "nonreflexive." At this point it seems apparent that Schön's practitioner who operates on the basis of "knowledge-in-action" is operating nonreflexively.

Linguistic-Conceptual Systems and Analytic Competence

Thus far we have concentrated on the information selection function of concepts, a function illustrated clearly by the example of perception being treated as a special case of communication, and by our own treatment of theories and conceptual frameworks as specialized linguistic-conceptual systems. Although we employed only the skeleton of a conception of communication in the first example, one scarcely deserving the appellation "conceptual framework," or "linguistic-conceptual system," it enabled us to select information that we would almost certainly have been unable to select without that framework; information about possible locations of the difficulty of concern. But that is only half the story. Recall Luhmann's words. He argued that ". . . processes capable of becoming reflexive in this way are always based on a selective *manipulation* of information." The other half of the story concerns the information manipulation function of concepts and linguistic-conceptual systems.

Having wittingly and purposefully selected the information selection mechanism, and having selected the information to which it directs our attention, how do we manipulate it? Although both answers are appropriate, it seems less than fully satisfying to say that we handle the symbols as if they were the things symbolized, or that we use the general case to select from the exemplar of the special case information to be manipulated. The question remains, what is it that specialized linguistic-conceptual systems enable us to do with the information?

In one set of terms, they enable us to engage in the exercise of *analytic competence*. In a discussion of language as an instrument of thought, Bruner (1975) distinguished between innate linguistic competence, communicative competence, and analytic competence. The latter, Bruner argued, goes beyond the former two in that it provides a basis for the invention of new modes of thought.

A general characteristic of language use is the manipulation of symbols according to the rules of the symbol system to express meanings, i.e., to generate additional meaningful symbols. All human linguistic symbols are sufficiently independent of contextual ties to permit relatively context-free use. However, preanalytic language usage is characteristically linked to immediate perceptual experience, and relative to analytic usage, context dependent. It tends to be concrete, intuitive, and limited to matters of fact. That is to say, thoughts tend to be closely related to concrete objects and actions, and words tend to be selected and ordered in response to what the user finds at the focus of perceptual attention. What tends to be symbolized, then, is the immediately relevant, concrete aspects of the "directly experienced" environment.

In contrast, analytic use " . . . involves the prolonged operation of thought processes exclusively on linguistic representations, on propositional structures, accompanied by strategies of thought and problem solving appropriate not to direct experience with objects and events but with ensembles of propositions" (Bruner, 1973, p. 72). *Analytic thought employs the permissible operations of the symbol system in use as a mode of thought,* not merely as a means of ordering symbols selected in response to the contents of direct experience. "The linguistic *system* and not external reality is what determines mental operations and their order" (Bruner, 1973, p. 80).

For this to occur, thought (the manipulation of symbols, in one of its aspects) must transcend the rigid constraints of perception, so that the productive rules of language, with their combinational richness, become available as a means of going beyond the givens of perception. Specifically, categories (concepts) must become more completely formalized and decontextualized. That is, they must encompass increasingly broad classes of environmental events, and be given increasingly precise definitions. As Bruner (1975, p. 76) points out, "Such categories have the characteristic that one can state reliably the diacritica (the defining properties) of a class of objects or events short of describing their use." Only with precise categories can one know what presuppositions are involved in, and what implications follow from, their use. An example from Bruner (1975) may be instructive:

> The development of formalization is gradual. From "things I can drive this tent stake with" we move to the concept "hammer" and from there to "mechanical force," each step being freer of definition by specific use than the former . . . The development of formal categories is tantamount to science making . . . Indeed, it is characteristic of highly elaborated cultures that symbolic representation of formal categories and formal category systems are eventually developed without reference to the classes of environmental events that the formal categories "stand for". Geometry provides a case in point . . . (p. 77)

Thought in which the contents of direct experience are symbolized within "natural" language can go beyond the information given through the application of transformational rules. However, it tends to deal only with the actual, i.e., the "reality," with which the thinker is confronted. Therein lies a further important difference between preanalytic and analytic thought. In the latter, with the use of decontextualized and formalized concepts and propositions in accordance with the rules of language, the emphasis shifts from the representation of "reality" as experienced directly, to "reality" as it might be, i.e., from reality to possibility. Thought is no longer limited to perceived realities, but rather, is extended to include hypothetical realities (Inhelder & Piaget, cited in Bruner, 1975, p. 77).

From the preceding it is clear that even the application of such a simple concept as "cup" selects a number of items of information about the object so categorized. And that information can be manipulated in accordance with the transformation rules of the language as illustrated in the dog bit the man quotation from Bruner. But the information manipulation function becomes particularly important when the conceptual framework employed comprises a specialized linguistic-conceptual system with its own vocabulary, concepts, semantic rules and grammar. Such systems permit the exercise of analytic competence so that not only may the success of the information selection process be enhanced, but also, that of the information manipulation process. Thus, when I employ the concepts of Euclidean geometry to select information about the distances between two of three points forming a right triangle, I can use the rules of that specialized linguistic-conceptual system to calculate the third distance. Or, when given a set of concerns about conflict, lack of coordination, and lack of accomplishment in a particular organization, I can use the Parsonian social system theory to select information about the values, norms, goals, and facilities of the organization. I can use the rules of that specialized linguistic-conceptual system to identify possible causes and courses of remedial action (not to mention hypotheses for testing).

Contexts of Linguistic-Conceptual System Application

It may be useful at this juncture to point out that the kinds of situations from which information may be selected for manipulation through the application of concepts and linguistic-conceptual systems may be sorted into three main categories that are particularly relevant to the present discussion. These are: (1) situations external to, and relatively independent of user; (2) situations pertaining to the actions and internal states of the user; and (3) situations involving interdependence between the actions and internal states of the user and external events. The point of making these distinctions here is that casual observations would suggest that skill in the application of linguistic-conceptual systems to situations external to the user, which appear to be developed the most readily, does not appear to transfer automatically to situations pertaining to the user him or herself, or to those involving systems of which he or she is a part.

Summary

We may summarize the preceding section by indicating, as in Figure 1, that the exercise of analytic competence through the application of specialized linguistic-conceptual systems may be analyzed within a framework of four variables. Reading from left to right across the top of the Figure[17], the first variable is the mode of representation, on which the values are enactive, iconic, and symbolic. Immediately below, still reading across the Figure, is the second variable—the type of symbol system. The four values on this variable are cognitive, expressive, evaluative, and constitutive. The third and fourth variables appearing at the extreme left hand margin of the Figure are the primary analytic referent, i.e., the object system analyzed initially, on which the values are external, internal, and interactive, and the secondary analytic referent. Here, by definition, the analytic referent is the outcome of a primary analysis, and the two values on the variable are reflexive and nonreflexive. The former identifies the case in which a process is being applied to itself, e.g., symbolizing cognitively the results of a cognitive primary analysis.

---

[17]This figure is intended to provide a schematic summary of the discussion contained in the section headed "A Linguistic-Conceptual System."

Figure 1: Types of Analytic Competence

2°	1°	Enactive				Iconic				Symbolic			
		Cog	Exp	Ev	Con	Cog	Exp	Ev	Con	Cog	Exp	Ev	Con
R	Ext												
	Int												
	IA												
-R	Ext												
	Int												
	IA												

(The header "Mode of Representation" spans the Enactive, Iconic, and Symbolic columns.)

Legend

Symbolic Systems	1° Analytic Referents	2° Analytic Referents
Cog = cognitive	Ext = external	R = reflexive
Exp = expressive	Int = internal	-R = nonreflexive
Ev = evaluative	IA = interactive	
Con = constitutive		

We have, in Bruner's terms, used the rules of the synthesized conceptual-linguistic system under development here to create a realm of possibility more complex than that represented by the separate constituent of linguistic-conceptual systems. It may well be that some aspects of the realm of possibility have no exemplars in "reality," e.g., it may be impossible to identify an exemplar of reflexive, enactive, internal cognition. Whatever may be the case at that level of detail, it is clear to us that the synthesized linguistic-conceptual system explicated here provides a useful context within which to clarify and to give alternative meanings to some of Schön's observations.

Reinterpreting Schön's Work

General Considerations

We turn now to the task of reinterpreting Schön's work within the linguistic-conceptual system assembled in the preceding sections. Specific suggestions of a general nature concerning reinterpretation have been made at various points in our discussion. However, it may be useful to bring those points together, amplify them, and add to them before proceeding to the next stage of our analysis. With that in mind, this section will deal with our conclusions regarding useful answers that might be given to questions concerning (1) the differences between the knowledge bases of technically rational performance, and the performances of Schön's competent professionals, and (2) what useful meanings might be given to such phrases as knowing-in-action, surfacing implicit understandings and reframing problematic situations. In the section to follow, we shall turn to a detailed analysis of Schön's mini-case study reports.

On the subject of differences between the kinds of knowledge that provide the basis for technically rational performance and the performances of Schön's competent professionals, we conclude that there are none of a fundamental sort. Both kinds of performances involve the utilization of specialized linguistic-conceptual systems. The degree of development of those systems available to practitioners of the minor professions and the greater complexity of the empirical systems of concern to them imposes limits on the extent to which technically rational norms can be met, but insofar as they are useful at all, it is through enhancing the rationality of aspects of the problem-solving process.

Even the nonreflexive exercise of analytic competence within linguistic-conceptual systems permits the practitioner to select information that would most likely not have been selected without them. He or she can formulate the problem in ways that are not possible without those systems. Moreover, the practitioner can manipulate the information selected within those systems to create hypothetical worlds that could not have been created without them. He or she can create alternative diagnoses and identify alternative solutions.

With the step to the reflexive exercise of analytic competence, the practitioner can achieve a level of mastery of the cognitive, expressive, evaluative, and constitutive meanings that guide his or her behavior higher than would otherwise be possible. Once that step is taken, it is possible to treat the unwittingly applied conception as a special case of the concept of linguistic-conceptual system and, in Vygotsky's terms, operate purposefully and deliberately within any known linguistic-conceptual system that is relevant to the situation at hand.

Through the reflexive exercise of analytic competence, specialized linguistic systems, even though underdeveloped relative to those in use in science-based professions, can enhance both the selection and the manipulation of the information on the basis of which problems are formulated, thus permitting the identification of a wider array of alternative solutions to problems than would be likely without them.

With respect to the question of what useful meanings might be given to such phrases as knowing-in-action, surfacing implicit understandings and reframing problematic situations, we suggest the following. Schön's knowing-in-action, clearly includes Bruner's enactive, iconic, and symbolic representations. In addition, within that same category, it is clear that we may distinguish between cognitive, expressive, and evaluative representations. Surfacing implicit understandings and reframing problematic situations may be no more than becoming conscious of one's own activities and adopting a different approach, perhaps taking a dialectical approach. However, in the most important cases it involves treating external phenomena, one's own activities or systems involving both as special cases of more general concepts. Specifically, it involves the exercise of analytical competence in the examination of the special case within the specialized linguistic-conceptual system associated with the general concept. Applied unwittingly to phenomena, this is Bruner's analytic competence. Applied wittingly, it is, in our terms, "reflexive."

Put another way, whether the object of the practitioner's attention is objects and events external to, and relatively independent of, him or herself, objects and events that are contingent on his or her actions, or his or her own actions, mental processes, or products considered apart from external objects and events, it is possible and useful to preselect the mechanisms, i.e., the concepts that will guide the selection of information on the basis of which the problem will be formulated and diagnosed. As noted above, through the distribution of complexity, preselection permits the successful handling of increased levels of complexity. Moreover, to the extent that the preselected mechanism comprises a specialized linguistic-conceptual system, thus permitting the exercise of analytic competence, the information selected can be manipulated according to the rules of the language to construct virtual worlds.

Analyzing and Reinterpreting the Case Studies

The language and concepts that Schön (1983) develops for talking and thinking about what his competent practitioner-subjects do is suggestive, but not particularly illuminating. It consists primarily of nongenerative (nonanalytic) metaphors, e.g. "surfacing," "making moves," "reflective conversation with the situation," and "reframing" which neither allow us to unify and make sense of his observations nor to formulate new sentences in the language. We have indicated at the general level, the meanings that we would assign to those terms, but it remains to be seen if we can usefully reinterpret the data reported in Schön's mini-case studies. That is the purpose of the present section.

Architecture

In his discussion of architecture Schön (1983) writes of the designer as one who employs a distinctive medium and language in making models of artifacts to be constructed by others. The designer "makes moves" within his model which, because "there are more variables—kinds of possible moves, norms, and interrelationships of these—than can be represented in a finite model," tend to produce unintended consequences.

> When this happens, the designer may take account of the unintended changes he has made in the situation by forming new appreciations and understandings and by making new moves. He shapes the situation in accordance with his initial appreciation of it, the situation "talks back," and he responds to the situation's back-talk.
> In a good process of design, this conversation with the situation is reflective. In answer to the situation's back-talk, the designer reflects in action on the construction of the problem, the strategies of action, or the model of the phenomenon, which have been implicit in his moves. (p. 79)

If we were to translate the above account into the language outlined in the preceding section, it would read as follows: the architect is one who employs distinctive linguistic-conceptual systems in making representations of artifacts (and the settings in which they are to be located), to be constructed by others. Representations of several types involved are cognitive-iconic and cognitive-symbolic comprising explicitly the proposed objective features of the artifact, and evaluative-iconic and evaluative-symbolic comprising the technical, aesthetic, functional, economic, and other standards, e.g., building codes, in relation to which the cognitive representations are to be evaluated. Operating within the rules of the cognitive language—those within which the artifact and its relation to the environment are represented objectively—and in accordance with his evaluative models—the designer constructs trial models of the artifact which are then judged in relation to the evaluative models. Because of the complexity of the artifact under design, e.g., the intricate relations among the components of the artifact, and because of the multiplicity and implicit status of some of the evaluative models, the consequences of a given design decision may not be apparent, and hence not accessible for evaluation, until it is incorporated into the model. Hence, they produce unanticipated consequences. Sometimes these unanticipated consequences are evaluated positively, sometimes negatively.

In his discussion of the case, Schön draws on the protocol of the dialogue between a studio master and a student architect. The latter has prepared preliminary drawings (iconic representations) with which she is dissatisfied, and which the master critiques. Schön notes here that reflection is partly reflection in interaction, and partly reflection-in-action. The student has acted; the master "reflects" on the student's action and on his own subsequent actions. That fact, plus the fact that the information provided is sketchy, makes the case less than fully useful for our purpose. While referring to "drawing" and "talking" as parallel ways of designing that together make up *the language of design* (p. 80), and to talk about the processes and principles of design as a *metalanguage,* Schön provides us with too little information about either to follow clearly the manner in which the master proceeds. Even so, it is possible to clarify some ambiguities in Schön's analysis of the case.

Schön describes the student as having encountered a problem in her attempt to fit the design of the building to the contours of the site, "the problem" being that she cannot "butt" the shape of the building into the slope of the site. In our terminology, this inability to butt the shape of building into the slope of the site is not the initial problem. Rather, it is a secondary problem arising from the failure of an attempted solution to the problem achieving a shape-slope fit. Put another way, it is clear that the student has not reflected on her efforts. She has not perceived her actions in a generalizing fashion, has not become conscious of the fact that butting a preselected shape into the slope is a special case of fitting the design to the contours of the slope. The studio master "reflects" for her by indicating implicitly that butting a preselected shape into the slope is a particular instance of a broader concept of fitting the design of the building to the contours of the slope. Having indicated that norm governing such efforts is "site coherence," i.e., the coordination of building shape with the contours of the site, the master suggests that the student "impose a geometry," a building shape on the site in accordance with that norm. That norm, in conjunction with a variety of others, e.g., cost, scale, functionality, aesthetic appeal, constitutes the syntax of the language of design.

Presumably, there are a number of geometries from among which one might select, but having selected one, it becomes the set of basic propositions in the specialized linguistic-conceptual system. Thereafter the task becomes one of formulating "sentences" in that language, evaluating them in relation to its syntactic rules, and, if necessary, revising basic propositions, i.e., "breaking the geometry open." Since neither the student nor the master is dealing directly with a situation, but rather with a specialized linguistic system, what Schön terms "a reflective conversation with the situation" might more usefully be termed "an exercise in analytic competence," *à la* Bruner. The master employs formalized, decontextualized concepts and symbols to explore the world of possibilities, formulating propositions that are evaluated in relation to a variety of implicit and explicit grammatical rules.

However, beyond implicitly seeing the student's attempt to butt the shape of the building into the slope of the site in a generalizing fashion, there is little evidence of either the student or the master behaving reflexively in Luhman's sense. As portrayed by Schön, neither reveals any consciousness of what he or she is doing; neither views his or her performances as particular instances of higher order concepts; and neither turns a process in which he or she is engaged back on itself. Like the person who is not conscious of operating within the decimal system, neither displays evidence of having mastered the "linguistic" skills he or she employs, but appears, on the contrary, to be bound to them.

Psychotherapy

Unlike the preceding case, in the psychotherapeutic case, the task confronting the participants was not one of creating a representation of a nonexistent entity. Rather, it was one of using a specialized linguistic-conceptual system to give higher order meanings to events already given meanings at an ordinary language level. From our alternate perspective, it involves the selection and use of a mechanism for the selection and manipulation of the information on which the problem formulation and solution are to be based. Here, Schön demonstrates unwittingly that even in psychoanalysis the practitioner exhibits a degree of technical rationality appropriate to the state of development of the specialized language in use. Neither the kind of "knowledge" on which competence is based, the use of that "knowledge" in problem solving, nor the kind of inquiry involved is fundamentally different from that of the science-based professions. Differences of degree are apparent, but not differences of kind.

The materials presented by Schön were taken from the record of verbal interaction between a psychiatric resident and his supervisor. During the session, the resident reports in such a way that it is apparent that, even though both he and the client can see a pattern in the relationship between the latter and her boy-friend, and in the relationship between the resident and the client, the former neither sees the similarity between the two patterns, nor "knows" what meanings to attribute to the relationship between himself and the client. The problem, as formulated by the resident, is that the client is "stuck" in both relationships; she can neither get emotionally involved nor withdraw. Evidently, the resident is operating at the natural language level, nonreflex-ively employing low level information selection, manipulation information selection, and manipulation mechanism which neither reduce complexity, systematize the selection of information, nor permit the exercise of analytic competence in its manipulation.

Having listened to the resident's initial comments, the supervisor says, in effect, "From what you have reported, I would suggest that what we have here is a *case* of *transference*. The client is repeating the pattern of her relationship with the boy-friend in her relationship with you." The supervisor has said, "What you have described to me sounds like a special case of the more general case of transference." Thus, we can tentatively talk and think about what you have described in ordinary language within the specialized language of psychoanalysis. (We can use the concept of transference and its associated concepts and propositions as an information selection and manipulation mechanism.) Since the word "transference" is not merely an empty label, like the name of an unfamiliar person, since it is a symbol for a conception (a model) comprising a complex of concepts and propositions that purport to represent underlying mechanisms, we can use that language in conjunction with the values that guide the therapeutic enterprise to select tentatively a course of treatment.

Schön characterized the action of the supervisor as follows: "He has reframed the problem in such a way as to locate it squarely in the transference . . . " (p. 124). Precisely. And whether one speaks of that as "reframing the problem," "reformulating the problem," or placing the problem within a diagnostic category, what is involved, from our point of view, is giving meanings ascribed at one level different, potentially more useful meanings within a higher order linguistic-conceptual system. Alternatively, it involves the adoption of an information selection and manipulation mechanism that reduces complexity, systematizes the selection of information, and permits the exercise of analytic competence. And in terms of fundamental cognitive operations, that does not differ significantly from what the physician does when he or she concludes on the basis of a variety of observations that a patient has diabetes.

In other parts of his presentation Schön revealed clearly the manner in which the supervisor exercises analytic competence. Having identified the circumstances described by the resident as a special case of transference, the supervisor employs the permissible operations of psychoanalytic language to formulate tentative propositions. Then he elicits and examines further evidence from the resident (selects information) which he manipulates to test the plausibility of his propositions. However, analytical thinking is not necessarily reflexive thinking. From the evidence available, we conclude that neither the resident nor the supervisor has behaved reflexively.

At one point in the discussion, the supervisor asks the resident, "Well, what's your understanding of why it's this way?" and responds to the anecdotal answers to that question with:

> You know, I don't get a sense of what you feel from seeing her. How would you characterize her problems in your own mind, psychodynamically? (p. 112)

Here the supervisor is asking the resident, "Of what general case do you see these circumstances as a special case?" Or, "Within what specialized linguistic-conceptual system might we give meaning to these observations?" The supervisor then answers his own question, using such terms as "aggression," "dependent," "guilt," "sexual wishes," and "self-punishment." In his own analyses of the case, Schön refers explicitly to ". . . the repertoire of meanings and psychodynamic patterns [information selection and manipulation mechanisms] accessible to the supervisor, but apparently not to the resident" (p. 119), which the former uses in the search for explanations. Clearly, to explain in this sense is to give the relevant observations, described in one set of terms, meaning within a higher order linguistic-conceptual system. If this kind of knowledge is different from that exhibited in technically rational performance, it differs only in the degree to which the relevant linguistic-conceptual system has been developed toward conceptual clarity and precision, logical consistency, and empirical validity and reliability, and in the degree to which it provides the basis for prescribing remedial action.

Not only is the "knowledge-in-practice" of the psychotherapist not fundamentally different from that employed in technically rational problem solving, but also Schön's assertions concerning uniqueness, the inapplicability of existing categories, and the setting aside of all preconceptions are misleading. The therapist who gives meaning to events within such categories as transference, aggression, dependency, etc., can scarcely be said to be ignoring existing categories, setting aside all preconceptions. To reframe a problem in Schön's sense is precisely to give it a meaning within an existing category. And to give a situation meaning within a category is to regard it, not as unique, but as similar in relevant respects to other situations. To be sure, giving events the meaning of transference does not enable the therapist to then apply standardized techniques. There appear to be none of a highly specific nature. But, as Schön observes, the client's interest in repeating the past in the present can provide access to information about his or her relationships outside therapy. Given that, the therapist can proceed in a loosely technical rational way to *diagnose* the problem. He does this in Schön's terms, by building and testing a chain of inferences which, in our terms, means that he operates within the specialized language of psychoanalysis, formulating propositions in that language that give more useful meanings to propositions describing the behavior and feelings of the client in a lower-order language.

As noted above, the process of building a chain of inferences, which Schön terms "a reflective conversation with the patient's materials," is not reflexive in our sense. In the present instance it is a process of selecting from among alternative meanings, categories, or conceptions within which to give meaning to reports of external events, not to the actions or thought processes of either the resident or supervisor. In response to the observation that the patient keeps herself frustrated, the supervisor suggests ways of giving that meaning in psychoanalytic terms. Either "they are in love with frustration," or "they're (so) guilty about getting something for themselves that they have to constantly put road blocks in the way" (p 122). Having concluded that these are not mutually exclusive categories, the supervisor suggests, "If she feels guilty, she wants punishment" (p. 122). The question then becomes, punishment for what?

> Again there are two alternatives, "aggressive, angry thoughts" or "sexual wishes." In order to decide between these alternatives, the supervisor conducts an experiment. He asks whether the punishing fights interfere with the patient's sex-life with her boy-friend. On being informed that they sometimes stimulate it, he infers that punishment responds to sexual wishes . . . (p. 122)

Here, working within the language of psychoanalysis, the supervisor appears to reason, "If the guilt and desire for punishment are responses to sexual wishes, then that should be evident in the patient's reports concerning her sex life. Since the patient reports that her sex life is sometimes stimulated by the punishing fights, which means that having been punished she can enjoy, the guilt and self-inflicted frustration are sex-related. Such reasoning presupposes careful empirical research establishing the relations in question. Given our (admittedly minimal) acquaintance with the field, this seems dubious. Nevertheless, the supervisor seems clearly to formulate sentences within the language of psychoanalysis in which the syntactic rules stipulate which sentences are "true," and hence admissible. How does this differ from technically rational performance? Insofar as we can tell, it differs only in the degree of elaboration and validation of the linguistic-conceptual system in use.

What the supervisor has done is display a high level of the sort of linguistic competence which Bruner (1975) termed "analytic." Far from eschewing existing categories and setting aside all preconceptions, as Schön would have it, the supervisor works systematically within the language of psychoanalysis, formulating hypotheses the plausibility of which he tests against further information elicited from the resident. And, far from treating the patient as a unique case (itself a contradiction in terms) to which standard diagnostic categories do not apply, Schön's supervisor does what anyone must do to make concrete application of a generalized linguistic-conceptual system. He applies standardized categories, e.g., transference, aggression, guilt, etc. These are some of the variables comprised by the theoretical system, variables that must be given values discovered in the specific context of application. The patient may be unique in a variety of irrelevant ways, and she may be unique in the sense that in no other application of the theory do we find precisely the same configuration of values on the several variables, but if she were literally unique, one could not talk about such processes as transference or self-frustration at all. The one sense in which a claim to a different kind of inquiry might be made relates to the manner in which hypothesis derived from the theory are tested. Such tests are based, not on objective evidence accessible to all observers, but on whether or not the patient finds the interpretation compelling (p. 123).

The Structure of Reflection-In-Action

In the chapter following the two in which the cases reviewed above were presented (Chapter 5), Schön "reflects" on "the structure of reflection-in-action." Here he reemphasizes points made earlier. Both practitioners approach the practice problem as a unique case. Both attend to the peculiarities of the situation. Neither appears to search for a standard solution. Both criticize and reframe the problem presented by the student. Neither deals with the problem by applying standard theories or techniques. Both engage in a reflective conversation with the situation, exploring the consequences of framing the problem in a particular way. Our response has been to observe that: (1) the emphasis on uniqueness is misleading; (2) even in the application of standard theories one must attend to the peculiarities of the situation, must assign values to the relevant variables; (3) there are few standard solutions in these and similar professions; (4) both practitioners reformulate or treat the problem as a special case of a more general specialized linguistic-conceptual system which, though perhaps not fully standardized, is generally applicable; (5) both nonreflexively explore the world of possibility within the limits of the specialized linguistic-conceptual system; and (6) in neither case is there evidence of either supervisor having preselected the relevant conceptual linguistic system by means of a higher order selection mechanism of the same kind. That is to say, both practitioners think reflectively in the sense that they exercise analytic competence but neither reflects on his reflections. Neither analyses his analysis, nor thinks reflexively.

In this discussion, Schön qualifies his earlier assertions by acknowledging the fact that both practitioners did use some general categories, e.g., parallels, classrooms, slope, self-assertion, transference, dependence, and guilt. "But" he argues,

> when it comes to the situation as a whole, each practitioner does not subsume it under a familiar category but treats it as a unique entity for which he must invent a uniquely appropriate description. (p. 137)

However, to say that an entity is unique, and that it calls for a unique description, is not to say that generalized categories and conceptions are inapplicable. It is to say only that particular values must be assigned to the relevant variables of the "theoretical" system in use, and the pattern of values assigned may be unlike any encountered previously.

Having acknowledged that the practitioner possesses a repertoire of examples, images, story types, understandings, interpretive explanations, etc., Schön poses a puzzle: "How can an enquirer use what he already knows in a situation which he takes to be unique?" (pp. 137-138). In an answer that undermines much of his own argument, Schön suggests that

> when a practitioner makes sense of a situation he perceives to be unique, he *sees* it *as* something already present in his repertoire . . .

Then, curiously, he proceeds to argue that

> to see *this* site as *that* one is not to subsume the first under a familiar category or rule. It is, rather, to see the unfamiliar, unique situation as both similar to and different from the familiar one, without at first being able to say similar or different with respect to what. The familar situation functions as a precedent, or a metaphor, or in Thomas Kuhn's phrase—an exemplar for the unfamiliar one. (p. 138)

The "somethings" in the practitioner's repertoire are representations, concepts and conceptions, models *of* things, and *for* actions. And to "see" a particular situation as an exemplar is often, but not always, to subsume it under a familiar category, to see it as a special case of a general case. Schön appears to hold to the view that the representations included in repertoires are all particulars; that the psychotherapist's repertoire contains an image of every instance of transference encountered, (which may be used analogically) but no concept of transference *per se*. When one allows that representations at higher levels of abstraction comprise sets of variables and propositions relating them to one another, then it is clear that "seeing this site as that one" may well be to subsume it under a familiar category, and that to see the "unfamiliar, unique situation" as different may be to emphasize its status as a special case with a particular configuration value on the relevant variables.

In the same chapter (5), Schön characterizes the performances of the two practitioners. "Each is operating in a virtual world, a constructed representation of the real world of practice" (p. 157). He also identifies the ability to construct and manipulate virtual worlds as a crucial component of professional competence, and acknowledges the architect's drawings and the analyst's "transference" as virtual worlds within which they reformulate problems, discover qualities, and relations unimagined beforehand, and formulate tentative solutions to be tested in action. Yet he concludes the discussion with the observation that the studio master and supervisor

> . . . reflect on their students' intuitive understandings of the phenomena before them and construct new problems and models derived, not from application of research-based theories, but from their repertoires of familiar examples and themes. (p. 166)

Questions concerning the nature and origins of these examples, images, understandings, and explanations, and how they came to be in the practitioner's repertoire, do not seem to occur to Schön.

Although we regard it as an hypothesis, we share Schön's view that the ability to construct and manipulate "virtual worlds" (Bruner's analytic competence) is a crucial component of professional competence whether one's profession is science, science-based or quasi-science-based. But, contrary to Schön's view, we regard these "virtual worlds" not as somehow independent of research-based theories, but as based upon more or less well-developed and tested linguistic-conceptual systems, specialized languages, conceptual frameworks, or frames of reference, which are the stock-in-trade of professional schools. Given that the minor professions have few research-based problem solutions to pass on to prospective practitioners, and given that the clinical knowledge of the practitioner will carry one only so far, the dissemination of such systems and the development of analytic competence in their use seems to us to be one of the most useful contributions that professional schools can make to professional practice. But it is only one contribution. A more advanced and equally important one is the development of reflexive analytic competence; competence in the witting preselection of the linguistic-conceptual systems employed. The problem is not that there is a mismatch between the knowledge purveyed by professional schools, on the one hand, and the problems of professional practice, on the other, not if by "mismatch" one means that the former is irrelevant to the latter. Rather, the problem is the failure of professional school faculty to ask and answer the questions, "What can the underdeveloped linguistic-conceptual systems available to the field contribute to professional practice?" and "What implications does our answer have for instruction?"

The Science-Based Professions

Schön's descriptions of practice in the "science-based" professions, e.g., medicine, agronomy, and engineering, add little to his previous discussion beyond introducing the concept of "generative metaphor." However, his approach to this discussion is particularly revealing in relation to several points. Having observed that, "faced with unexpected and puzzling phenomena, the inquirers (the practioners whose actions have been described) made initial *descriptions* which guided their further investigations" (p. 182), Schön returns to his concept of "seeing as." When the mechanical engineers concerned with developing a new method of bluing the metallic parts of guns "described" the process as one involving the removal of oxygen from the surface of the metal, they were, in Schön's terminology, seeing it as similar to a problem they had already encountered, or modelling one problem solution on another. Schön then refers to the role of analogies in science, and finally suggests that

> When two things seen as similar are initially very different from one another, falling into what are usually considered different domains of experience, then *seeing-as* takes a form that I call "generative metaphor". (p. 184)

We would argue that to see two things as similar is to see both as special cases of a more general case. However, if the general case is ignored, or if it does not symbolize a complex of concepts and propositions, and if one special case is used as a paradigm for the analysis of the other, then we are thinking analogically or metaphorically. In the case of both analogical and metaphorical thinking, the process can be generative only if it provides the basis for the exercise of analytic competence. On the other hand, if the label of the general case is a symbol for a complex of concepts and propositions, a specialized linguistic-conceptual system, then both special cases may be seen as instances of the broader conception and, as such, eligible for analyses within it. Most, but not all, of Schön's examples seem to be of this sort.

Schön's discussion in this chapter (6) is revealing in relation to another point—the phenomenon to which we refer as "problem-solution reversal." In describing the approaches taken by practitioners of different professions to a problem of child malnutrition, he reported that nutritionists saw it as a problem of agricultural productivity; public health personnel saw it as a problem of sanitation; economists saw it as a problem of economic development; politically oriented personnel saw it as a problem of resource distribution; and still others saw it as a problem of population control.

To our way of thinking, what has happened here is this. Having created or formulated a malnutrition problem—created in the sense that problems are never objective states of affairs on which all competent observers can agree, but are discrepancies between perceived and valued states—each group reformulated the problem analytically within its own specialized linguistic-conceptual system. Having come to see increasing agricultural productivity as *the* problem, rather than as a proposed solution to the original problem, and having failed to see their own actions reflexively, the agronomists were unable to consider the possibility that there might be alternative and/or complementary ways of reformulating the problem, and hence of identifying solutions.

When we say that each group diagnosed the problem nonreflexively, we mean to suggest that they did not "know" what they were doing when they did what they did. That is to say, having no linguistic-conceptual system within which to think and talk in a generalizing fashion about their own activities, they could not see their proposals as a special case of a more general case—a special case of how to solve the problem of malnutrition. Hence, they could not ask, "What other special cases might be useful?" "Within what alternative linguistic conceptual systems might we examine this problem?" Again, Schön's practitioners think analytically, but not reflexively.

Town Planning

In the case of the town planner (Chapter 7) Schön traces the evolution of role of the town planner and illustrates the consequences of framing the role in a particular way for the problem setting, knowledge selection, and strategy selection activities of the planner. Beyond suggesting that the evolution of the planning role may be seen as the outcome of "a global conversation with the planning situation" (p. 234), the chapter yields no additional observations concerning "reflection-in-action."

Management

As in other professional contexts, reflection-in-action in management takes the form of " . . . on-the-spot surfacing, criticizing, restructuring and testing of intuitive understandings of experienced phenomena" (p. 241). However, for us, the case with which Schön illustrates the process is neither analytical, nor reflexive. Having listened to two plant managers and a vice-president for manufacturing express their views regarding the relationship between the plants of the two managers (one of which supplies parts for the other), the corporation president concludes that the problem has two parts: (1) a lack of effective communication among the several parties; and (2) a split between the new plant and central operations. While it may be that "communication" and "split" are elements of the specialized linguistic-conceptual system of management, it seems more likely to us that the manager in question has exemplified a form of problem obfuscation common among managers of our acquaintance. From the evidence presented in the discussion, it would appear to us that the president has done little more than *label* the problem. Perhaps formulating the problem as one of ineffective communication counts as problem framing in Schön's sense, but for us he has done no more than name it. That seems evident in the fact that the process established by the president to effect a solution to the problem—send a team to the troublesome plant to " . . . trace the source of delays, to review and repair reporting systems, to fix whatever problems in operations they discover" (pp. 250-51)—has little to do with communication.

Our point is not that the mechanism established by the president was inappropriate—it may have been entirely appropriate. Rather, it is that useful problem formulations go beyond labeling the phenomenon. They invoke the complex of concepts and propositions, the specialized linguistic-conceptual system, symbolized by the label. Depending on the conception of communication that one adopts, formulating a problem as a communication problem may be to reason as follows. Since all communication involves five components, an encoder, a transmitter, a medium, a detector, and a decoder, the problem may involve a breakdown of anyone of all of these.

In his discussion on the patterns and limits of reflection-in-action (Chapter 9), Schön emphasizes the importance of skill in the manipulation of the media, languages, and repertoires of the field in question. Competent practitioners develop "a feel for the media and languages of their practice" that permits them to "construct virtual worlds in which to carry out imaginative rehearsals of action" (p. 271). Precisely. But what does it mean to say that one has developed a feel for, or skill in the manipulation of, media, languages, and repertoires? Our answer is that they have developed analytic competence in Bruner's sense. They are able, at appropriate times, to detach themselves from the control of environmental stimuli and operate within the transformative rules of specialized linguistic-conceptual systems, thereby achieving an approximation to technical rationality. And if they have acquired the capacity to think reflexively, then they can select deliberately among alternative conceptual-linguistic systems within which to think analytically. The communication problem may also be a problem of organizational culture, a problem of malintegration, a problem of value conflict, etc.

From the evidence presented in the several case studies, one might conclude that Schön's practitioners have developed reasonable levels of analytic competence. They are reasonably fluent in the use of their own specialized linguistic systems. But one might also conclude that rather than having mastered those languages, they are bound by them. Nowhere in the material presented do we find any suggestion of reflexive processes or the attendent ability to shift at will from one "notation system" to another.

To the extent that the practitioner behaviors described by Schön are characteristic of individuals and representative of competent professionals, and to the extent that reflexive thinking are positively related to competence, competent professionals would appear to be a good deal less competent than they might be.

Implications for Preparation Programs
The implications of our analysis of preparation programs seem fairly obvious. Assuming that practitioners who are analytically competent and reflexive are, other things being equal, more competent than those who are not, then students in preparation for practice should acquire whatever variety of relevant specialized linguistic-conceptual systems is available, and they should develop analytical competence on their application. In addition, in order to be able to operate deliberately within alternative and/or complementary systems, they should come to see each system as a particular instance of such systems. That is to say, in order that their performances be witting as opposed to unwitting, they should learn to act reflexively. Although it may not need to be said, we might add that little of this is likely to happen until their mentors come to "know what it is they do when they do what they do."

REFERENCES

Bellah, R. (1970). *Beyond belief: Essays on religion in a post-traditional world*. New York: Harper and Row.

Bronowski, J. (1961). Science as foresight. In J. R. Newman, (Ed.). *What is science (pp. 408-461)*. New York: Washington Square Press.

Bronowski, J. (1962). *The common sense of science*. Hammondsworth, Penguin Books.

Bronowski, J. (1966). *The identity of man*. Garden City, N.Y.: American Museum Science Books.

Bronowski, J. (1977). *A sense of the future*. Cambridge, MA.: The M.I.T. Press.

Bronowski, J. (1978). *The origins of knowledge and imagination*. New Haven, CT.: Yale University Press.

Bronowski, J. & Bellugi, U., (1970). Language, name and concept. *Science, 168,* 669-673.

Brown, H.I. (1977). *Perception, theory and commitment: The new philosophy of science*. Chicago, The University of Chicago Press.

Bruner, J.S. (1964). The course of cognitive growth. *American Psychologist, 19*(1-5).

Bruner, J.S. (1973). *Toward a theory of instruction*. Cambridge, MA.: Harvard University Press.

Bruner, J.S. (1975). Language as an instrument of thought, in A. Davies, (Ed.). *Problems of language and learning*. London, Heineman.

Geertz, C. (1973). *The interpretation of cultures*. New York: Basic Books.

Hanson, R.N. (1965). *Patterns of discovery: An inquiry into the conceptual foundations of science*. Cambridge: Cambridge University Press.

Holzner, B. (1972). *Reality construction in society*. Cambridge, MA., Schenkman Publishing Co.

Kuhn, A. (1963). *The study of society: A unified approach*. Homewood, IN.: Irwin Dorsey Press.

Luhmann, N. (1982). *The differentiation of societies*. New York: Columbia University Press.

Northrop, F.S.C. (1959). *The logic of the sciences and the humanities*. New York: Meridian Books.

Parsons, T. (1961). Introduction. In T. Parsons, E. Shils, K. Naegele, and J.Pitts (Eds.), *Theories of society*. Vol. II (pp. 963-993). New York: The Free Press.

Schön, D.A. (1983). *The reflective practitioner: How professionals think in action*. New York: Basic Books.

Smith, E.E., & Medin, D.L. (1981). *Categories and concepts*. Cambridge, MA.: Harvard University Press.

von Bertalanffy, L., (1966). The tree of knowledge. In G. Kepes, (Ed.). *Image and symbol: Vision and value series*. Vol. 6 New York: George Braziller.

Vygotsky, L.S. (1962). *Thought and language*. Cambridge, MA.: The M.I.T. Press.

11

SCHÖN'S GATE IS SQUARE: BUT IS IT ART?

Mark Selman
University of British Columbia

Donald Schön has proposed a new epistemology for professional practice and used it to draw conclusions about how education for professionals should be conducted. This paper begins with an examination of the assumptions underlying Schön's project. Discussion of these assumptions calls into question a conceptual argument which is central to Schön's thesis that the design studio should be accepted as a model for professional education in general. Various questions regarding the use of technical terms are raised and consideration is given to the very limited role of ethics in Schön's account. The conclusion describes some commonplace examples of "learning a practice," making the point that there are many different strategies which may be useful, depending on the nature of the practice. In many cases, a practice is constituted by concepts, rules, and standards. Making explicit these elements is an important part of education for reflective practice.

Three Assumptions

To consider the assumptions embodied in Schön's framing of the problem, it is helpful to consider his project in its simplest formulation. In opposition to the prevailing, but inadequate epistemology of professional practice, Schön constructs a new epistemology. Based on the central role of the concepts "design" and "artistry" in his epistemology, he determines a preferred teaching methodology for those aspects of professional practice which are not adequately captured under the description, "teaching of applied science." Such a formulation gives rise to the following three sets of rather basic questions:

1. How are epistemology and educational practice linked? or: What inferences can be drawn for educational practice from an epistemological theory?
2. Why do we need a new epistemology? . . . and the related question: What exactly is wrong with "technical rationality"?
3. What reasons are there for supposing that professional practice marks off an epistemologically significant category?

Philosophers and educators have long realized that there are important relationships between epistemology and educational practice. Given the close relationship between "knowing" and "learning," this is not surprising. But it is important to keep in mind the nature of our knowledge about the conditions under which people learn to do various things and our knowledge of epistemology. Everyone has firsthand experience of the sorts of things which are helpful, or irrelevant, to learning how to do any number of things. These experiences may result in knowledge which is unsystematic, but it is closely tied to experience. Epistemic theories, on the other hand, are far removed from experience. To use Lakatos's terminology, there is a broad protective belt of auxiliary hypotheses between epistemological claims and experiences which could serve to support or disconfirm them.

Because epistemology and education are related, philosophers have often used educational experiences as evidence for or against epistemic positions. Schön provides an example of this strategy when he quotes from the *Meno* in which Socrates used the evidence of the slave boy who was able to discover a theorem to support his theory that knowledge exists in the mind prior to experience. But Schön wishes to do the opposite, that is, he wishes to use an epistemic theory to derive a form of educational practice. Given the abstract and contested nature of epistemic theories, and their logical "distance" from confirming or disconfirming evidence, our confidence in any conclusions drawn from this sort of argument should be rather faint. Even as a method for deriving plausible hypotheses about educational practices, this form of argument seems unnecessarily convoluted. Given that Schön identifies a number of exemplary practicing professionals, it would seem that interviews about significant experiences might be a more reliable, if rather more mundane approach. While interviews of exemplary practitioners are not without their own limitations, they have a distinct advantage in that they are grounded in firsthand experiences rather than derived by necessarily speculative chains of theoretical reasoning.

This argument is not meant to show that Schön is without evidence for his claims about the role of the reflective practicum in professional education. Rather, it shows that the empirical evidence, which he offers mainly in the form of case studies, must provide the grounds which would convince us that the reflective practicum plays such a role. Nor is the argument meant to imply that epistemology is irrelevant to decisions about educational strategies. Epistemological theories may be useful in illuminating educational practices by identifying both goals and categories which are pedagogically significant. An epistemology developed for the purpose of informing educational practice ought to make explicit those elements which are essential or important for competent (or exemplary) performance. For example: the realization that "knowing," in many of its uses, implies "being able to justify," suggests that teachers who want their students to know something ought to encourage them to believe the claim in question on the basis of relevant reasons whenever possible. It suggests that the giving of reasons has particular significance as an educational practice. It says little, however, about the ways in which students are best encouraged to see the importance of reasons or to insist on having good reasons before becoming committed to a belief. To the extent that Schön uses his theory to illuminate goals and significant features of educational practice, he is employing his theory in a responsible manner, however, it should be clear that a case for any particular approach to educational practice will require more than argument from an epistemic theory.

The second question to be asked about Schön's project is: why do we need a new epistemology? Schön provides an answer by suggesting that "technical rationality" creates an intolerable dichotomy between the rigor of the high ground of theory and the relevance of the swampy areas of practice (1987, p. 3). Practitioners have come to see that assumptions imbedded in this approach are not credible. Problems do not arrive predefined, nor are most problems amenable to technical solutions based on the unproblematic application of scientific theory to individual cases. It is not my intention to question this characterization of "technical rationality," the extent to which it continues to hold sway in professional schools, or its deficiencies. However, it is important to realize that this conception of rationality has been under criticism for some time. If one traces "technical rationality" to a positivist philosophy of science, as Schön does, it is worth mentioning that numerous alternatives have been proposed. Some of them are rather well developed. Horkheimer wrote *The End of Reason* in 1941 as an indictment of instrumental rationality. The tradition of Horkheimer and other members of the Frankfurt School has been continued by many writers, most notably, by Habermas. Popper and Lakatos provide another alternative tradition, as do Wittgenstein, and post-Wittgensteinians like Kuhn, Toulmin, and Winch. Dewey and other American pragmatists pose yet another alternative, one which has influenced Schön significantly. Charles Taylor has consistently opposed what he refers to as "reductionist theories" with an "interpretive" or "hermeneutic" approach. There are many more. My point here is that there is widespread agreement at the level of social theory and epistemology that "instrumental rationality" is not all there is to rationality, in scientific endeavors or in "ordinary life."

When Schön proposes an alternative to "technical" or "positivist" approaches, he enters a contested field. His approach must be compared not only to that of "technical rationality," but to the range of competing alternatives. While this might seem obvious, it bears stating because Schön frames his theory in opposition only to "technical rationality" without differentiating his theory from the field of alternatives. As Fenstermacher points out (1987, p. 417), Schön seems in some ways to maintain the dichotomies he sets out to destroy: dichotomies between the "high" and the "swampy" ground; between science and practice; and between "bad" instrumental approaches and "good" ones based on "artistry." For purposes of rational evaluation of Schön's project, it is essential to avoid getting caught up in an "either/or" kind of discussion when we are faced with a multiplicity of competing theories of human competence with varying degrees of compatibility.

It might be useful to consider briefly the reasons why one might object to what Schön calls "technical rationality," as one's reasons for objecting may well illuminate the standards we would expect an adequate theory to meet. Schön points out that practitioners find that many of the issues confronting them are not technical ones. He cites the example of civil engineers who face both technical problems ("how to build roads suited to the conditions of particular sites and specifications") and problems which are not amenable to technical solutions ("deciding *what* road to build, or whether to build at all"). This is an important point. Technical rationality is not wrong in itself or on its own ground; there are situations in which technical solutions are possible and desirable. It is, however, a mistake to think that all rationality takes the form of technical rationality or to try to subsume all issues under the model of a technical problem. Theories such as positivism in philosophy of science, emotivism in the field of ethics, and behaviorism as an explanation of human action are criticized in that they are radically incomplete theories posing as complete explanations.

But, going beyond Schön's point about incompleteness, we can ask: for what kinds of issues is a technical approach inadequate? If we examine the kinds of examples Schön offers, we can see that issues involving a consideration of people's interests, intentions, and values are problematic. If the criteria or standards by which the solution to a problem are not given in the formulation of the problem itself, technical approaches are not much help. And, this gives us a clue as to why "technical rationality" is not only incomplete, but dangerous. It is dangerous because problems involving competing interests or competing formulations based on conflicting values are pushed outside the sphere of rational consideration. The consequence of such a move is that answers to such questions can be legislated, chosen, or imposed, but not negotiated or justified on the basis of reasons or rational argumentation.

Underlying virtually all objections to "technical rationality" is the conviction that theories of knowledge or competence must be able to account for the important role of rational considerations in issues involving conflicting interests or value claims. Therefore, it seems reasonable to assume that an important criterion which any competing epistemological theory must meet would be to make possible a coherent account of those issues as objects of rational consideration. This criterion will play a central role in the evaluation of Donald Schön's theory below.

The third question which could be asked of any attempt to reformulate our conception of knowledge in the field of professional practice is: What reasons are there for supposing that professional practice marks off an epistemologically significant category? If a field of knowledge is constituted, at least in part, by concepts, exemplars, norms, and forms of explanation, then there are arguments in favour of identifying disciplines like history, aesthetics, or the physical sciences as epistemologically significant categories. Each of these disciplines is constituted, in part, by shared nature of the concepts and forms of explanation, and the standards by which they are judged. This line of reasoning might serve as justification for suggesting that certain individual professions with developed standards, concepts, exemplars, and forms of practice had a claim to epistemic significance, but not the claim that the professions in general do. Given that education, medicine, engineering, psychotherapy, law, and urban planning do not share many of these epistemologically significant features, what reason is there for thinking it is possible to develop a theory of knowledge which applies usefully to the practice of the professions in general?

A Conceptual Argument

Schön does suggest that there is a significant feature which unites the professions. He claims that all professional practice is "design-like" and it is the artistry of designing which is left out of "technical rationalist" understanding of the professions. In trying to understand and explain this productive, or "design-like" aspect of the professions, Schön takes up examples which have a strong aesthetic component. He introduces his ideas with examples drawn from architecture, a profession which has a special relationship to aesthetics. He studies that part of architectural training which is most directly concerned with aesthetics as opposed to those more prosaic parts like building codes, principles of engineering, properties of materials, construction procedures, or the sociological and legal implications of architectural practice. The design studio is used as an exemplar for what education in any profession should be. In arguing that this particular part of training for this particular profession should serve as a model for all of the professions, Schön (1987) relies on the way in which "designing," "building," and "making" have a role in all of the professions. In Schön's words:

> Artists make things and are, in this sense, designers . . . Professional practitioners are also makers of artifacts. Lawyers build cases, arguments, agreements, and pieces of legislation. Physicians construct diagnoses and regimens of testing and treatment. Planners construct spatial plans, policies, regulatory arrangements and systems for the orchestration of contending interests. (p. 42)

We could continue Schön's list by saying that bees build hives, photocopiers create copies, and we all make mistakes. The fact that some product (or performance) is designed, planned, or constructed is a very general sort of claim, one which does not narrow the field in a very informative way. As Schön goes on to say, "[Practitioners] construct situations suited to the roles they frame and they shape the very practice worlds in which they live out their lives." For Schön, following Nelson Goodman, all acts, including acts of perception, are "ontological" in the sense that they "create" reality. However, if all human actions are creative (in this sense), the claim that "designing" typifies professional practice is rather hollow. On this account everything we do involves design, creation, and construction. It fails to point to anything distinctive about the professions, anything which would incline us to believe that we should regard them as being different from anything else, in a way which is relevant to epistemological or, indeed, educational purposes. If Schön's argument is a good one, it follows from his constructivist premise that education for any area of human competence ought to be modelled on the design studio. Surely such a position is no more tenable than a position which subsumes all rationality under "technical rationality."

The notion that we use the word art or artistry to describe something important about professional practice is similarly uninformative. It seems reasonable to assume that Dickens had no aesthetic judgment in mind with the epithet, "The Artful Dodger." The Concise Oxford Dictionary suggests a number of meanings for the word "art," including "cunning," and more relevantly, 1) "skill, especially human skill as opposed to nature." This is in contrast to, 2) "imitative or imaginative skill applied to design, as in paintings, architecture, etc." If these are separate meanings, as I believe they are, it does not follow that because the word "art" can be correctly used to describe a variety of types of practice in a general sense, we must accept that the more specific aesthetic sense applies also. We cannot conclude that educational strategies which have been found to be effective in bringing about competent aesthetic performances should be similarly effective in developing artistry in enterprises which are less obviously aesthetic.

Many of Schön's examples, especially the ones which he offers as exemplars of professional practice, are from situations in which aesthetic standards are central to judging the quality of practice. We have special problems in trying to understand issues involving aesthetics which have different sources from the other problems Schön considers. Two quotations illustrate this point:

Stanley Cavell, in *Must we mean what we say*, interprets Kant as saying:

> that apart from a certain spirit in which we make judgments we could have no concepts of the sort we think of as being aesthetic. (1976, p. 89)

and goes on in a footnote to explain,

> Kant . . . describes . . . "[speaking] of beauty as if it were a property of things." Only "as if" because it cannot be an ordinary property of things: its presence or absence cannot be established in the way that ordinary properties are; that is, they cannot be established publicly, and we don't know (there aren't any) causal conditions, or usable rules, for producing, or altering, or erasing, or increasing this "property". (p. 89)

Wittgenstein (cited in Pitkin, 1972) suggests:

> Thus to study esthetic judgment, one must concentrate not on the words "good" or "beautiful" . . . but on the occasions on which they are said—on the enormously complicated situation in which the esthetic experience has a place, in which the expression has a negligible place. (p. 224)

If Cavell, Kant, and Wittgenstein are right about the peculiar or minimal role that concepts, causal conditions, rule formulations, or theory have in the field of aesthetic judgment, there seem to be obvious implications for both epistemology and education in this area. But these implications are warranted only for practices, products, and performances which are judged aesthetically.

It might be suggested that, aesthetic or not, there is a style, a manner, or an approach which can be brought to our professional practice. There is a way of doing things which can make the difference between good practice and ordinary practice and is not captured by an "applied science" or "technical" understanding of the professions. This claim is (given Schön's definition of "technical rationality") surely true. Things can be done carefully, intelligently, creatively, exquisitely, coarsely, etc., but as Wittgenstein points out, it is not the concepts but the context which make these judgments aesthetic, or not. There may be any number of norms which are important in judging the way in which something is done but some of these norms are connected explicitly and essentially to concepts, theories, and rules in ways which aesthetic norms are not. In legal, political, and ethical enterprises, explicit use of concepts and rules plays a role of central significance. Subsuming these sorts of enterprises under either a "technical rationality" model or an aesthetic "design-like" model, is surely misleading. As was pointed out earlier, the general motivation for abandoning "technical rationality" as an encompassing theory of rationality was to "make room" for rational consideration of issues involving intentions, competing interests, and values. Schön's solution seems to consider only aesthetic values, leaving a range of other value standards to be overlooked or excluded.

It may be suggested that these arguments misconstrue Schön's theory by taking a very narrow interpretation of "art" or "artistry." But if one reads "artistry" as referring to the special manner which is associated with skillful practice, the argument for the special significance of the design studio is unfounded. Many educational practices are typically employed to bring about skillful performance, including performance at typing, operating a table saw, playing chess, public speaking, analyzing data, and evaluating epistemological theories. According to the "skillful practice" interpretation of "artistry" any one of these practices would have equal claim to significance. But, of Schön's examples, only the aesthetic ones are clearly convincing.

To make this point, I will offer an alternative description of the building of his gate. His description showed that he (as an admittedly amateur carpenter) could learn by doing, if he paid attention and reframed the situation as he acted. He was able to build an adequate gate even though he had no conscious understanding of the kinds of problems he would run into as he built it, and he had no technical training to provide solutions. In particular, he had not thought out the problem of keeping the gate square until he was surprised by the wobble which existed in the partially constructed gate. Schön attributes his success in this project to having engaged in the "process of reflection-in-action."

Alternatively, one might argue that he brought two standards to the situation from outside. These standards were stability and squareness. He also brought some knowledge of theory, in this case geometry. He knew that the diagonals of a rectangle are equal. He also knew that the triangular shapes created by placing a diagonal reinforcement across the rectangle were inherently stable in a way which the simple rectangle was not. It was not the wobble which surprised him. It was the realization that his procedure for building the gate (as conceived so far) was not likely to produce a gate which would meet his standards. What distinguished Schön's successful gate building from that of someone who ignored, or failed to notice, the gate's instability was either the appreciation of relevant standards or the care and attention with which the task was done.

Notice that concepts, theories, and rules can play an intelligible part of an account of building a gate in a way in which they cannot be used (at least according to Cavell) in explaining the production of an original piece of design work. It would be difficult to redescribe some of Schön's examples in a similar manner, but surely an account which refers explicitly to the relevant standards and principles is desirable (whenever possible) for pedagogical purposes. These elements are an important part of thinking clearly about what is required to teach someone to be competent at gate building, and many other activities. Obviously, my alternative account of Schön's gate building is incomplete. Neither it nor Schön's account address the issue of the manual skill involved, for example. But, as educators, we must consider whether what we are teaching seems similar to carpentry, in which explicit references to theories, procedures, propositions, value standards, concepts, and rules can play a significant role in explaining competent performance, or to more purely aesthetic enterprises, in which concepts and rule formulations play a significantly reduced role.

I would argue that many aspects of many professions are like carpentry in that they can be learned by learning procedures and standards, and reasons for both. Of course, prospective carpenters will need to practice the manual aspect of their trade, and will need a variety of opportunities to confront problematic situations if they are to become competent, but I think that we can talk sensibly about this using quite ordinary language. At its heart, the learning of a practice involves developing appreciation of relevant standards, that is, coming to care for and discriminate according to relevant standards, and learning procedures and strategies for coping with varied situations.

Some Central Concepts

When Schön employs the notion of a "process of reflection-in-action" to explain his success at gate building, he raises several serious difficulties. Two of the most important have been associated with philosophers referred to in his book. The first we might call Ryle's problem and the second, Goodman's problem. Each will be dealt with in turn.

Schön (1987) quotes Ryle as saying:

> . . . "thinking what I am doing" does not connote "both thinking what to do and doing it". When I do something intelligently . . . I am doing one thing and not two. My performance has a special procedure or manner, not special antecedents. (p. 22)

Given these comments, one has to wonder about the status of the "process of reflection-in-action" and its relation to what is being done intelligently. If Schön was engaged in the process of building a gate and in a "process of reflection-in-action," was he not engaged in two processes in exactly the way that Ryle has denied? If this is not the case, if "building" and "reflecting" are alternative descriptions of the same "process," then what does it add to the account of his building the gate to say that he was engaged in a "process of reflection-in-action"? If it is the manner in which the gate building was approached which makes it a case of reflection-in-action, that is, if reflection-in-action "really means" that the task is approached "with care and an open mind," then positing a special process seems misleading.

While this point may seem to some to be unnecessarily "analytic," or even picky, it does have pedagogical significance. It is important to know whether Schön is urging teachers of professional practitioners to encourage a certain attitude on the part of their students, or perhaps, to foster certain virtues, habits, or skills. As Passmore has argued so cogently, there are different logical requirements for each of these categories and different criteria for judging their adequacy (1967). Most importantly, teachers need to know how the procedures, standards, theories, and knowledge referred to in my alternative account of gate building, are related to one's ability to engage successfully in Schön's "process." Without having a relatively clear idea of these relationships, teachers are somewhat at sea in trying to implement a strategy aimed at developing successful practice in Schön's terms. Merely attempting to replicate Schön's examples of exemplary practice would hardly be feasible without a rather more complete account of the knowledge and experiences of budding professionals to add to Schön's extensive account of their emotional states.

The Goodman problem is also related to this question of specifying the criteria for reflection-in-action, but it applies more generally to Schön's specialized terms. To express the elements of successful practice in terms like "the process of reflection-in-action," "knowing-in-action," "tacit theories," and "tacit sensations" is problematic, not merely because the labels sometimes are inconsistent with our everyday use of words like "process" or "tacit," but also because such terms have not been entrenched in our language sufficiently to assure a uniform interpretation. As Nelson Goodman has pointed out, our ability to make sensible statements of a conditional or counterfactual nature, which most theoretic statements are, depends on our use of predicates which have established interpretations or criteria for use (1983). In the physical sciences, criteria for use can often be clearly specified according to a rule linking the new concept (or revised interpretation) to established concepts. It would be unreasonable, however, to expect Schön to define the concepts in question with explicit rules, and he does not. He does offer examples and nonexamples in an effort to show, rather than say what he means. Unfortunately, the examples offered are insufficient to fix the boundaries of the concepts, and I feel confident in predicting that enthusiastic admirers of Schön's ideas will interpret them "all over the map."

Given the limited range of examples, the reader is unable to establish exactly what constitutes "reflection-in-action." Does it, like "knowing-in-action" imply a criterion of success? Certainly all of Schön's examples of "reflection-in-action" are examples of successful practice. Each of Schön's examples also share the feature that no clear idea of the end product can be specified at the outset by the student or practitioner. Is this an essential characteristic? Can one engage in "reflection-in-action" if one has a clear objective, like getting to the top of a mountain, or even a clear idea about the route one intends to follow? Is "reflection-in-action" possible only in the conditions of uncertainty which Schön associates with professional practice or can one engage in it while doing research or some other "theoretic" activity? The list of questions could be continued, but the point is that the examples are insufficient to fix even some of the central features of the concept. This being the case, we can expect considerable disagreement amongst various practitioners attempting to employ Schön's approach to education for professional practice. One can well imagine approaches which take an "anti-theory," "anti-science," and even "anti-rationality" stance, under the label of "reflection-in-action." While Schön would, no doubt, hope that readers would imbue the terms "action" and "reflective" with their full Deweyan connotations, it is probably more than one can reasonably expect.

The problem of "lack of entrenchment" is compounded by the use of several specialized terms within the same theoretic structure. Reflection-in-action is partly defined by its relation to "knowing-in-action," but, as I have suggested, it is unclear whether the connection is analytic or empirical, whether reflection-in-action is discovered by finding out what processes lead to "knowing-in-action" or whether reflection-in-action has other criteria for use and has been found (empirically) to bring about "knowing-in-action." But apart from this, the use of "knowing-in-action" seems to have an unfortunate consequence. This is not, I might add, that one's actions can serve as evidence for knowledge claims. Nothing could be more commonplace. But by calling something "knowing-in-action," there is an obvious implication that there is some other kind of knowing which is irrelevant to action. But, while it is true that one may know something without having an opportunity (or need) to display that knowledge in doing something (either verbally or physically), this is a matter of happenstance, not a matter of different categories of "knowing." Wittgenstein's example of knowing how to play chess may say it best:

> Suppose it were asked: "When do you know how to play chess? All of the time? or just while you are making a move? And the *whole* of chess during each move? How queer that knowing how to play chess should take such a short time, and a game so much longer! (1953, p. 59n)

Surely the label "knowing-in-action" is an invitation (however unintended) to say that someone displays knowing-in-action while playing chess but some passive form of knowing chess at all other times. Should this be the case, then "knowing-in-action" seems likely to undermine, rather than bolster, the increasingly pragmatic view of knowledge, truth, and justification which has reemerged in much recent philosophy.

There is one final category of terms which bears examination. It is Schön's use of "tacit" as in "tacit knowledge," "tacit theory," "tacit claim," and "tacit sensation." To consider "tacit sensation" first: in what sense can a sensation be other than "tacit"? While the possession of many manual skills involves being able to adjust one's actions on the basis of sensations, which is apparently the sort of case in which Schön intends this concept to be applied, there is no room in such an account for anything like "tacit" in the sense we use it in "tacit understanding" or even Polanyi's "tacit knowledge." In a similar vein, one might ask if a "tacit claim" is something other than an assumption.

In what sense does a "tacit theory" exist? By endorsing Ryle's view that intelligent practice is not two things but one, Schön has denied the need for a "bit of theory" to precede each bit of intelligent practice. When I drive a car intelligently (or well), it need not be the case that I know Newton's laws in a statable or a "tacit" form. What I must know is that certain actions on my part are connected with certain results in terms of the car's performance. I need to know that turning the key starts the engine but do not need a theory about how the turning causes the starting. If all that is meant by tacit theory is that I need not think consciously of this connection between my action and the resultant performance of the car in order to accomplish my objective, so be it, but the concept seems destined to make readers think of "unstated bits of theory" in our heads. Once one gets started this way, one is tempted to posit "tacit calculations" and a host of other tacit objects and operations.

This point is an important one in social theory and epistemology. A great deal of confusion surrounds the use of theories, rules, and norms, and their role in determining human action. There are many examples of tasks in which competence is determined by adherence to rules or norms and for which no complete set of explicit rules is available. The use of language is, of course, the ubiquitous example. In order to make sense, one's language must conform to rules, yet few competent language users can make many of the rules explicit. One must ask whether it makes sense to say that the rules exist in some tacit sense (or subconscious state) in the language user's mind, or whether competent language users merely know how to speak according to rules without knowing how to express them. In this latter formulation, rules need not be thought of as some special kind of abstract objects which exist unperceived in competent language user's minds, but rather as part of a way of talking about intentional regularities in the practices of individuals and groups. While Schön, Polanyi, and others, may find it useful to speak of "tacit knowledge" in describing such situations, there are alternative formulations. Habermas, for instance, contrasts the "pre theoretic understanding" of rules of the competent language user with the "theoretic understanding" of the linguist or grammarian (1979, p. 14). While no formulation of this issue seems ideal, Habermas's way of talking seems to avoid the temptation to understand rules as being a particularly mysterious set of entities.

Apart from the problem of the multiplication of entities, "tacit knowledge" and other sets of tacit things often seem to become junk categories of the kind for which Schön expresses explicit contempt. The fact that competent bicycle riders are often unable to state which way to turn the wheel to avoid falling when they would have no difficulty deciding "in practice" is a different sort of problem from that of an artist who can produce great art without being able to tell others how to. Different again is the case in which one knows and may be able to state a procedure for arriving at a particular answer without being able to state the answer. Yet again, one's claims may rest on evidence which cannot be made explicit because it is based on an intuition or on faith in something inexpressible. As has been suggested, some things can be shown but not said. Any of these examples can be referred to as instances of "tacit" forms of knowledge, yet they are of diverse status according to any epistemological theory. One might well ask what purpose it serves to subsume all, or even some, of these cases under a single label. Sometimes it merely creates an apparent paradox around the perfectly commonplace phenomenon that one can often do something without having a theory which is sufficient to explain it.

The Appeal of Schön's Case Studies and What Is Left Out

Given that Schön's conceptual argument for the distinctive "artistry" of the professions is suggestive, rather than providing clear reasons for adopting the reflective practicum as a model for teaching each of the professions, the weight of responsibility falls on his examples and his appeals to common sense and common knowledge. His examples can be quite appealing in that we sense the give and take of the teaching situation and feel the excitement that is associated with new insights and capabilities. We can feel the contrast between this, and the sense of rejection and exclusion associated with the failure to become a part of an enterprise which one cares about. It is important to remind educators of the ways in which these emotions may affect students, not merely in terms of educational, but also broader social and ethical ideals. But, we ought not be so distracted by the details of each case that we lose perspective on the breadth of the claims being made and the specificity of the evidence cited. Schön's case studies are very special cases. As I have pointed out, the most convincing cases of "reflection-in-action" involve specifically aesthetic enterprises. Most examples include extended periods of one-on-one interaction between student and teacher. Many are of exemplary teachers and a good number are of exemplary students. It is worth remembering that many teachers of professional practitioners are not exceptional, have average students in their classes, have limited opportunities for interactions with individual students, and are not expecting their students to produce art. They have their own challenges, standards, satisfactions, goals, and likely require their own educational strategies which may or may not be similar to a design studio or a master's class for musicians.

Of course, Schön points out many common sense features of educational situations which are sometimes forgotten. His example of teaching the violin reminds us of the importance of treating each student as an individual and his discussions of dialogue remind us of the ways discussion can be opened up or closed off. But, as useful and necessary as such reminders may be, they are not what is attracting all the attention to Schön's work. Schön has promised a new epistemology of professional practice which will stand the prevailing conception on its head. He has suggested that his new epistemology implies a new approach to education for professional practice. However, from the evidence he has provided so far, one would only adopt his strategy if one had outside evidence for the success of the practicum approach in achieving one's own particular educational goals.

Before making a few remarks about the ways in which certain epistemological factors are important in thinking clearly about education, I would like to consider some of the aspects of professional practice which are not discussed at any length in Schön's account. It is surely significant that Schön's account of the professions is remarkably devoid of consideration of the political, economic, legal, and other social ramifications of professionalism. Even the obvious differences between the rights and responsiblities of educators working as private tutors, and educators working in publicly funded-institutions, are barely noted. While Schön recognizes that the professions are invested with significant power to define and control aspects of people's lives, the aesthetic and individualistic focus of his examples draws attention away from these questions. Even the obviously "loaded" distinction between "major" and "minor" professions is adopted without comment. Given recent challenges to the role of professional knowledge in shaping individuals and society, it is surprising to see no consideration of these issues. One thinks, for example, of Michel Foucault's writings on the role of architecture and psychiatry in shaping human life. Schön's examples of education for reflective practice emphasize the cloistered feel of a limited community pursuing interests largely separate from those of society. He describes the exclusiveness of the small world of which budding practitioners wish to become a part. But while such an environment may typify the world of design studios, it does not exemplify the conditions under which many professionals practice, or perhaps, should learn to practice.

Ethical issues (which are, of course, related) are also, for the most part, set aside. As Schön (1987) states:

> I say little here about wisdom in response to ethical dilemmas of practice in bureaucratic institutions where professionals spend increasing amounts of time. Nevertheless . . . I am concerned with institutional forces that restrict discretionary freedoms essential to the exercise of wisdom and artistry alike. And I believe that education for reflective practice, though not a sufficient condition for wise or moral practice, is certainly a necessary one. (p. xiii)

Without a more clearly defined conception of reflective practice, one is hardpressed to evaluate this claim, but it does seem that "coming to be moral" can take place in an unspecifiable variety of ways, requiring only the presence of a community, with moral rules, sentiments, and practices as a necessary condition. But more seriously, one might notice that this passage, one of the few explicit references to moral issues, identifies a very narrow range of ethical concerns. Schön refers to "freedoms essential for wisdom and artistry," but not to the way in which professionals come to have responsibility for their clients, how they move from a position of, for example, medical expertise into a role of counsellor or moral advisor, how the norms created by a practice like psychology are used to control and justify the control of individuals and social groups, and the many ways in which institutions of professional practice produce, as well as restrict, forms, and categories of behavior.

Given the widespread interest in professional ethics, especially in schools of medicine, law, and business, it is surprising not to see more attention to these matters. And it is all the more surprising given Schön's obvious concern for developing ethical, rather than merely effective, conditions for dialogue. Yet it is ethical values, fully as much as aesthetic ones, which are excluded from the arena of rational consideration by the approach Schön refers to as "technical rationality."

Conclusion

If one considers a range of practices in which people learn to engage, one notices that there is a multiplicity of factors which have varying degrees of importance, depending on the nature of the practice and the relevant experiences of the person learning. When one learns to ride a bicycle, very little theory and only a few simple strategies are involved (Keep pedalling! Look where you're going!). Becoming competent is largely a matter of "developing a feel for it" or internalizing a set of reactions to certain sensations. Typically, there is little that can be said when teaching someone to ride which is helpful other than by way of encouragement. Criteria of success, in the initial stages of learning to ride, are as completely obvious to the novice as they are to the teacher. Thus the novice is in a good position to be able to correct her performance on the basis of obvious differences between success and failure.

Learning to be polite is, however, quite different. Although it also involves coming to have certain habitual responses, the responses are linked to relatively explicit sets of rules. It is difficult to imagine children, or people who had a very different set of social conventions from our own, coming to be polite members of our sort of society without some explicit instruction in the conventions and standards of politeness. (This is not to deny, of course, that many aspects of polite behavior are simply "picked up" in daily life.) While much of "coming to be polite" is a matter of being reminded to act in certain ways, what counts as "acting in certain ways" or what counts as an appropriate occasion for such "acting," is determined by rules which cannot be explicated simply according to physical behaviors or particular sensations. Unlike learning to ride (at least in the sense of learning to stay up), learning to be polite requires coming to appreciate certain standards or norms that are not obvious.

Becoming competent at long division is different again. Long division is done by following a certain procedure, completing a certain sequence of operations in a particular order. While it seems perfectly plausible that a person could learn the practice of long division simply by watching those competent at long division, nothing would seem more natural than for a teacher to start by describing the various steps involved in doing the various operations. A good teacher would be able to explain the operations accurately and clearly, and be sensitive to the ways in which the procedures can be misunderstood. Notice that strategies play an extremely limited role in competence at practices of this sort, in that the procedure is adequate to deal with the range of possible cases without much room for questions of technique.

Learning to play a game like chess is different from all the previous examples. It involves learning the rules which govern chess playing (which are analagous to the procedures which are long division) and the strategies which make the difference between simply making a legal move and making an intelligent move. A large part of being competent at chess is learning the extended consequences of a move or line of play. With experience, one may develop a large repertoire of strategies which can be invoked and varied to fit particular sorts of situations. These strategies are typically learned through a combination of instruction and/or study, and through practice. One comes to see how certain situations can be utilized in pursuing one's objectives.

Clearly, one could continue this sort of list at some length, noticing how various practices differ in their degree of reliance on rules of various kinds and at various levels of explicitness. Any complex human activity involves the application of a variety of procedures, strategies, standards, and/or techniques. How each particular practice can be learned, or, is best learned, depends on a variety of factors, including: the adequacy of relevant explanatory theories, the degree of physical skill involved, the complexity of the constituitive rules and strategies required, whether there are "usable rules" to guide practitioners, whether the standards for adequate performance are obvious, and the degree to which beginners may be familiar with any of the above mentioned aspects. One of the ways in which educators may err is in trying to assimilate the teaching of all practices under the strategies appropriate for a narrow range of practice. Thus, under the influence of the "technical rationalist" model, educators might tend to approach education for all practices as if it involved the application of comprehensive theories onto individual cases. Schön, on the other hand, wishes to emphasize the extent to which the practice of all professions is like the practice of riding a bicycle or producing a work of art, in that what must be learned cannot be expressed very adequately in language, or conveyed by "usable rules." I want to suggest that this is only one of the many ways in which practices fail to conform to "technical rationalist" models.

To think clearly about these issues, it is necessary to distinguish "theories" from "rules," including standards or norms. Consider the role of standards of conduct in "being polite" or the role of rules in the game of chess. If one tries to understand the way rules determine actions in these circumstances in the same way that theoretically derived physical laws determine whether a bicycle remains upright, confusion is bound to result. As Baker and Hacker (1984) put it:

> The normative guidance of a rule is not a form of causality. Even mandatory rules do not causally necessitate action. Of course, if one wishes to effect certain normative consequences, one *must* follow the rule compliance with which *normatively* (not causally) produces them. (p. 251)

They go on to say that: "Normative activities are normally taught and explained by citing the rules which govern them. We *formulate* rules." (p. 252)

Given that all professional practices are normative activities in this sense, it is an important feature of any relevant epistemic theory that it provide an adequate account of "knowing" in the sense that one knows a rule or can act according to a rule. While such rules are conventional, they are not chosen or constructed independently by individuals. They are social constructions. While it is very important to realize that most human activity is not well explained under the hypothetical deductive model, this should not lead us to downplay the importance of rules epistemologically, or as elements in educational strategies.

One of the ways of understanding professional (or other human) practices better is to conduct a careful examination for the purpose of making explicit the concepts, standards, and rules which constitute given practice. Rather than formulating a "new paradigm" which will overturn established views in one sweep, we could describe, criticize, and reconstruct our practices at a local level. Educating the reflective practitioner, on this account, would involve analysis of the central concepts and standards of a practice. It would also involve encouraging and equipping the "would-be" practitioner to take part in this criticism and analysis. While Schön's account does break with an unacceptable "theory" of professional practice, his desire for a global solution and his willingness to employ a rather ambiguous terminology obscure some of the critical questions.

REFERENCES

Baker, G.P., & Hacker, P.M.S. (1984). *Language, sense and nonsense.* Oxford: Basil Blackwell.

Cavell, S. (1976). *Must we mean what we say?* Cambridge: Cambridge University Press.

Fenstermacher, G.D. (1987). A reply to my critics. *Educational Theory, 37,* 413-421.

Goodman, N. (1983). *Fact, fiction and forecast.* (4th ed.) Cambridge, Mass.: Harvard University Press.

Habermas, J. (1979). What is universal pragmatics? In *Communication and the evolution of society.* (trans. by T. McCarthey). Boston: Beacon Press.

Horkheimer, M. (1941/1982). The end of reason. In A. Arato & E. Gebhdt (Eds.), *The essential Frankfurt School reader.* New York: Continuum Press.

Passmore, J. (1967). On teaching to be critical. in R.S. Peters (Ed.) *The concept of education.* London: Rutledge & Kegan Paul.

Pitkin, H.F. (1972). *Wittgenstein and justice.* Berkeley: University of California Press.

Schön, D.A. (1987). *Educating the reflective practitioner: Toward a new design for teaching and learning in the professions.* San Francisco: Jossey-Bass.

Wittgenstein, L. (1953/1976). *Philosophical investigations* (trans. by G.E.M. Anscombe). Oxford: Basil Blackwell.

CONCLUSION

EXPLORATIONS IN THE FIELD OF REFLECTION: DIRECTIONS FOR FUTURE RESEARCH AGENDAS

Gaalen L. Erickson
University of British Columbia

This book focusses upon an exploration of the utility of Schön's recent writings on the nature and the role of reflection in teaching and supervision contexts. In these writings, Schön presents a language and an analysis of professional knowledge which has stimulated considerable debate in the recent educational literature. The chapters in this book add an important contribution to this ongoing debate in several ways. First, Schön's chapter itself expands upon some of the themes and issues he has addressed in his earlier books and has applied this analysis more explicitly to the areas of teaching and supervision. Second, a number of these chapters offer critical assessments of various aspects of Schön's analysis thus providing the reader with several alternative frames for evaluating the conceptual credibility of his account. Finally, a number of the chapters offer exemplary analyses of issues and problems encountered in a variety of teaching and supervision situations using Schön's basic framework, and thus provide the reader with an expanded repertoire of "cases" which could serve to exemplify and clarify the application of this framework in practice and research settings. It is to be hoped that these accounts will, in turn, lead to further reflection by the educational community and will result in the continued conceptual and empirical scrutiny of Schön's ideas in contexts of concern to the readers. Given the general agreement by all of the authors in this collection of the importance of some type of "reflection" in and on educational practices, it is also to be hoped that the book will serve as a starting point for initiating a continuing and more detailed inquiry into the nature and the role of reflection in educational practice.

The primary purpose of this chapter is to examine the content of the arguments and issues raised by the chapter authors with the intent of identifying some of the common pathways that are interwoven through their accounts of this challenging terrain. In so doing I shall try to identify those territories which still require further charting and clearing of the conceptual landscape and those which may prove to be more hospitable to settlement. While the authors of these chapters have turned over many stones and marked many trees for trails or cutting, I have narrowed my reconstructed map of the terrain to three major features. The first is the persistent uneasiness that many of Schön's critics feel over the distinction he makes between "technical rational" approaches and "reflective" approaches to the framing and resolving of many problems of practice. The second is the viability of his conceptualization of the nature and the process of reflection as it pertains to acting in a problem setting. And the third is the extent to which the empirical work that has been conducted in this terrain serves to extend and clarify Schön's perspective.

The Dichotomy of Technical Rationality Versus Reflective Practice

By far the most common and problematic issue identified by all of Schön's critics is the dichotomy that he establishes between a "technical rational" approach and a "reflective" approach to problem solving in a practice setting. Shulman is the first, chronologically in the book at least, to warn us of the "dangers of dichotomies," even though he recognizes its primary use in Schön's writing as a "marvellous rhetorical device." Citing Dewey as his inspiration, the challenge he sets for Schön in particular, and the educational community in general to address is to develop a "deeper set of principles through which the dichotomy could be resolved."

A number of authors begin to take up this challenge, in varying degrees of specificity and completeness. Shulman, himself, suggests that the reflection that occurs in the context of "the giving of reasons to the learner" (one of the major themes in Schön's chapter) must also be mediated by a consideration of what is "reasonable" in a particular learning situation. And it is precisely in this mediation process between these two principles that Shulman claims "the traditions of technical rationality . . . and reflection and action must come together. These are not competing principles."

Fenstermacher also focusses much of his attention on this dichotomy in posing the question: "How does science find its way into the thinking and practice of teachers?" His conjectured solution takes the form of "practical arguments" wherein the empirical premises in this "coherent chain of reasoning" could be, in part at least, the products of educational research. Although Fenstermacher recognizes the uniqueness, the uncertainty, and the value conflicts which Schön claims to be typical of the practice setting, he argues that the knowledge required to address these issues is to be found in the "situational premises" of a teacher's repertoire. But, he argues, teachers also require empirical premises such as the way that students learn, how best to diagnose and remediate difficulties, how to teach a certain content to certain children, etc., in order to act in a "reasonable" and competent manner. While he appears to recognize that any of these empirical premises could have been constructed by the practitioner as a result of experience in the practice setting, he argues that the role of research is "to alter the truth value of existing empirical premises, . . . to complete or to modify empirical premises, or . . . to introduce new empirical premises into the practical arguments in the minds of teachers.'' Through this notion of practical arguments, then, Fenstermacher claims that a teacher's knowledge-in-action can be informed by a variety of empirical findings emanating from a vast array of studies in the "scientific tradition.''

Thus Fenstermacher claims that practical arguments not only represent a reasonable bridge between the swampy lowlands of practice and the high, firm ground of research, but they may also serve as useful analytic devices by which teachers might examine their own practice more carefully and so achieve Schön's desired end-state of becoming more reflective practitioners.

Other critics in this book also take Schön to task for the over-extension and over-simplification of this "rhetorical device.'' Hills and Gibson, for instance, argue that there is no dichotomy to be found in the problem-solving behavior of competent, professional practitioners versus those in the scientific disciplines—only a difference "in the degree of development of the linguistic-conceptual systems available'' to these respective practitioners. They devote their entire chapter to clarifying the nature and functioning of these systems as a basis for thought and action and end up with a reinterpretation of a number of Schön's cases in terms of their own "linguistic-conceptual system.'' Thus, for Hills and Gibson, the types of problems of practice faced by practitioners in the professions, especially those in the "minor'' professions, are not different in kind from those faced by the practitioners in other disciplinary fields, but they are simply disadvantaged by an immature or underdeveloped linguistic-conceptual system.

Selman takes a somewhat different approach from the others in considering the search for Shulman's "underlying principles'' that would resolve the dilemma posed by this dichotomy. In analyzing the relationships that exist between epistemology and educational practice, he questions whether there is indeed a need to posit an alternative epistemology of practice. He argues, basically in agreement with Schön, that while a technical rational approach may be quite appropriate for certain types of well-formed and stable problem situations, it is "radically incomplete'' when applied to many situations of practice—situations which typically involve a consideration of people's interests, intentions, and values. In spite of this agreement, Selman claims that it is similarly mistaken to try and account for most of the practitioner's thinking and actions strictly in terms of a reflective model.

One of the major issues that Selman addresses is whether the general domain of professional practice "marks off an epistemologically significant category,'' as suggested in Schön's claim of elucidating an alternate "epistemology of practice,'' from the one which currently dominates professional schools. The only central feature that Selman can find in Schön's writing that might characterize "professional practice'' in general is the notion that it is "design-like'' and involves a form of "artistry.'' After analyzing Schön's account of artistry and its accompanying concepts, Selman asserts that there is an incredible diversity of practices both within and between different professions. He argues that since the concepts, exemplars, norms, and rules which characterize these practices are different, there are few grounds for concluding that there is a unique epistemology of professional practice. Hence, where Schön has argued for a dichotomy, Selman claims that Schön's analysis of "reflective practice" represents "only one of many ways in which practices fail to conform to technical rationalist models."

It is apparent that this dichotomy is clearly a source of considerable concern and debate. Furthermore the critics, in this volume at least, have proposed a diverse set of "deeper principles" advanced to resolve this dichotomy as called for by Shulman in his chapter. For example, one could opt for the more pluralistic approaches of Fenstermacher's "practical arguments" and Selman's multiplicity of practices argument or for the more formalistic approach of developing more mature linguistic-conceptual systems as advocated by Hills and Gibson. This choice, of course, will greatly influence the design of preparation and continuing education programs as well as the type of research studies one would conduct on the nature of the practice itself. While Schön has identified a number of research questions and agendas which would follow from his analysis of professional practice, it remains for others to examine the above positions to determine if and how his questions might be altered in the light of these critiques.

The Language of Reflection

A second major feature which pervades many of the contributions to this book is the orientation towards clarifying Schön's use of the term "reflection" in its many contexts. While both Shulman and Fenstermacher see the potential value "in providing us with a new rhetoric . . . to talk about the practical activity of teaching," this optimism is not shared by all.

At the level of practice Gilliss has two quite different concerns. On the one hand she questions whether teachers have to discover everything themselves, thus creating "wholly idiosyncratic practitioners whose primary way of operating is to invent unique solutions to problems that (to them at least) are unique." This she sees as a barrier to the sharing and development of a professional knowledge base and hence argues for focussing on the similarities rather than the differences of practice. A second concern is that most teachers do not have the time to engage in reflection-in-action as they are "caught up in the hurly-burly of instructing twenty or thirty active children."

A different type of critique of Schön's notion of reflection comes from the chapters written by Hills and Gibson, and Court. In the case of the former authors, they end up arguing for a different conceptual frame by which to characterize the process of reflection. Drawing extensively upon Luhmann (1982), who defines reflection as "the process through which a system establishes a relationship with itself," they argue that a primary condition for reflection to occur requires that the system, presumably a practitioner's cognitive system in the present case, must be consciously "demarcated from or discontinuous with its environment" so that multiple relations between itself and its environment may be developed. In their subsequent reanalysis of some of Schön's cases using their own "linguistic-conceptual system" they claim that this condition of conscious detachment from the frame used to address a given problem is not met in the examples Schön gives of reflective practice. Hence they argue that, while these "competent practitioners" may have been thinking "analytically" within their own specialized linguistic-conceptual systems, they were not thinking "reflectively or reflexively." It should be noted, however, that the primary aim in Hills and Gibson's chapter is to argue that Schön's notion of reflection is basically an application of a technical rational approach *but* using an "underdeveloped linguistic-conceptual system." Thus it is not surprising that their conception of reflection emerges as being somewhat different from that of Schön's.

Court adopts yet another approach to the other commentators in her critique of Schön's analysis of reflection. In analyzing Schön's use of the term reflection-in-action she argues that he applies the term to several different types of activities; but all of these "appear to involve *removing* oneself from the action in order to reflect" (emphasis hers). Court asks: In what sense should these types of activities be called reflection-in-action? Clearly the question hinges around clarifying the concept of "action". Schön appeals to the notion of an "action-present—a zone of time in which action can still make a difference to the situation—to further elucidate what he means by reflection-in-action. However, Court argues that, since the "action-present" could range in time from a school period to a whole year, in dealing with a difficult pupil for instance, this term is also ambiguous and does not distinguish between being in "the thick of things" which can lead to more immediate problem solutions and the more leisurely kinds of reflection carried out at home or in discussion with a colleague which could lead to longer term problem solutions. Court clearly wishes to maintain the former attribute for action and so concludes her chapter by suggesting that the reflecting-in-action that does occur in the "thick of things" might create less confusion if we returned to Dewey's notion of deliberation leading to a decision. And the sort of reflection carried out by practitioners that may occur over a period of days or months might more clearly be called "reflection on practice."

Schön's notion of reflection, and particularly reflection-in-action, is clearly problematic for several contributors to this volume. If these constructs are to play an important role in the development of a professional language to describe and discuss the practice of teaching as Schön and others in this volume are suggesting, then it seems clear that further conceptual and empirical work is required to stipulate and demonstrate the meaning of these terms in this particular "language game." This will entail becoming clearer about those situations where one can distinguish between reflection-in-action versus reflection-on-action and in so doing clarify the dynamic nature of the implied "mechanism" that Schön attributes to these constructs in accounting for continued professional growth.

Research Programs and Future Directions

While the above two issues have focussed on several of the thorny conceptual problems raised by Schön's perspective, this final section outlines some of the empirical implications of his work. First I will look at some of general research questions that Schön outlines in his chapter and then I will briefly review the match between these questions and the various chapters in the book which utilize a Schönian framework. Finally I will close the chapter with some directions for future work.

In the chapter on "Coaching Reflective Teaching" Schön identifies a family of research questions—some fairly specific, others quite general—in addition to orienting us to a preferred methodological stance which would be necessary in pursuing these questions. Of the more specific questions that he poses is the call for a closer examination of "the nature of kids' spontaneous understandings and know-how, the substance of their confusions, difficulties that arise at the juncture of everyday knowledge and school knowledge." As it turns out, in some curricular fields such as science and mathematics education, this type of research agenda has been a burgeoning, growth industry for the past eight to ten years (see the discussion on "Children's Science" in MacKinnon and Erickson's chapter). It should be pointed out, however, that much of this work has been and still is being done outside of the classroom context where one cannot readily examine the "juncture of everyday knowledge and school knowledge." And it is precisely this juncture which now needs to be seriously addressed.

While none of the chapters specifically address this issue of systematically identifying students' spontaneous reasoning in a school setting, Kilbourn's chapter, in arguing strongly for the "giving of reasons" to student thinking, illustrates one technique which could be used to identify and communicate this type of knowledge to other teachers. Glickman's conceptual distinction between knowledge and certainty could also be extended to students' reasoning and understanding in an interesting way. Thus, in a pedagogical context, one would make a distinction between students' personal knowledge or children's science as it has been called by some, and scientists' public knowledge which most philosophers would agree should still not be considered as representing certainty. Finally, MacKinnon and Erickson's chapter is set in a supervisory context where attending to the importance of the students' spontaneous reasoning is one of the important dispositions being discussed and deliberated upon by the novice teacher and the supervisor.

A second family of research questions that Schön proposes would examine the conditions around which "reflective teaching" might flourish. He suggests that the structures and strategies of reflective teaching that are used by competent teachers be documented with particular attention being directed towards "the forms of rigor appropriate to it." It seems to me that, as we begin to grapple seriously with this latter issue of "the forms of rigor," we will begin to reveal some of the tensions encountered by teachers and also some of the practical resolutions used by teachers in coming to grips with the dichotomy between "science" and "artistry" discussed earlier in the chapter. As we begin to look at the criteria of "reasonableness" that teachers employ in the practice setting we may be able to see some evidence of the sorts of practical judgments that teachers use to guide their actions in various practice settings.

Two very important questions must be addressed if we are to attend to this latter research agenda. The first is: What is the type of knowledge that might be generated by these sorts of inquiries? And secondly, what methodological stance might best be utilized to conduct studies of this sort? Schön's own writing, both in this book and in his earlier books, represents one response to these crucial questions. He relies exclusively upon case studies or "carefully documented stories" as he refers to them in the present chapter to present and then illustrate the analytical framework that he and his colleagues have constructed over the past fifteen years. This type of knowledge is something akin, then, to what Shulman refers to as "case knowledge." Provided these cases are accompanied by an analytical frame they are more than just descriptions; they are also capable of generating "theories that offer perspectives on practice." In order for these perspectives on practice to be functional, however, the case knowledge must be written in a language and format that is directly accessible to teachers (not just university researchers). This is crucial because the primary purpose of this knowledge is to provide teachers with potential interpretive frames that could be "tested" in the course of their own practice. Using case knowledge in this manner requires that teachers incorporate it into their repertoire (much in the same way as they might learn from their own experience) so that it might function, as Schön argues "like metaphors, projective models to be transformed and validated through on-the-spot experimentation in the next situation." He refers to this kind of learning as a type of "reflective transformation."

Is there a preferred method for incorporating this crucial feature of accessibility into case knowledge? This question leads us to the issue of the methodological stance which might best be used in a research program on reflective teaching. Since most of the knowledge claims are focussed upon describing and theorizing about phenomena occurring in the practice setting, it is essential to have the full cooperation and preferably the collaboration of teachers in the research program. In other words this type of research must be done "with teachers" and not "on teachers." This is the case for several reasons, the most obvious being the privileged access which teachers have to the practice setting; furthermore, it is the type of access which outside researchers cannot easily obtain because claims about the "juncture of everyday knowledge and school knowledge" require one to be immersed in the action-setting and to possess a "rich," interpretive framework that could account for the actions of the participants in this setting. A second important and related reason is that teachers are required to provide a "validity check" on the language and the basic coherence of the episodes used to tell the "stories" that will serve as the basis for the type of "reflective transformation" described above. Ideally it would be desirable, if institutional support were forthcoming, for teachers to engage directly in generating much of this case knowledge. As it stands at present, this notion of having teachers define and contribute to an expanding professional knowledge base is neither encouraged nor valued by our educational institutions. There are some indications, however, that this may be changing as there is increasing attention being directed toward more collaborative models of professional development and research (Elliott, 1988; Lieberman, 1988; Miller and Lieberman, 1988; Stenhouse, 1976; Tickle, 1987).

How do the contributions in Section II of this volume address these issues? Kilbourn's chapter is devoted to providing a rationale and some interesting exemplars of the sort of case knowledge discussed by both Shulman and Schön. The argument advanced by Kilbourn for the use of "vignettes" as a basis for bringing new understandings and new ways of seeing to present and future practice settings parallels that made by Schön. The theme which pervades all of Kilbourn's vignettes is that of "the place of *reasons* in the classroom" (emphasis his). In the process of describing and analyzing several vignettes, Kilbourn identifies three distinguishing criteria which he suggests should contribute to their effectiveness in enhancing "reflective transformation." These are: (1) the necessity to focus upon specific and relevant detail in telling the story so as to get the point of the story across to the readers; (2) the action can be slowed down, and even repeated several times if necessary, thus allowing one to reflect at leisure, so to speak, as opposed to the rapid reflection often required in the practice setting itself; and (3) the vignette should display something of both the moral and the educational character of teaching. These criteria are illustrated in varying degrees by each of the vignettes described by Kilbourn. These criteria, however, provide only the skeletal structure; the real, substantive issues can only be realized through a careful analysis of a vignette. Through Kilbourn's eye these vignettes yield a variety of interesting conjectures concerning the role played by the teacher's knowledge of subject matter in carrying out class discussions, the various forms of classroom constraints that limit teacher's actions in important ways, e.g., class size, control problems, content coverage, etc., and the negative impact on a class discussion when the teacher's primary interest is in receiving "correct responses." Like Schön, Kilbourn also argues that the potential in reflecting on these vignettes rests on the degree to which they provide insight into our own teaching for the purpose of considering future actions. That is, these vignettes cannot be treated in a prescriptive manner; in order for them to be functional, the readers must engage in their own "reflective transformation" so that they may be of possible use in subsequent reflections-in-action.

Glickman also draws upon a vignette or a story, in his case a personal recollection of a problematic situation more than a decade ago, to develop and illustrate a particular point of view about the supervision of instruction. The message in the story is the importance of distinguishing between knowledge and certainty. He argues that the knowledge that teachers have constructed about teaching allows them to explore rather than control with certainty a problem situation. Just as Schön and Kilbourn warn us about the dogma of right answers with respect to teaching subject matter, so Glickman reminds us of a similar point as it pertains to professional knowledge. He also sees in this uncertainty a certain liberating quality in that it forces us to explore new situations, make decisions, and then reflect upon the results (both positive and negative aspects) with a view towards enhancing our knowledge and acting more wisely in future situations.

The research program at Queen's University as described in the Russell et al. chapter begins with very similar assumptions to the other contributors in this section, but adopts a significantly different set of methods to pursue their aims. Their primary aim is to try to understand the knowledge that teachers, with varying degrees of experience, have constructed about the nature of practice in general and more specifically about the relationship between theory and practice. Their method consists of conducting a series of interviews with one teacher at various times throughout the school year. The transcripts of these interviews for several teachers are then analyzed for their metaphorical content. They are interested in speculating about how particular metaphors become a part of teacher's ordinary speech, the roles these metaphors play in particular teaching situations, and finally whether a teacher's preferred metaphors change with experience. While the results that Russell et al. report are still very preliminary, the aim of the research is to attempt to unpack some of the underlying conceptual structures and linguistic patterns that teachers employ when discussing their craft. Unlike Hills and Gibson who argue for the development of formalized "linguistic-conceptual systems" to orient and guide practice, these authors are concerned with unpacking the actual language used by teachers to describe their practice, with particular reference to the metaphorical foundations of their conceptual frames.

An interesting aside in their chapter is the point they make about the interview itself being a method for stimulating reflection in these teachers. The fact that some of their teachers regarded these interviews as a useful form of "therapy" may say something very significant about the need for teachers to discuss and reflect upon their practice in a nonthreatening environment and the extent to which this need is not being met in their day-to-day professional lives, except for their involvement in this project.

The chapter by MacKinnon and Erickson utilizes the context of a teaching practicum setting to explore many of the complex issues about the construction of professional knowledge raised by Schön and the other contributors to this volume. The predominant focus of their analysis is oriented towards examining the nature of supervisory practice as exemplified in several transcripts of conversations between Brian, a novice teacher, and Mr. Kelly, an experienced science teacher. While claims are made about the potential fruitfulness of Schön's three "coaching models" in describing the various supervisory moves made by Mr. Kelly, the substantive principles and techniques that were being communicated to Brian about an important aspect of science teaching are described in terms of the notion of developing an "intellectual empathy" for pupils. This notion entails the "giving of reasons" to the pupils' cognitive as well as social behavior in the classroom. It seems evident, from this dialogue at least, that an important factor in developing and sustaining this disposition for seeing many classroom events from the perspective of the pupils is the extent to which teachers can draw upon a rich repertoire of exemplary problem situations and potential solutions which they have constructed from their previous experiences. These "pedagogical exemplars" (Erickson, 1987) constitute that part of the teacher's practical knowledge base which deals with what Schön describes as the "juncture of everyday knowledge and school knowledge." Examples of this kind of knowledge were displayed in Mr. Kelly's discussion of Beth's interpretation of how to draw a straight line of "best fit" through a series of data points in order to calculate the slope, or the students' frequent confusion over interpreting a distance-time graph in terms of acceleration. This repertoire of exemplars, then, is a product of a teacher's reflections on previous actions in similar situations which subsequently have become codified so that they are readily accessible for use as conjectures on hypotheses in the "hurly-burly," as Gilliss described it, of the action setting. MacKinnon and Erickson argue that the context of practicum supervision may be an ideal setting for identifying some of the structures and strategies in the repertoire of experienced teachers since this knowledge has to be made explicit to some degree when the experienced teacher and novice teacher are reflecting on the classroom actions of the latter, or in some instances when they discuss the performance of the supervisor in a "follow-me" strategy. Not surprisingly, Schön also recognizes the fruitfulness of this type of approach since many of his most telling cases involve supervisory-type situations.

In concluding this chapter, it seems very apparent from the preceding chapters that Schön's analysis of the status and the development of teachers' professional knowledge has had a considerable impact upon a number of scholars representing a wide range of interests and perspectives in the domain of educational inquiry. The collective wisdom generated by this volume—both the critiques and the exemplary case studies—should provide either the casual visitor or the seasoned traveller with a much more detailed map of this terrain by highlighting some trails where caution should be exercised and other areas which show considerable promise in terms of their potential for further exploration.

While it is impossible to determine the source of the recent interest in Schön's writings, one aspect of this appeal surely stems from his perspective on professional knowledge which offers an explanation of how practitioners become competent by acting and reflecting in the practice setting. In laying out a language and a set of constructs to bolster his position, Schön not only validates the type of knowledge that derives from a practitioner's experience, but he also lays a foundation for addressing a set of issues that have plagued educational researchers for generations—often characterized as the theory-practice interface. As such, the forum of debate and discussion that has been generated by Schön's writing transcends the specific issues raised in this book and points us in some interesting directions in such crucial areas of concern as teacher preparation, staff development, and collaborative research models.

As indicated earlier, accompanying this ambitious program of inquiry into professional knowledge are several caveats. These can perhaps best be described in terms of the tension that exists between those theoretical perspectives which focus primarily upon the personal context versus the social context of knowledge construction. Schön, in grappling with the problem of *how* it is that individual practitioners can act competently in an uncertain and complex practice setting, has clearly opted for the former. This position, however, should not be construed in such a manner that it is vulnerable to either of the standard solipsistic or relativistic critiques. That is, we must not proceed along a path which leads in a direction that would indicate that *all* professional knowledge must be constructed by each practitioner in the isolation of his or her practice setting. Or, we must not move in a direction which assumes that the knowledge constructed by individual practitioners is not subject to external criticism because no one else is familiar with the context in which it was constructed. Both of these paths (which incidentally are rooted in a naive, inductivist, epistemological tradition) tend to ignore the extremely powerful influence, or constraints if you like, of the socio-cultural setting in which teachers, pupils, and the school community at large are firmly enmeshed. Hence this dominant cultural template provides a very powerful set of constraints upon the conceptual and the linguistic categories that are available to teachers in their endeavors to construct meaning out of classroom/school phenomena. The most interesting problems emerge as we seek to find a resolution to this tension between the personal and social influences on knowledge construction. This will entail the development of a research program aimed at:

1. uncovering and making explicit the preferred language and exemplars used by teachers to describe and make sense out of classroom phenomena;
2. examining the extent to which their practice is subjected to critical scrutiny by themselves and others in the community;
3. elucidating the norms and also the rigor with which the practice is examined by its most competent practitioners; and
4. developing models of professional growth which would incorporate these attributes and features of a community of educators into existing preservice and inservice settings.

Such a research program is a very ambitious undertaking and it faces many conceptual and practical barriers. Its potential value, however, in legitimizing or "giving reason" to teachers' knowledge and contributing to the knowledge base upon which many teachers stand, would seem to be well worth the resources expended. Because this program will require fairly specialized conceptual/analytical skills and will require access to and insights into the action setting, both university and school personnel must be involved in this type of endeavor. If significant progress is to be made in obtaining a better understanding of the types of issues raised in this book, then ways must be found to bring these communities together in a cooperative and collaborative relationship rather than to have them continue to exist in isolation.

REFERENCES

Elliott, J. (1988). *Teachers as researchers: Implications for supervision and teacher education*. Paper presented at the annual meeting of the American Educational Research Association, New Orleans.

Erickson, G. (1987). *Constructivist epistemology and the professional development of teachers*. Paper presented at the annual meeting of the American Educational Research Association, Washington, D.C.

Lieberman, A. (1988). *Building a professional culture for teaching*. New York: Teachers College Press.

Luhmann, N. (1982). *The differentiation of societies*. New York: Columbia University Press.

Miller, L. and Lieberman, A. (1988). School improvement in the United States: Nuance and numbers. *International Journal of Qualitative Studies in Education I* (1), 3-19.

Stenhouse (1976). *An introduction to curriculum research and development*. London: Heinemann.

Tickle, L. (1987). *Learning teaching, teaching teaching: a study of partnership in teacher education*. London: Falmer Press.

NOTES ON CONTRIBUTORS

Deborah Court is a Doctoral Candidate in the Centre for the Study of Curriculum and Instruction at the University of British Columbia.

Gaalen L. Erickson is an Associate Professor in the Department of Mathematics and Science Education, and a Research Program Coordinator in the Centre for the Study of Teacher Education at the University of British Columbia.

Gary D. Fenstermacher is Professor and Dean of the College of Education at the University of Arizona.

Carol Gibson is a Doctoral Candidate in the Department of Administrative, Adult, and Higher Education at the University of British Columbia.

Geraldine Gilliss is the Director of Research and Information Services for the Canadian Teachers' Federation in Ottawa.

Carl D. Glickman is a Professor in the Department of Curriculum and Supervision, and Head of the Center for Educational Reform at the University of Georgia.

Peter P. Grimmett is an Assistant Professor in the Department of Administrative, Adult, and Higher Education, and Director of the Centre for the Study of Teacher Education at the University of British Columbia.

Jean Hills is Professor and Acting Head of the Department of Administrative, Adult, and Higher Education at the University of British Columbia.

Brent Kilbourn is an Associate Professor in the Department of Curriculum at the Ontario Institute for Studies in Education, Toronto.

Phyllis Johnston is a Research Associate on the project *Metaphor, Reflection, and Teachers' Professional Knowledge* in the Faculty of Education, Queen's University, Kingston, Ontario.

Allan MacKinnon is an Assistant Professor in the Faculty of Education at the University of Toronto, and a Doctoral Candidate in the Department of Mathematics and Science Education at the University of British Columbia.

Hugh Munby is a Professor in the Faculty of Education at Queens University, Kingston, Ontario, and Principal Investigator of the project *Metaphor, Reflection, and Teachers' Professional Knowledge*.

Tom Russell is an Associate Professor in the Faculty of Education at Queen's University, Kingston, Ontario, and Co-Investigator of the project *Metaphor, Reflection, and Teachers' Professional Knowledge*.

Donald A. Schön is Ford Professor of Urban Studies and Education at the Massachusetts Institute of Technology, and an Honorary Fellow of the Royal Institute of British Architects.

Lee S. Shulman is Professor of Education, an affiliated Professor of Psychology, and Director of the Nationally-funded Teacher Assessment Project at Stanford University.

Mark Selman is a Doctoral Candidate in the Department of Social and Educational Studies at the University of British Columbia.

Charlotte Spafford is a Research Associate on the project *Metaphor, Reflection, and Teachers' Professional Knowledge* in the Faculty of Education, Queen's University, Kingston, Ontario.

INDEX